The ROSETTA STONE in the British Museum (Southern Egyptian Gallery, No. 24), inscribed in Greek, Demotic, and hieroglyphs, with a copy of the Decree which was promulgated at a great General Council of the priests from every part of Egypt, who assembled at Memphis to celebrate the first commemoration of the accession of Ptolemy V Epiphanes to the throne of Egypt in the year 197–196 B.C., *i.e.* in the ninth year of his reign.

THE ROSETTA STONE

E. A. WALLIS BUDGE

DOVER PUBLICATIONS, INC.
NEW YORK

This Dover edition, first published in 1989, is an unabridged and unaltered republication of the work originally published in 1929 by The Religious Tract Society, London, under the title *The Rosetta Stone in the British Museum: The Greek, Demotic and Hieroglyphic Texts of the Decree Inscribed on the Rosetta Stone Conferring Additional Honours on Ptolemy V Epiphanes (203–181 B.C.) with English Translations and a Short History of the Decipherment of the Egyptian Hieroglyphs, and an Appendix Containing Translations of the Stelae of Ṣân (Tanis) and Tall al-Maskhûṭah*. For reasons of space, a number of plates have been moved to different locations in the present edition. A few obvious typographical errors have been tacitly corrected.

Manufactured in the United States of America
Dover Publications, Inc., 31 East 2nd Street, Mineola, N.Y. 11501

Library of Congess Cataloging-in-Publication Data

Budge, E. A. Wallis (Ernest Alfred Wallis), Sir, 1857–1934.
[Rosetta stone in the British Museum]
The Rosetta Stone / E. A. Wallis Budge. — Dover ed.
p. cm.
Reprint. Originally published: The Rosetta stone in the British Museum. London : Religious Tract Society, 1929.
Bibliography: p.
Includes index.
ISBN 0-486-26163-8
1. Rosetta stone. 2. Egyptian language—Writing, Hieroglyphic. I. Title.
PJ1531.R5B78 1989
493'.1—dc20

89-33495
CIP

CONTENTS

LIST OF PLATES

PREFACE

IN the ninth year of the reign of PTOLEMY V EPIPHANES, who reigned from 203–181 B.C., the priests of all the gods of UPPER and LOWER EGYPT assembled at MEMPHIS, presumably in the great temple of PTAḤ, the Blacksmith-god of that city, the capital of the northern half of the kingdom. By whose wish or order they assembled is not known, but the definite object of this great Council of Priests was the commemoration, for the first time, of the accession of PTOLEMY V to the throne of EGYPT. The King was then only about twelve years of age, but during the six years of his reign under the direction of AGATHOCLES, SOSIBIUS, TLEPOLEMUS, ARISTOMENES, SCOPAS and others, the affairs of the kingdom had on the whole prospered. The abuses of the misgovernment of PTOLEMY IV had been corrected, revolts had been crushed, and important reforms in the administration of the Army and Navy had taken place. The King had spent his royal revenues lavishly on behalf of the State and his people, he had abolished many taxes and substantially reduced others, he had given bounties to every grade in the Army, he had restored law and order in the country, and had restored all the ancient rites and privileges and revenues of the priests, and had shown himself to be pious and a devout worshipper of all the gods of his country. All these facts were universally admitted.

One of the first acts of the priests was to celebrate the ancient SEṬ Festival, 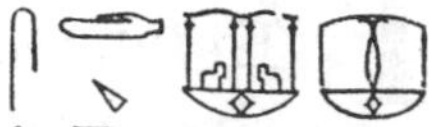, *i.e.* the "Festival of the Tail." This Festival was celebrated every thirty years, or after any very great event, or whenever the King wished to obtain a renewal of his life from the gods, and the physical and spiritual power to rule with justice and righteousness, the highly symbolic ceremonies of this Festival being duly performed according to ancient use and wont. This solemn Office having been performed, the Council of Priests proceeded to review the good works which the boy King had performed, and they decided that the services which he had rendered to EGYPT and to the clergy and laity were so valuable that additional honours should be paid to him in all the principal temples of the country. They then drafted in Greek a Decree in which the good deeds of the King and the honours which they proposed to pay him were carefully enumerated. They further ordered that a copy of it, together with translations, written both in the modern language and script of EGYPT (*i.e.* in Demotic or, New Egyptian), and in the ancient language and script (*i.e.* the hieroglyphs or, Old Egyptian) should be engraved upon a tablet of hard stone, and set up in every temple of the first, second and third class in EGYPT. This Decree, as found on the ROSETTA STONE, is dated on the fourth day of the Greek month Xandikos = the eighteenth day of the second month (MECHIS) of the Egyptian season of PER-T = March 27, 196 B.C. It is doubtful if this Decree was carried out literally.

We owe our knowledge of the Decree of the Council of Priests at MEMPHIS to the lucky blow of the pick of a French soldier called BOUSSARD, who in 1798 was engaged in digging down a ruined wall of FORT ST. JULIEN at ROSETTA. Whilst engaged on this work he dislodged a large slab of basalt, which, when cleaned and brushed, was seen to be covered with three different kinds of writing. According to the late Dr. BIRCH, who received his information from Mr. HARRIS, H.B.M.'s Consul at ALEXANDRIA, General MENOU, who was in command of the French troops at ALEXANDRIA, had the slab taken to his tent and carefully cleaned, and thus saved it from further injury. The French *savants* who were attached to NAPOLEON'S Army wrote of it and spoke of it as the "Pierre de Rosette," and to-day the ROSETTA STONE is one of the best known and most famous monuments in the world.

But the real importance of this Stone was not proved until twenty years later. In 1818 THOMAS

YOUNG succeeded in deciphering the name of PTOLEMY EPIPHANES which is found on it, and he assigned correct phonetic values to most of the hieroglyphs which formed that name, and through these HENRY SALT identified and partly read the name of CLEOPATRA, which he had seen on the Obelisk of PHILAE. The supreme value of the ROSETTA STONE to the early decipherers was due to the fact that it contained a BILINGUAL inscription, and that one of the two languages of the inscription, viz. Greek, was a well-known language. YOUNG was the first to grasp the idea of the existence of a phonetic principle in reading the Egyptian hieroglyphs, and, as CHABAS said, "cette idée fut, dans la realité, le FIAT LUX de la science" (*Inscription de Rosette*, p. 5). Better equipped with the knowledge of Coptic and other Oriental languages than YOUNG, the great French scholar CHAMPOLLION LE JEUNE promptly appreciated YOUNG's discovery at its true value, and applied his system of decipherment to the names and titles of the Ptolemies and the Roman Emperors, and produced the hieroglyphic alphabet which is the base of that used by Egyptologists to-day.

The Decree of Memphis was drafted in Greek, and about the general meaning of its contents there was never much doubt. But with the translations in Demotic and in Hieroglyphs the case is different. The early decipherers knew very little about their contents, and the so-called "translations" of ÅKERBLAD and YOUNG were based on guesswork. BRUGSCH'S translation of the Demotic text (published in 1848) was the first real translation of it ever made. As for the translation of the Decree written in hieroglyphs, it is sufficient to point out that the phonetics and the characters and meanings of many of the words of the hieroglyphic version were unknown in 1820, and they remained so until the present century.

A new impulse was given to the study of the inscriptions on the ROSETTA STONE through the discovery in 1887 of a large granite stele inscribed in hieroglyphs with a copy of the Decree of Memphis. The text is full of faults, it is true, and the transcripts published by BOURIANT, BAILLET and myself were unsatisfactory. But it has since been submitted to an intensive examination by SETHE and SPIEGELBERG, and we now know as much as we are ever likely to know about the Decree of Memphis.

In the present volume an attempt has been made to incorporate the results of the recent labours of HESS, SETHE and SPIEGELBERG. In the transcript of the Greek text the words have been separated for the convenience of the beginner. In the early Chapters an account of the discovery of the ROSETTA STONE will be found, and in the later a short history of the decipherment of the Egyptian hieroglyphs. Hieroglyphic type has been used freely so that the reader may make himself familiar with the Egyptian hieroglyphs. As the Decree of Memphis is the last of a series of three Decrees which were promulgated by the priests of Egypt in honour of PTOLEMY V and his father and grandfather, I have given in the Appendix translations of the Decrees which concern PTOLEMY IV and PTOLEMY III. The series supplies a very instructive illustration of the growth of the power of the priesthood in fifty years, *i.e.* between 247 and 196 B.C.

The decipherment of the Egyptian texts on the ROSETTA STONE opened up a new and vitally important field of study to the historian and philologist, and above all to the students of the Bible. During the past century Egyptologists have made a study, ever more and more intensive, of the literature of Egypt, both sacred and profane; and nearly all the principal works which help to explain, or which supplement the Bible narrative, have been published and translated. The information which has been derived from the monuments and papyri of Egypt supports the sections in the historical books of the Bible which describe the relations of the Hebrews with the Egyptians in a very remarkable manner, and attests their general accuracy even in details. The papyri have given us access to "all the wisdom of the Egyptians" in which MOSES was learned, and we can now perceive the greatness of the administrative and financial ability of JOSEPH, the Viceroy of Pharaoh. And the historical foundation of the tradition of the EXODUS, and of the story of the wanderings of the ISRAELITES in the deserts parallel with Egypt declare themselves. The historical inscriptions of the New Kingdom throw great light on the intrigues which the Hebrew and Egyptian Kings carried on against the BABYLONIANS and ASSYRIANS, and help us to realize the political condition of PALESTINE and EGYPT when ISAIAH was hurling his denunciations against the Hebrews, and prophesying the downfall of their heathen allies.

For the use of those who wish to gain familiarity with the inscriptions on the ROSETTA STONE and to study them from a palaeographic point of view, the Trustees of the British Museum have prepared plaster casts, both white and coloured, which can be purchased from the Department of Casts at the Victoria and Albert Museum, South Kensington. An excellent coloured facsimile in plaster, measuring 13½ inches by 10½ inches, on which all the inscriptions have been reproduced accurately by mechanical means, has been specially prepared for the use of lecturers and private students. It can be obtained from Mr. R. B. FLEMING, photographer, of Bury Street, W.C.1. The best small photographic reproduction of the ROSETTA STONE ever published is that published by the British Museum in the pamphlet *The Rosetta Stone*, with the letterpress, price 6*d*.

My thanks are due to the Trustees of the British Museum for permission to photograph the portraits of THOMAS YOUNG and CHAMPOLLION LE JEUNE, the ROSETTA STONE, and several of the objects which are illustrated in this book. The two Plates (XII, XIII) of Ptolemaïc coins have been made from casts kindly given to me by Mr. A. P. READY of the British Museum. I am indebted to my friend, the Rev. C. H. IRWIN, D.D., General Editor of the Religious Tract Society, for the helpful suggestions which he had made and which I have adopted, whilst writing this volume and the other five volumes which the Society has published. The excellence of the material forms of these volumes is due to Mr. H. R. BRABROOK, the General Manager of the Society, whose knowledge of paper, printing and binding is unrivalled. Messrs. Harrison and Sons, Ltd., have reproduced the Oriental texts and inscriptions with great success, and more than a word of acknowledgment is due to Mr. George Crane and Mr. S. J. Wadlow of their staff. The latter set the hieroglyphic type, and is ably continuing the work of his predecessors, the great Oriental compositors Messrs. Mabey, Fisher and Fish.

E. A. WALLIS BUDGE.

48, Bloomsbury Street, London, W.C.1

July 27, 1929.

CHAPTER I

I.—THE DISCOVERY OF THE ROSETTA STONE

THE famous, irregularly-shaped slab of black basalt in the BRITISH MUSEUM (Southern Egyptian Gallery, No. 24), which is now universally known as the " ROSETTA STONE," was discovered at a spot which lies a few miles to the north of the little town of RASHÎD which Europeans generally call " ROSETTA." RASHÎD stands on the left bank of an arm of the Nile, which in ancient days was called the " Bolbitinic arm," in the WESTERN DELTA, about 5 miles from the mouth of the river, and some 30 miles from ALEXANDRIA, which lies to the west. The name RASHÎD is that by which the town is known to the Arab geographers (*e.g.* YÂKÛT, ii, p. 781), and it is probably of Arab origin, for " RASHÎT," the name given to the town by the COPTS is, as AMELINEAU thought (*Géographie*, p. 405), undoubtedly a mere transcription of RASHÎD. Whether the Bolbitinic arm of the Nile was artificial or not matters little ; it is tolcrably certain that a seaport town of considerable importance has always stood on the site of RASHÎD, and that its inhabitants have always thrived on its sea-borne trade. The Egyptian inscriptions tell us nothing about the history of the towns which must have stood successively on the site, and the early Coptic writers are silent about them.

In the second half of the IXth century the ARABS realized the importance of the place as the site for a seaport, and they founded RASHÎD. Though after the conquest of Egypt by 'AMR IBN AL-'ÂṢI in 641 the Arab general treated the Alexandrians with great consideration, the prosperity of ALEXANDRIA declined rapidly, and much of her trade passed into the hands of the merchants in the other seaports of the DELTA. In 969, the Khalîfah MU'IZZ founded the city of AL-ḲÂHIRA, or CAIRO. ALEXANDRIA ceased to be a great trading centre, and most of her maritime commerce found its way to the newly founded Arab towns of RASHÎD and to DAMIETTA, in the EASTERN DELTA. The trade of RASHÎD grew rapidly, her merchants became wealthy, and the outskirts of the town became filled with large houses, many of which stood in gardens and plantations filled with vines and fruit-bearing trees. Several mosques were built, and many learned men founded their homes at RASHÎD, and wrote voluminous works on the ḲUR'ÂN and Muḥammadan traditions. The prosperity of the town was abruptly arrested by the discovery of the new route to INDIA round the Cape of Good Hope, by VASCO DA GAMA in 1497, and by the Portuguese victories in the Red Sea. But the trade of the port was very considerable during the XVIth, XVIIth, and XVIIIth centuries. The death-blow to the prosperity of the town was given by MUḤAMMAD 'ALÎ, who in 1819 began to dig the Maḥmudîyah Canal, which connected CAIRO with ALEXANDRIA, and so caused the diversion of the trade of RASHÎD to ALEXANDRIA.

At the present time the inhabitants of RASHÎD are about 15,000 in number, and are chiefly MUSLIMS and GREEKS. In some of the larger houses the visitor will see ancient stone columns and slabs built into the walls, and in the Mosque of SAKHLÛN there are many more pillars. These were never hewn by the Arabs, and an examination of them shows that they were brought to their present places from some Egyptian or Egypto-Ptolemaïc buildings in or near one of the ancient towns that stood on the site. It is well known from classical sources that the branch of the river which flows by the town was called the "Bolbitinic arm" of the NILE, and we may therefore assume that these pillars came from buildings in the town of BOLBITINE, which is mentioned by HECATAEUS and DIODORUS as having stood on the river. Of the town of BOLBITINE nothing is known, and we can only speculate as to the causes which led to the disappearance of a populous and apparently well-to-do town. The inscribed remains of Egyptian buildings found in the neighbourhood suggest that the town called BOLBITINE by the Greeks was a flourishing market-centre under the Pharaohs of the XXVIth Dynasty, and its downfall may well have been brought about by the founding of ALEXANDRIA, some 35 miles distant. And again, the silting up of the arm of the NILE may have made it impossible for sea-going ships to reach the town. From the phrase *βολβίτινον ἅρμα*, which is quoted by STEPHANUS of BYZANTIUM (Vth century), it would seem that the chariots made there were famous throughout the East. A town of the size and importance of BOLBITINE must have had at least one temple, and it is very possible, as CHAMPOLLION thought (*L'Égypte sous les Pharaons*, vol. ii, p. 241), that the ROSETTA STONE stood in the great temple of that town.

The exact circumstances under which the Stone was discovered are not known, and there is some doubt as to the name of its discoverer. There is no doubt that it was found in August, 1799, whilst the French, who had occupied ROSETTA in 1798, were engaged in repairing or adding to the fortifications which lay to the north of the town. One account says that the discoverer was a French Officer of Engineers called BOUSSARD, who may perhaps be identified with the distinguished French General Baron A. J. BOUSSARD, who played a prominent part in NAPOLEON'S Expedition to Egypt, and who died in 1812. Another account says that it was found by one BOUCHARD, who discovered the Stone by striking it accidentally with his pick; if this be so, BOUCHARD was probably one of the soldiers who were working at the reconstruction of FORT ST. JULIEN under the direction of General BOUSSARD. It has been stated that BOUCHARD found the Stone lying loose on the ground, but it is also said that when he struck it with his pick it was built into an ancient wall, the demolition of which had been decided upon. In either case it seems tolerably certain that the Stone had been removed from the temple in which it had been set up, and used in building the wall which the French were demolishing. When this was done it is impossible to say, but the fortifications of ROSETTA were old and in a ruined state when the French came there, and it is probable that they formed part of a famous system of defence works which the Khalîfah AL-ASHRAF ḲÂNṢÛH AL-GHÛRÎ constructed at ALEXANDRIA and RASHÎD between 1501 and 1516. The late Dr. BIRCH said, "The Stone appears to have been placed in a temple dedicated to TUM or TOMOS, the setting Sun, originally erected in the reign of NECTANEBO" (*i.e.* during the first half of the IVth century B.C.), but I cannot find out what his authority for the statement was. On the other hand, Mr. HARRIS, formerly H.B.M.'s Consul at ALEXANDRIA, repeating a tradition current in his day, said that the Stone had originally stood in a temple built by NECHO, the PHARAOH NECHO of the Bible (XXVIth Dynasty).

II.—REMOVAL OF THE ROSETTA STONE TO CAIRO

Soon after its discovery the ROSETTA STONE was taken to CAIRO and placed in the INSTITUT NATIONAL, where a considerable number of large and important antiquities had been collected by the *savants* whom NAPOLEON had taken to Egypt with him, and by native agents throughout the country. As soon as the *savants* returned from UPPER EGYPT to CAIRO they examined the Stone, and quickly realized its importance. NAPOLEON the Great, who was among the first who saw it, regarded it with the keenest interest, and "in order to satisfy the curiosity of the *literati* in every country, gave orders to have the inscription engraved immediately" (*Gentleman's Magazine*, vol. lxxi, 1801, p. 1194). Two expert lithographers "Citoyens MARCEL et GALLAND" were summoned from PARIS in haste, and they made copies of the texts on the Stone by inking it with printer's ink and rolling sheets of paper over it. Not content with this, "Citoyen RAFFINEAU" was ordered by NAPOLEON to make a sulphur cast of the Stone for the use of Professor AMEILHON of Paris, whom NAPOLEON ordered to translate the Greek text. In the autumn of 1801, General DUGUA,[1] "l'un des guerriers qui, dans la mémorable expédition d'Égypte, ont si glorieusement

[1] Charles François Joseph Dugua was born at Toulouse in 1740, and died as the result of a wound received at St. Domingo in 1802.

servi sous les Héros de la France"; returned to Paris and took with him two copies of the inscriptions on the Rosetta Stone made by "Citoyens Marcel et Galland," and presented them to the Institut National of Paris.

III.—SURRENDER OF THE ROSETTA STONE TO THE BRITISH

Meanwhile the British forces had gained many victories over the French in Egypt, and after the capitulation of Alexandria, all the antiquities which the French had collected in Cairo and Alexandria, and had packed up ready for transport to Paris, were surrendered to them. Under Article XVI of the Treaty of Capitulation, General Hutchinson took possession of them, and despatched them to England at the end of the year 1801. The famous Stone, which even at the time was generally known as the Rosetta Stone, was among them, and it arrived in England in February, 1802; and, as a result of the description of it published in Paris by "Citoyen Du Theil," created a great sensation. The copies of the inscriptions which General Dugua had taken to Paris were committed to the care of "Citoyen Du Theil," who read the Greek text at once, and forthwith declared that the Stone was a "monument of the gratitude of some priests of Alexandria, or some neighbouring place, towards Ptolemy Epiphanes." He went on to say that the first and second texts on the Stone contained repetitions of the contents of the Greek, and that, as the last line but one of the Greek text ordered that a copy of the decree of the priests was to be inscribed upon a hard stone stele "in sacred letters, and in letters of the country, and in Greek letters," **ΤΟΙΣ ΤΕ ΙΕΡΟΙΣ ΚΑΙ ΕΓΧΩΡΙΟΙΣ ΚΑΙ ΕΛΛΗΝΙΚΟΙΣ ΓΡΑΜΜΑΣΙΝ**, the first text on the Stone must be written in HIEROGLYPHS, and the second in ENCHORIAL characters. These statements at once drew the attention of learned men throughout the world to the Stone, for it was clear that by means of the Greek text it would probably be possible to decipher the Egyptian hieroglyphs and also the enchorial script of EGYPT.

IV.—HOW THE ROSETTA STONE CAME TO LONDON

The story of the transport of the Stone to England was told by Major-General H. TAYLOR in a letter addressed by him to NICHOLAS CARLISLE, Secretary to the Society of Antiquaries, London, and printed in *Archaeologia*, vol. XVI, London, 1812, pp. 212 ff. This letter reads:—

"The ROSETTA STONE having excited much attention in the learned world, and in this Society in particular, I request to offer them, through you, some account of the manner it came into the possession of the British Army, and by what means it was brought to this country, presuming it may not be unacceptable to them.

"By the sixteenth article of the Capitulation of Alexandria, the siege of which terminated the labours of the British Army in Egypt, all the curiosities, natural and artificial, collected by the French Institute and others, were to be delivered up to the captors. This was refused on the part of the French General to be fulfilled, by saying they were all private property. Many letters passed; at length, on consideration that the care in preserving the insects and animals had made the property in some degree private, it was relinquished by Lord HUTCHINSON; but the artificial, which consisted of antiquities and Arabian manuscripts, among the former of which was the ROSETTA STONE, was insisted upon by the noble General with his usual zeal for science. Upon which I had several conferences with the French General MENOU, who at length gave way, saying that the ROSETTA STONE was his private property, but, as he was forced, he must comply as well as the other proprietors. I accordingly received from the Under-Secretary of the Institute, LE PÉRE, the Secretary FOURIER being ill, a paper, containing a list of the antiquities, with the names of the claimants of each piece of Sculpture; the Stone is there described as black granite, with three inscriptions, belonging to General MENOU.

"From the French sçavans I learnt, that the ROSETTA STONE was found among the ruins of Fort ST. JULIEN, when repaired by the French and put in a state of defence ; it stands near the mouth of the Nile, on the Rosetta branch, where are, in all probability, thc pieces broken off. I was also informed, that there was a stone similar at MENOUF, obliterated, or nearly so, by the earthen jugs being placed on it, as it stood near the water ; and that there was a fragment of one, used and placed in the walls of the French fortifications of Alexandria. This Stone was carefully brought to General MENOU'S house in Alexandria, covered with soft cotton cloth and a double matting when I first saw it. The General had selected this precious relic of antiquity for himself. When it was understood by the French Army that we were to possess the antiquities, the covering of the Stone was torn off, and it was thrown upon its face, and the excellent wooden cases of the rest were broken off ; for they had taken infinite pains in the first instance to secure and preserve from any injury all the antiquities. I made several remonstrances, but the chief difficulty I had was on account of this Stone, and the great sarcophagus, which at one time was positively refused to be given up by the CAPITAN PASHA, who had obtained it by having possession of the ship it had been put on board of by the French. I procured, however, a centry on the beach from Mon. LE ROY, prefect maritime, who, as well as the General, behaved with great civility ; the reverse I experienced from some others.

"When I mentioned the manner the Stone had been treated to Lord HUTCHINSON, he gave me a detachment of artillerymen, and an artillery-engine, called from its powers a devil-cart, with which that evening I went to General MENOU'S house, and carried off the Stone, without any injury, but with some difficulty, from the narrow streets to my house, amid the sarcasm of numbers of French officers and men; being ably assisted by an intelligent sergeant of artillery, who commanded the party, all of whom enjoyed great satisfaction in their employment; they were the first British soldiers who entered Alexandria. During the time the Stone remained in my house some gentlemen attached to the corps of sçavants requested to have a cast, which I readily granted, provided the Stone should receive no injury; which cast they took to Paris, leaving the Stone well cleared from the printing-ink which it had been covered with to take off several copies to send to France, when it was first discovered.

"Having seen the other remains of Egyptian sculpture sent on board the Admiral by Sir RICHARD BICKERTON'S ship, the Madras, who kindly gave every possible assistance, I embarked with the ROSETTA STONE, determining to share its fate, on board the Egyptienne frigate, taken in the harbours of Alexandria, and arrived at Portsmouth in February, 1802. When the ship came round to Deptford, it [*i.e.* the Stone] was put in a boat and landed at the Custom House; and Lord BUCKINGHAMSHIRE, the then Secretary of State, acceded to my request, and permitted it to remain some time at the apartments of the Society of Antiquaries, previous to its deposit in the British Museum, where I trust it will long remain, a most valuable relic of antiquity, the feeble but only yet discovered link of the Egyptian to the known languages, a proud trophy of the arms of Britain (I could almost say *spolia opima*), not plundered from defenceless inhabitants, but honourably acquired by the fortune of war.

[Signed] "H. TURNER, *Major-General.*"

An interesting note on the other antiquities sent to LONDON may be quoted from the *Gentleman's Magazine* (vol. lxxii, 1802, p. 726). "The various Egyptian antiquities collected by the French Army, and since become the property of the conquerors, have been lately conveyed to the British Museum, and may be seen in the outer court of that building. Many of them were so extremely massive, that it was found necessary to make wooden frames for them. They consist of an immense bath of granite, about 10 feet long, and 5 feet deep and over, covered within and without with hieroglyphics; another bath of smaller dimensions equally adorned; a granite coffin with the shape of the head, and covered all over with hieroglyphicks; a hand clenched, the statue belonging to which must have been 150 feet high; two statues in white marble, in Roman habits, one of them without a head, the features of the other much defaced; the head of a ram, in reddish stone, measuring about 4 feet from the nose to the crown of the head, and every way proportionate, the right horn broken off; several human figures sitting, with the heads of beasts, and in the left hand the *crux ansata*, or cross, with a handle and ring; similar heads without bodies; two marble obelisks, the four sides charged with hieroglyphicks; a large cylindrical pillar of granite, measuring 12 feet in length, and 3½ feet in diameter. The smaller bath weighs about 11 tons, and there were 11 horses to draw it to the Museum; the larger only 9 tons, the stone not being so massive, required only 9 horses. The whole weight of the collection is calculated at about 50 tons."

The granite "bath" referred to above is the sarcophagus of ḤAP-MEN 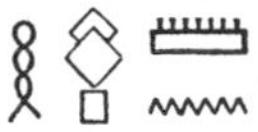, a royal scribe and director of granaries. Its length is 9 feet, width 4 ft. 7 in., height 3 ft. 11 in., and it weighs about 7 tons 4 cwts. It was found in CAIRO, where it had been used as a tank, and a hole was cut in one end of it to allow the muddy sediment to run out. [B.M. No. 826 (23).] The other "bath" is the sarcophagus of NEKHT-ḤER-ḤEBIT MERI AMEN , King of

Egypt, about 378 B.C. It has often been called the "sarcophagus of ALEXANDER THE GREAT." The two obelisks [B.M. Nos. 523 and 524] were made by the same king, and having been taken to CAIRO from a town in the DELTA stood for some years before one of the mosques. The granite coffin, "with the shape of the head," is now No. 882 (66); the "hand clenched" is the left fist from a colossal statute of RAMESES II (No. 596); the "head of a ram" is the head of a ram-headed sphinx from the AVENUE OF SPHINXES at KARNAK [B.M. No. 550 (7)], and the "figures with the heads of beasts" are statues of the goddess SEKHMIT from KARNAK [No. 405 (88), etc.]. These and many other objects were presented to the British Museum by KING GEORGE III in 1802; a list of them is given in *A Guide to the Egyptian Galleries* (*Sculpture*), London, 1900, p. xv.

V.—THE ROSETTA STONE AND THE SOCIETY OF ANTIQUARIES

We have seen above (p. 23) that "Citoyen DU THEIL" informed the learned world in PARIS about the nature of the contents of the inscriptions on the ROSETTA STONE as soon as he received the copies of them, which were brought to him from EGYPT by General DUGUA, and that he described correctly the three kinds of writing found on the Stone. This he did apparently before any English scholar had the opportunity of reading the texts, and the credit of being the first to discover why, and when, and where, and in whose honour the Stone was set up, undoubtedly belongs to the French.

We may now see what steps were taken by the British to make the Stone available for study when it arrived in London. In his "Account of the Rosetta Stone, in three languages, which was brought to England in the year 1802" MATTHEW RAPER says: "On the eleventh of March in the year 1802 the Society of Antiquaries received a letter from GRANVILLE PENN, Esq., informing them that, by the desire of Lord HOBART, he had forwarded two cases for the inspection of the Society, and that he wished them to remain in their custody till he could give further directions for the removal of them to the British Museum. On the same day a letter was received from Colonel TURNER, stating that he had brought the Stone, together with the statues, all contained in the two cases above mentioned, from EGYPT; and describing the means by which they came into his possession. [For this letter, see above, p. 24 f.] In the month of April following, the Rev. STEPHEN WATSON (a Fellow of this Society) presented a short translation of the Greek inscription on the Stone, with some critical remarks thereon. In July the Society ordered four casts of the Stone to be made by Mr. Papera, in plaster of Paris, and these were to be sent, properly packed up in cases, to the Universities of OXFORD, CAMBRIDGE, EDINBURGH, and DUBLIN, accompanied by a letter to each from the Secretary. A facsimile of the Greek inscription was engraved and a copy of it was sent to General Garth, for His Majesty. Copies were also distributed to the Fellows of the Society, and others were forwarded to the following places, in addition to those foreign Universities, to which the Society usually sent presents of their works. To the Vatican. To the Society de Propagandâ Fide. To Cardinal Borgia at Rome. To the Imperial Library at Vienna. To the Imperial Society of Petersburgh. To the Academy at Berlin. To the National Institute. To the National Library at Paris. To the Royal Society of Antiquaries at Copenhagen. To the University at Upsala. To the Academy at Madrid. To the Royal Library at the Escurial. To the Academy of Science at Lisbon. To the Philosophical Society at Philadelphia. To the University at Leyden.

" The Society hoped to have been favoured, in return, with some translations or communications on so valuable a relic of antiquity ; containing so much matter for remarks, on the circumstances mentioned in the inscription ; at least it might have been expected that some Members of the learned foreign Societies would have endeavoured to fill up the lacunae occasioned by the fracture of the Stone. No intelligence, however, of any kind being received, Mr. WESTON presented a full translation of the Greek inscription, which was read to the Society at their Meeting on the fourth day of November, 1802, wherein the deficiencies, occasioned by the fractures, were very ably supplied. On the eleventh of November following, the Secretary received a letter, written in the French language, enclosing one to the Society, in Latin, accompanied by a Latin version of the Greek inscription, with a considerable number of learned remarks thereon, from Professor HEYNE, of the University of Göttingen. This translation comes very near, but it is not exactly the same, with that presented by the Rev. STEPHEN WESTON; as both translations will be printed at length, the reader will have an opportunity of forming his own opinion which of the two comes nearer to the original.

"On the second day of December of the same year [1802], our learned Member, TAYLOR COMBE, Esq., sent a letter, with a most elaborate and instructive dissertation on the inscription, which were read to the Society at their Meetings, proving that the Decree of the Priests, in honour of Ptolemy Epiphanes, was not published in his lifetime. Mr. COMBE also sent a portrait of Ptolemy Philometor, taken from a unique coin in the French Cabinet, as a proper accompaniment to his memorial. On the thirteenth of January, 1803, Mr. WESTON presented to the Society a paper, containing the words, and parts of words, which he supposed had filled up the vacancies occasioned by the fractures on the Stone; and on the same day Professor PORSON presented one similar to it, accompanied by the Latin letter engraved on the plate of the facsimile of those letters, written thereon by the Professor himself, as his conjectural restorations of the lost parts of the Greek inscription; either of which might serve to supply what is wanting; but as only one is necessary, Mr. Professor PORSON'S was delivered to the engraver in order to its being executed in such a manner as to correspond with the former facsimile engraving of the Greek inscription . . .

"Seven years having now elapsed since the receipt of the last communication to the Society on this subject, there is little reason to expect that any further information should be received: the Society therefore resolved to gratify the curiosity of the learned, by publishing in their next volume of *Archaeologia*, all the particulars relating to this very interesting monument. It would have appeared sooner, had it not been judged advisable to give sufficient time for any additional matter to come in, in order that the publication might be rendered as complete as possible. They now present it to the public, with the hope that it may fully answer their expectation; and, in order to accommodate such persons as may be desirous of possessing so curious a piece of ancient history, the Society have determined to print, separate from the *Archaeologia*, so many copies of it, as may be supposed necessary for the supply of such demand.

[Signed] "MATT. RAPER."

[From *Archaeologia*, London, 1812, vol. xvi, p. 208 f.]

VI.—DESCRIPTION OF THE ROSETTA STONE

The ROSETTA STONE is an irregularly shaped slab of compact black basalt which is about 3 ft. 9 in. in length, 2 ft. 4½ in. in width, and 11 inches in thickness. The top right- and left-hand corners, and the right-hand bottom corner are wanting; the missing portions of the slab were carefully sought for immediately after its discovery, but were never found. This fact suggests that the slab was broken in transit from the place where it stood to the wall in which it was found built up. How much of the upper part of the Stone is missing cannot be said, but judging by the proportion which exists between the lengths of the inscriptions which are preserved upon it, we may assume that when the Stone was complete, it was from 18 to 24 inches longer than it is at present. There is every reason for believing that the Stone, when complete, resembled in general form and appearance the other Stelae which were set up in honour of Ptolemy III, and Ptolemy IV, and Ptolemy V by the priesthood of Egypt assembled at MEMPHIS and CANOPUS. And all these in turn resembled the famous STELE OF PITHOM, which PTOLEMY II set up to record his triumphs and exploits.

[THE RELIEFS SCULPTURED ON THE STELAE OF PTOLEMY II, PTOLEMY III AND PTOLEMY IV]

On the flat surface of the rounded top of the STELE OF PITHOM are sculptured two scenes :—

1. PTOLEMY II, in official regal attire, offering a figure of the goddess MAAT  to TEM  the great god of THEKU (SUCCOTH). Behind him stand OSIRIS, the god of PER-QEḤRT  or PI-HAHIROTH (Exod. xiv. 2; Num. xxxiii. 7), HORUS, ISIS, and ARSINOË, the Queen of PTOLEMY II, who is identified with the goddess ISIS-HATHOR.

2. PTOLEMY II offering an Utchat  to the god of the Utchat, *i.e.* THOTH. PTOLEMY offering vases of milk to TEM, behind whom stand ISIS, and Queen ARSINOË, who is identified with the goddess ISIS-HATHOR. [*See* Plate 8 in NAVILLE, *Store-City of Pithom*, London, 1885, and the photograph in AHMED BEY KAMÂL, *Catalogue*, 2 vols., Cairo, 1905.]

On the Stele of Canopus, from KOM AL-HISN, which was set up in honour of PTOLEMY III, the founder of the great temple of Edfû (**Plate I**) we

PLATE I.

The Entrance and Colonnade of the Temple of Edfû founded by Ptolemy III.
(From a photograph by the late A. Beato of Luxor.)

PLATE II.

The great Temple at Philae on which a copy of the hieroglyphic version of the Decree on the ROSETTA STONE was cut by the priests. Many portions of the text were obliterated by one of the later Ptolemies who had figures of the gods, etc., cut on the wall on which it was engraved. (From Colonel Lyons' *Philae*, Plate 31.)

have the vaulted heaven and the Winged Disk on the flat surface of the rounded top. From the Disk are suspended two uraei, the one wearing the crown of the South 𓋑, and the other the crown of the North 𓋔; attached to each uraeus is a fly-flapper or fan 𓋻. The Disk is called "giver of life," 𓏙𓋹. Below these is a row of figures, the centre one of which is the king wearing the double crown 𓋖, and holding a sceptre and the symbol of life 𓌀𓋹. Facing the king are the goddesses NUT (or ISIS ?), HATHOR and BAST, and the gods APIS, AMEN, and HORUS. Behind him stand Queen BERENICE, THOTH who holds a stilus 𓆳 and a palm branch, on which he inscribes the number of the years of the king's life. Next follows the goddess SESHETA 𓋇𓏏𓆇, "the lady of books" and counterpart of THOTH, and then we have figures of two PTOLEMYS and two Queens ARSINOË who represent the king's parents and grandparents. Thus we see that the PTOLEMIES and their Queens were deified and made to rank as equals with the gods.

The Stele from TALL AL-MASKHUṬAH, which was set up in honour of PTOLEMY IV PHILOPATOR, is also sculptured with a figure of the Winged Disk; immediately below this is the prenomen of

PTOLEMY IV, and on each side of it are the signs , and the figures of HORUS of the South (EDFÛ) and HORUS of the North  (MESEN). To the left we see PTOLEMY IV standing in a chariot, with the horses at the galop, and driving a long Macedonian spear into the body of a prisoner, who is kneeling with his arms tied at the elbows behind his back, and is being thrust towards the king's spear by the god ÅTEM, or TEM. Behind the king stands his sister-wife ARSINOË. Behind ÅTEM stand OSIRIS, lord of the door of the East, ḤER-SMAI-TAUI, *i.e.* "Horus, unifier of the two hands," the god of THEKUT (SUCCOTH), HORUS, lord of ĀNT , Chief of PER-QEḤRT (PI-HAHIROTH), and the goddesses HATHOR and ISIS. For PTOLEMY V and his ancestors, and the great gods and goddesses, who were worshipped by them, see the translations of the ROSETTA STONE in the following pages.

[DUPLICATES OF THE ROSETTA STONE]

The priests who drew up the Decree on the ROSETTA STONE ordered that a copy of the Decree, cut on a hard stone tablet, was to be set up in each of the temples of the first, second, and third classes in EGYPT, and that their order was carried out is proved by the fact that portions of some of these duplicates have been found. The most important of these is the STELE OF DAMANHÛR, or the Stele of Annobairah, as it is sometimes called. This monument is 4 ft. 2 in. in height, and nearly 1 ft. 8 in. in width, and is inscribed with 31 lines of hieroglyphic text. Immediately above the inscription, and under the Winged Disk, is sculptured a scene in which the king, Ptolemy V, is represented in the act of spearing an enemy, who kneels before him and has his arms tied together at the elbows behind him. Behind the king stands a royal lady wearing the disk and plumes of Isis. Facing him is a god who has the feather of Maat 𓆄 upon his head, and is presenting to the king a scimitar of victory. Behind him stands a lioness-headed goddess (Bast ?), and behind her are figures of three of the Ptolemies and their Queens, and close to their heads are the cartouches containing their names. These probably represent the parents, grandparents and great-grandparents of Ptolemy V. (A photographic reproduction of the Stele is given by Ahmed Bey Kamâl, in his *Catalogue général des Antiquités Egyptiennes du Musée du Caire*, 2 vols., Cairo, 1905, plates LXII and LXIII ; and by Sethe in the *Nachrichten* of Göttingen, Berlin, 1916, Heft 2.) There is then, no good reason for thinking that the Rosetta Stone differed in respect of its general scheme of decoration from the Stelae set up in honour of Ptolemy III and Ptolemy IV.

VII.—THE INSCRIPTIONS ON THE ROSETTA STONE

The bilingual (not trilingual) inscription on the ROSETTA STONE is written from right to left in the two forms of EGYPTIAN writing and in GREEK. It was the fashion at one time to compare the inscription on the ROSETTA STONE with the great Inscription which DARIUS I had cut upon the rock at BAHISTÛN in PERSIA, and to describe each of these documents as trilingual. But it must be remembered that the DECREE on the ROSETTA STONE is BILINGUAL, though written in three kinds of *writing*, and that the BAHISTÛN Inscription is TRILINGUAL, and written in three *languages* (PERSIAN, SUSIAN, and BABYLONIAN) in three different kinds of cuneiform character. The GREEK portion of the inscription on the ROSETTA STONE is written in uncials; it contains 54 lines of text, the last 26 of which are imperfect at the ends. In the transcript given on p. 124 f. the words are divided by spaces for the convenience of the beginner. The EGYPTIAN portion of the text is written in—

1. The HIEROGLYPHIC character, that is to say in the old picture writing which was employed in Egypt from the earliest dynasties in making copies of funerary and religious texts, and in nearly all state and ceremonial documents that were intended to be seen by the public. The invention of hieroglyphic writing was attributed to the god THOTH, who is

described as the heart and tongue of Rā, the Sun-god, and the scribe or secretary of the gods. The texts written on the walls of the chamber and corridors of the pyramids at Ṣaḳḳârah (VIth Dynasty) are in hieroglyphs, and the spells which they form were considered to be more efficacious when so written. The Hieroglyphic text on the Rosetta Stone consists of 14 lines, not one of which is complete; it corresponds roughly to the last 28 lines of the Greek version, and more than one-half of this version of the Decree is wanting.

2. The Demotic character, that is to say the conventional, abbreviated, and modified form of the Hieratic character, or *cursive form* of hieroglyphic writing, which was in general use for literary and commercial purposes during the Ptolemaïc period, and for some centuries earlier. The Demotic version contains 32 lines of text, and the first 14 of these are imperfect at the beginnings.

VIII.—THE CONTENTS OF THE INSCRIPTIONS ON THE ROSETTA STONE

The Decree inscribed on the Rosetta Stone was promulgated at a great General Council of Egyptian priests from Upper and Lower Egypt, who assembled at Memphis, presumably in the great temple of Ptah and Apis, to celebrate the first commemoration of the accession of Ptolemy V

EPIPHANES to the throne of Egypt in the year 197–196 B.C., *i.e.* in the ninth year of his reign. The DECREE summarizes the benefactions which PTOLEMY V had bestowed upon the priesthoods, and upon the soldiers and sailors and civilians of Egypt, and orders an augmentation of the honours to be paid to the king as a token of their gratitude. The opening lines contain the date, and describe the assembling of the priesthoods at MEMPHIS, and then follows the list of the King's benefactions, which include :—

1. Gifts of corn and money to the temples.
2. Gifts to the officers and men in the King's Army.
3. The remission of taxes to increase the comfort and prosperity of all classes.
4. The withdrawal of claims to arrears of taxes.
5. The release of offenders who had been in prison for a long time.
6. The restoration to the temples of sacrosanct lands and revenues.
7. The reduction of the taxes paid by the priests.
8. The abolition of the obligation of the priests to visit ALEXANDRIA annually.
9. The abolition of the press-gang for the Navy.
10. The remission of two-thirds of the tax on the byssus due from the temples to the king.

11. The restoration of peace and order throughout EGYPT, and of the ceremonies connected with the worship of the gods.
12. The forgiveness of those who had rebelled, and the granting to them of permission to return to their homes, and to resume possession of their lands and property.
13. The formation of an Army and a Navy to defend EGYPT at the King's expense.
14. The siege and capture of the City of LYCOPOLIS which had been fortified by the rebels.
15. The punishment of the ringleaders of the rebellion against PTOLEMY IV PHILOPATOR, the father of the King. Some of the rebels were impaled at MEMPHIS.
16. The remission of the contributions of corn and money due to the King from the temples, and of the tax on byssus.
17. The remission of the tax of one *artaba* per *arura* of land, and one jar of wine per *arura* of vineyard.
18. The endowment of the temples of APIS and MNEVIS and the other sacred animals, and payment of all charges connected with their burials, and the maintenance of their cults.
19. The maintenance of cults of the gods throughout Upper and Lower Egypt.

Having summarized the King's religious and patriotic benefactions, the priests go on to point out that in return for all these noble deeds the gods and goddesses have given to the king power and victory, life and health and strength, and good things of every kind, and that they have, moreover, established his throne, and secured the possession of it by his posterity. The priests also recognized that it was their duty to mark their sense of gratitude to the king for the benefits which they and their temples had received in some unmistakeable way, and they therefore decreed that—

1. Additional honours should be paid to PTOLEMY V EPIPHANES and his ancestors.
2. A statue of PTOLEMY V as the " Avenger of Egypt " should be set up side by side with a statue of the chief local god in the most prominent place in every temple in EGYPT.
3. Worship of these statues should be performed thrice daily, and every ceremony which would gratify their KAU (*i.e.* Doubles) should be performed with the same care and attention to ancient use as was shown to the great gods of the country.

4. A wooden figure of the king, in a gilded shrine, should be set up in every temple, side by side with the statues and shrines of the other gods.
5. Both the figures of the king, and their shrines, should be carried out with the figure and shrines of the other gods on the holy days when sacred processions were made.
6. Each shrine should be decorated in an unusual manner, and with a series of crowns arranged in such a way that the shrine of PTOLEMY V should be the most prominent in every group of shrines in every temple.
7. The birthday of PTOLEMY V and the day of his accession to the throne should be observed monthly as days of festival.
8. The first five days of the month of THOTH should be observed as a festival, during which the people should wear garlands.
9. The title "Priest of the god Epiphanes Eucharistus" should be added to the other titles of the priests, and should be inscribed on the ring of each priest.
10. Private persons should be permitted to associate themselves with the priests in paying honours to PTOLEMY V.

11. The Decree should be inscribed in the old hieroglyphic character, in Demotic, and in Greek on a slab of hard, black basalt, and a copy of it, inscribed on hard stone, should be set up side by side with the image of the king in every temple of the first, second, and third class in EGYPT.

How far the priests gave effect to their Decree is not known. If they took care that a hard stone tablet inscribed with the Decree in Greek, Demotic, and hieroglyphs was set up in all the temples of the first, second, and third orders in UPPER EGYPT and LOWER EGYPT, a very considerable number of copies would have to be made. But it is very doubtful if their decision was carried into effect literally, for the only two complete copies of the Decree inscribed on stelae known to us are those of ROSETTA and AN-NOBAIRAH. No copy of the Decree has been found at THEBES or ABYDOS, or even at MEMPHIS, and it seems as if the priests contented themselves with setting up copies of it in the towns of the DELTA, which lay at no great distance from ALEXANDRIA, the seat of the Government of the PTOLEMIES. The copy cut on the walls of the temple at PHILAE (**Plate II**) was mutilated by a successor of PTOLEMY V, who paid scant respect to the fame of his predecessor, and was chiefly concerned with glorifying himself.

THE DECREE CONFERRING ADDITIONAL HONOURS ON PTOLEMY V EPIPHANES (B.C. 203–181) WHICH WAS PASSED BY THE PRIESTHOOD OF ALL EGYPT ASSEMBLED AT MEMPHIS ON THE EIGHTEENTH DAY OF THE MONTH MECHIR, IN THE NINTH YEAR OF THE REIGN OF THE KING

CHAPTER II

I.—EARLY PUBLICATIONS OF THE ORIGINAL GREEK TEXT OF THE DECREE ON THE ROSETTA STONE

Half a century ago several distinguished Egyptologists thought that the bilingual Decree inscribed on the ROSETTA STONE was drafted by the priests, assembled at Memphis in the year B.C. 197–196, in Demotic, and that the Greek text was merely a translation of it. This view seemed reasonable enough at that time, for few Egyptologists then possessed a competent knowledge of Demotic. But the studies made by Demotologists during the last twenty years have proved that the original draft of the Decree was written in Greek, and that the Demotic text on the Stone is a translation made from the Greek, which it does not always represent accurately.

The first facsimile of the texts on the Stone was made by the French lithographers, who were sent to Cairo from France specially for this purpose, and they took their facsimiles back to Paris with them. The earliest published facsimiles of the Stone will be found in *Vetusta Monumenta*, vol. iv, plates VIII and IX (published by the Society of Antiquaries of London); *Description de l'Égypte,* tome v, plates V, VI and VII; and LEPSIUS, *Auswahl,* plates XVIII and XIX. Among the early editions of the Greek text which were published with elaborate commentaries and translations, may be mentioned those of "Citoyen AMEILHON" (in Latin and French, Paris, *Floréal,* an XI (1803), 4to, Imprimé par Baudouin); DUANE, *Coins of the Seleucidae,* London, 1803; C. G. HEYNE (in *Comment. Soc. R. Sc. Gött.,* tome xv, pp. 260–80), Göttingen, 1804; W. DRUMANN, *Inschrift von Rosetta,* Königsberg, 1923; LETRONNE and C. MÜLLER (in DIDOT'S *Fragmenta Hist. Graec.,* tome i, Appendix); LETRONNE, *Recueil,* Paris, 1842; BOECKH, *Corpus Inscriptionum Graecarum,* tome iii, Berlin, 1853, No. 4697. Recent editions of the Greek text will be found in J. P. MAHAFFY, *The Empire of the Ptolemies,* p. 316 f.; M. R. STRACK, *Die Dynastie der Ptolemäer,* Berlin, 1897, p. 240 f.; and W. DITTENBERGER, *Orientis Graeci Inscriptiones Selectae,* 2 vols., Leipzig, 1903.

The earliest ENGLISH TRANSLATION of the Greek text was made by PLUMPTRE (Prebendary of Gloucester), and was published in the *Gentleman's Magazine,* 1802, vol. 72, p. 1106 f. Later translations are those of DUANE (*Coins of the Seleucidae,* London, 1803, p. 190 f.); PORSON, published by E. D. CLARKE in *Greek Marbles,* p. 58; S. BIRCH (in ARUNDALE and BONOMI'S *Gallery of Antiquities*, p. 114 f., and in *Records of the Past*, London, 1825, vol. iv, p. 71 f.); MAHAFFY (in *Empire of the Ptolemies*, pp. 316–27, and *The Ptolemaïc Dynasty*, p. 152 f.); and E. BEVAN, *A History of Egypt under the Ptolemaïc Dynasty*, London, 1827, p. 263 f. The earliest FRENCH TRANSLATION published was that of AMEILHON, *Éclaircissements*, Paris, 1803, pp. 108–16. The translation made by M. DU THEIL before this date was never published. LETRONNE made a French translation for the use of CHAMPOLLION LE JEUNE, and it was published in DIDOT'S *Fragmenta Hist. Graec.*, vol. i, Paris, 1841. Good LATIN TRANSLATIONS are those of AMEILHON (1803), C. G. HEYNE (1804), and J. BAILEY (1816). The GERMAN TRANSLATION made by W. DRUMANN was published in 1822–4, and was a good piece of work. An ITALIAN TRANSLATION by F. RICARDI appeared at Genoa in 1833.

II.—ENGLISH RENDERING OF THE GREEK TEXT ON THE ROSETTA STONE

[THE DATING OF THE DECREE]

1 In the reign of the YOUNG [GOD], who hath received the sovereignty from his father, the Lord of Crowns, who is exceedingly glorious, who hath stablished EGYPT firmly, who holdeth

2 in reverence the gods, who hath gained the mastery over his enemies, who hath made the life of man to follow its normal course, lord of the Thirty-year Festivals,[1] like HEPHAISTOS[2] THE GREAT, a King, like HELIOS,[3]

3 great king of the UPPER COUNTRY[4] and of the LOWER COUNTRY,[5] offspring of the gods PHILOPATORES,[6] whom HEPHAISTOS hath chosen,[7] to whom HELIOS hath given the victory, the Living Image[8] of ZEUS,[9] the son of HELIOS (RĀ), PTOLEMY,

[1] *I.e.* the Seṭ Festivals. The Seṭ Festival, , or "Festival of the Tail," was celebrated by the king every 30 years, or after any great event, however frequent, or whenever he wished to obtain a renewal of his life from the gods.

[2] *I.e.* PTAḤ, , the great handicraftsman-god of Memphis. PTAḤ like IEMHETEP, the god of medicine, also of Memphis, was originally a deified citizen of Memphis.

[3] *I.e.* the Sun-god RĀ, 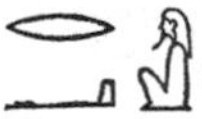, *par excellence* of Heliopolis.

[4] *I.e.* all Egypt south of Memphis.

[5] *I.e.* the Delta.

[6] In Egyptian, .

[7] The Kings of Egypt were selected or chosen by RĀ, or ÅMEN, or PTAḤ; the candidate for the throne was introduced into the shrine of the god, and the hand of the god stretched itself out and rested on the god's chosen one.

[8] In Egyptian, *Sekhem ānkh,* .

[9] The equivalent of the Egyptian god ÅMEN, 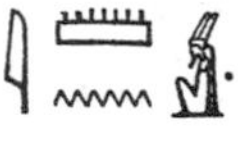.

PLATE III.

Crowning the Athlophoros. (From a Roman terra-cotta relief in the British Museum.)
(See the translation of the Greek text, line 5 (p. 53).)

PLATE IV.

Canephoros, or Priestess of Demeter, bearing on her head a basket for the fruits of the earth. (From a statue in the British Museum.) (See the translation of the Greek text, line 5 (p. 51).)

4 the everliving, the beloved of PTAḤ.

In the IXth year, when AETOS, the son of AETOS, was priest of ALEXANDER, and of the gods SOTERES,[1] and of the gods ADELPHOI,[2] and of the gods EUERGETES,[3] and of the gods PHILOPATORES, and

5 the God EPIPHANES[4] EUCHARISTOS[5]; PYRRHA, daughter of PHILINOS, being the Athlophoros[6] **(Plate III)** of BERENIKE EUERGETES, and AREIA, daughter of DIOGENES, the Kanephoros[7] **(Plate IV)** of ARSINOË PHILADELPHOS, and EIRENE,

6 the daughter of PTOLEMY, being priestess of ARSINOË PHILOPATOR; the IVth day of the month XANDIKOS,[8] which corresponds to the XVIIIth day of the Egyptian month of MEKHEIR, the second month of the season PERT, 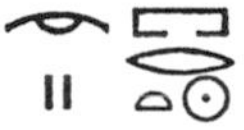.

[1] In Egyptian, .

[2] In Egyptian, .

[3] In Egyptian, .

[4] In Egyptian, , P-NETER-PERI, *i.e.* the "god who cometh forth" [like the Sun-god RĀ ?].

[5] The hieroglyphic version has no equivalent for this title: it is a translation from the Demotic words.

[6] *I.e.* bearer of the gift of victory.

[7] The priestess of Demeter.

[8] The Macedonian month of April.

[Introduction to the Decree]

The High-priests, and the Prophets, and those who go into the shrine to dress
7 the gods, and the Bearers of Feathers, and the sacred Scribes, and all the other priests who have gathered themselves together from the temples throughout the country before the king in Memphis, for the commemorative festival of the reception of the
8 kingdom, by Ptolemy, the everliving, the beloved of Ptaḥ, the god Epiphanes Eucharistos,[1] which he received from his father, being assembled in the temple of [Ptaḥ] in Memphis, on this day, declared [thus] :—

[Ptolemy V as benefactor of the temples of Egypt]

9 (1) "Inasmuch as King Ptolemy, the "everliving, the beloved of Ptaḥ, the "God Epiphanes Eucharistos, the off- "spring of King Ptolemy (IV) and Queen "Arsinoë, the Gods Philopatores, hath "given many benefactions, both to the "temples, and
10 "to those that dwell therein, and to all those "who are subject to his dominion, being a

[1] An Egyptian equivalent is perhaps *neb neferu*, , "lord of beneficent actions."

" God born of a god and goddess—even like
" HORUS, the son of ISIS and OSIRIS, who
" avenged his father OSIRIS— ;

11 (2) " and towards the gods
" being full of benevolent piety, hath dedicated
" to the temples revenues in money and in
" grain ;

(3) " and hath incurred great expenses in
" order that he might bring EGYPT into a
" state of prosperity, and might establish the
" temples ;

12 (4) " and hath given away freely of all the
" moneys which were his own ;

(5) " and of the taxes and dues which come
" to him from EGYPT, some he hath finally
" remitted, and others he hath reduced, so
" that the people (*i.e.* the native EGYPTIANS)
" and all the others (*i.e.* foreigners domiciled
" in the country)
13 " might be prosperous during his reign ;

(6) " and hath remitted to the natives of
" EGYPT and to all the other people [domiciled]
" in his kingdom, the debts which were due to
" the royal treasury and which were indeed
" very many in number ;

(7) " and hath set free from the charges
" against them those who were in the prisons,
14 " and who had been there for a long time
" because of the [non-settlement of their
" cases].

[PTOLEMY V CONFIRMS THE REVENUES OF THE TEMPLES, AND RESTORES THEIR FORMER REVENUES]

(8) "and hath ordered that the revenues of
" the temples, and the grants which are made
" to them annually, both in respect of grain
15 " and money, and also the proper portion
" [which is assigned to the gods from the vine-
" yards, and from the gardens, and the other
" possessions of the gods, should, as they were
" in the reign of his father,
16 " remain the same;

(9) "and in respect of the priests also, he " hath also commanded that they should pay " no more as their fee for consecration, than " what they had been [formerly] assessed in " the time of his father and up to the first year " [of his reign].

[ABOLITION OF THE PRIEST'S ANNUAL JOURNEY TO ALEXANDRIA AND REDUCTION OF THE TARIFF]

(10) " And further he hath released
17 " members of the priestly class [from the
" obligation] to sail down [the NILE] annually
" to ALEXANDRIA.

(11) " And he hath likewise commanded that " men shall no longer be seized by force [for " service] in the Navy;

(12) " and of the tax upon cloth of byssus
" which is paid to the royal treasury by the
" temples
18 " he hath remitted two-thirds.

[THE RESTORATION OF PEACE IN THE COUNTRY AND THE GRANTING OF AN AMNESTY]

(13) " and whatsoever things had been
" neglected in times past he hath restored,
" and set in the order in which they should
" be ;

(14) " and he hath taken care that the
" ceremonial obligations to the Gods should
" be
19 " rightly performed ;

(15) " and moreover, he hath administered
" justice unto every man, even like HERMES,[1]
" the Great Great ;

(16) " and he hath further ordered that those
" of the soldiers who returned, and of the
" others
20 " who had held rebellious opinions in the
" troubled times, should, having come back,
" be allowed to keep possession of their own
" property.

[1] The equivalent of the Egyptian god THOTH, , who in hieroglyphic texts is called " twice great," , and " thrice great," .

[Ptolemy V protects Egypt from enemies from without]

(17) "And he hath made provision that
"forces of cavalry and infantry, and ships also,
"should be despatched against those who were
"about to invade
21 "Egypt, both by sea and by land, [thus]
"incurring great expenditure in money and
"grain, so that the temples and all who were
"in the country might be in a state of security.

[Ptolemy V punishes the rebels of Lycopolis]

(18) "And having gone
22 "to Lycopolis,[1] which is in the Busirite nome,
"which had been occupied and fortified against
"a siege with an arsenal well stocked with
"weapons of war and supplies of every kind—
"now of long standing
23 "was the disaffection of the impious men who
"were gathered together in it, and who had
"done much injury to the temples, and to all
"those who dwelt in Egypt—and having
"encamped
24 "against them, he surrounded it with mounds,
"and trenches, and marvellous engines; and
"when the Nile made a great rise (*i.e.*
"inundation) in the VIIIth year, and being
"about, as usual, to flood out

[1] The ΚΟΥΝΟΥ (Cuno) which Strabo and Pliny join to Busiris; it lay between Thmuis and Tawa.

25 "the plains, he (*i.e.* the King) held [the river]
"in check, having dammed up in many places
"the mouths of the canals, and in carrying
"out this work spent no small sum of money;
"and having stationed cavalry and infantry to
"guard [the dams]
26 "he took by storm the city in a very short
"time, and destroyed all the impious men who
"were therein, even as HERMES (THOTH), and
"HORUS, the son of ISIS and OSIRIS, in those
"very same places, reduced to subjection
27 "those who had rebelled.

[PUNISHMENT OF THE LEADERS OF THE REVOLT AGAINST PTOLEMY IV PHILOPATOR]

"And the men who had led astray the
"rebels in the time of his father, and had stirred
"up revolt in the country, and had committed
"sacrilege in the temples, having come into
"MEMPHIS for the purpose of avenging
28 "his father and his own sovereignty, he
"punished according to their deserts at the
"time when he came there to perform the
"duly appointed ceremonies for his reception
"of the crown.

[REMISSION OF ARREARS OF TAXES AND CONTRIBUTIONS FROM THE TEMPLES]

(19) "And moreover he hath remitted to
29 "the temples that which was due to the royal
"treasury up to the VIIIth year of his reign,

" which was no small amount of corn and
" money ;

(20) " and moreover, he hath remitted the
" dues upon byssus cloth which had not been
" paid into the royal treasury,
30 " and also the charges made for the examina-
" tion (?) of those which had been sent in
" during that same period ;

(21) " and he hath also freed the temples
" from [the tax of] one *artaba* for each *arura* of
" land [held by the temples], and also [the tax
" of] one jar of wine
31 " for each *arura* of vineyards.

[PTOLEMY V PROVIDES FOR THE SACRED ANIMALS, AND THE WORSHIP OF THE GODS ; HIS REWARD FOR THE SAME]

(22) " And to [the Bull] APIS, and to [the
" Bull] MNEVIS he hath given many gifts, and
" to the other sacred animals in EGYPT, far
" more indeed than the kings who were before
" him, and he was careful in respect of what
" belonged to them in
32 " every matter whatsoever, and for their
" burials he gave all that was needed with
" splendid generosity, and that which was
" necessary for private shrines, and for sacri-
" fices, and for commemorative feasts, and for
" the ordinances as by law (or, custom) pre-
" scribed ;

33 (23) " and the honourable estate of the
" temples and of EGYPT he hath maintained in
" a fitting manner, according to traditional
" custom;

(24) " and he hath decorated the Temple of
" APIS with fine work, expending upon it gold,
" and silver, and
34 " precious stones in no small quantities;

(25) " and he hath founded (refounded ?)
" temples, and shrines, and altars, and hath
" restored those which needed repairs, having
" the zeal of a beneficent god in matters which
" relate to
35 " divine service, and having discovered which
" of the temples were most held in honour, he
" hath restored the same during his reign, as
" was meet.

" In return for all these things the gods have
" given him health, and victory, and power,
" and all other good things, and his
36 " sovereignty shall remain with him, and with
" his children for all time.

[THE PRIESTS DECREE ADDITIONAL HONOURS FOR PTOLEMY V AND HIS ANCESTORS]

" WITH THE FORTUNE (OR LUCK) WHICH FAVOURETH.

" It hath seemed good to the priests of all
" the temples in the land, that the honours
" which have been bestowed upon

37 " King PTOLEMY, the everliving, the beloved
" of PTAḤ, the God EPIPHANES EUCHARISTOS,
" and likewise those of his parents, the Gods
" PHILOPATORES, and those of his ancestors,
" the Gods EUERGETES, and
38 " the Gods ADELPHOI, and the Gods SOTERES,
" should be greatly added to [viz.] :—

[STATUES OF PTOLEMY V AND THE LOCAL CHIEF GODS ARE TO BE SET UP IN ALL THE TEMPLES]

(1) " To set up to the God PTOLEMY, the
" everliving, the God EPIPHANES EUCHARISTOS,
" an image in the most prominent part of every
" temple,
39 " which shall be called (inscribed ?) ' PTOLEMY,
" THE AVENGER OF EGYPT.' And close by this
" image shall stand [an image of] the chief god
" of the temple presenting to him the weapon
" of victory, which shall be constructed after
" the Egyptian
40 " fashion.[1] And the priests shall do homage
" to the[se] image[s] three times each day. And
" they shall array them in sacred apparel, and
" they shall perform [for them] ceremonies
" similar to those which they are wont to
" perform for the other gods during the
" festivals which are celebrated throughout
" the country.

[1] In Egypt the gods gave to the kings a sword or scimitar of victory shaped thus, .

[A WOODEN STATUE OF PTOLEMY V IN A GOLDEN SHRINE IS TO BE SET UP IN THE TEMPLES]

41 (2) "And they shall set up for King "PTOLEMY, the God EPIPHANES EUCHARISTOS, "the offspring of King PTOLEMY (IV) and "Queen ARSINOË, the Gods PHILOPATORES, a "statue and a golden shrine in each of the "temples,

42 "and they shall place it in the inner chambers "[of the sanctuary] with the other shrines. "And during the great commemorative fes-"tivals, wherein the shrines go forth [in pro-"cessions], the shrine of the God EPIPHANES "EUCHARISTOS shall

43 "go forth with them. And in order that the "shrine may be readily distinguished now and "in after time, it shall be surmounted by the "ten golden crowns of the King, and an asp "(*i.e.* cobra) shall be affixed thereto, even as "there is on all the other

44 "crowns with asps which are on other shrines, "but in the centre of them shall be [placed] "the crown which is called PSCHENT, which he "(*i.e.* the King) put on when he went into the "Temple [of PTAḤ] in MEMPHIS to perform "therein

45 "the prescribed ceremonies connected with "[his] assumption of sovereignty. And there "shall be placed on the [faces of the] square

" [cornice ?] which is round about the crowns,
" side by side with the above-mentioned
" crown

46 " [PSKHENT] ten golden phylacteries (*i.e.* scrolls
" or tablets ?) which shall bear the inscription
" 'This is [the shrine] of the KING who maketh
" manifest the UPPER COUNTRY and the LOWER
" COUNTRY.'

[SPECIAL FESTIVALS ARE TO BE ESTABLISHED IN HONOUR OF PTOLEMY V]

" And inasmuch as the XXXth day of the
" month of Mesore,[1] whereon the birthday of
" the KING is celebrated, and likewise the
" XVIIth day of the

47 " month of PAOPHI, whereon he received the
" sovereignty from his father, have been
" recognized as name-days in the temples, for
" they were the sources of many benefits for
" all people, on these days a festival and a
" panegyry shall be celebrated in the temples
" of

48 " EGYPT each month, and sacrifices and liba-
" tions, and all the other rites and ceremonies
" which are prescribed shall be duly performed

49 " as on other festivals. [Here a few words are
" wanting.]

[1] The Stele of Damanhur has , " fourth month of the season Shemu."

(3) "And a festival and a panegyry shall
" be celebrated yearly for King Ptolemy, the
" everliving, the beloved of Ptaḥ, the God
" Epiphanes Eucharistos, in all the temples
" throughout the
50 " country, from the first day of the month of
" Thoth, for five days. And they shall wear
" crowns (*i.e.* garlands), and shall offer up
" sacrifices and make libations, and do every-
" thing which it is customary to do.

[The priests of Ptolemy V shall assume a new title]

51 (4) "And the priests of the other gods shall
" adopt the name of 'Priests of the God
" 'Epiphanes Eucharistos,' in addition to the
" names of the other gods to whom they
" minister.

(5) "And in all the decrees and [ordinances]
" promulgated by them shall be mentioned
52 " his order of priests.

[Private individuals may participate in paying these honours to Ptolemy V]

(6) "And members of the laity shall be per-
" mitted to celebrate the festival, and to set up
" and maintain in their houses shrines similar
" to the aforesaid shrine, and to perform the
" ceremonies which are prescribed for the
" festivals, both monthly

53 " and annually, in order that it may be well
" known that in EGYPT men magnify and
" honour the God EPIPHANES EUCHARISTOS,
" the King, as they are bound to do by law.

[THE PROMULGATION OF THE DECREE]

(7) " And this Decree shall be inscribed upon
" stelae
54 " of hard stone, in holy, and in native, and in
" Greek letters, and [a stela] shall be set up
" in each of the temples of the first, second, and
" third [class] near the image of the everliving
" KING."

III.—GREEK TEXT OF THE DECREE OF THE PRIESTS ON THE ROSETTA STONE

1 ΒΑΣΙΛΕΥΟΝΤΟΣ ΤΟΥ ΝΕΟΥ ΚΑΙ ΠΑΡΑΛΑΒΟΝΤΟΣ ΤΗΝ ΒΑΣΙΛΕΙΑΝ ΠΑΡΑ ΤΟΥ ΠΑΤΡΟΣ ΚΥΡΙΟΥ ΒΑΣΙΛΕΙΩΝ ΜΕΓΑΛΟΔΟΞΟΥ, ΤΟΥ ΤΗΝ ΑΙΓΥΠΤΟΝ ΚΑΤΑΣΤΗΣΑΜΕΝΟΥ ΚΑΙ ΤΑ ΠΡΟΣ ΤΟΥΣ

2 ΘΕΟΥΣ ΕΥΣΕΒΟΥΣ, ΑΝΤΙΠΑΛΩΝ ΥΠΕΡΤΕΡΟΥ, ΤΟΥ ΤΟΝ ΒΙΟΝ ΤΩΝ ΑΝΘΡΩΠΩΝ ΕΠΑΝΟΡΘΩΣΑΝΤΟΣ, ΚΥΡΙΟΥ ΤΡΙΑΚΟΝΤΑΕΤΗΡΙΔΩΝ, ΚΑΘΑΠΕΡ Ο ΗΦΑΙΣΤΟΣ Ο ΜΕΓΑΣ, ΒΑΣΙΛΕΩΣ ΚΑΘΑΠΕΡ Ο ΗΛΙΟΣ,

3 ΜΕΓΑΣ ΒΑΣΙΛΕΥΣ ΤΩΝ ΤΕ ΑΝΩ ΚΑΙ ΤΩΝ ΚΑΤΩ ΧΩΡΩΝ, ΕΚΓΟΝΟΥ ΘΕΩΝ ΦΙΛΟΠΑΤΟΡΩΝ, ΟΝ Ο ΗΦΑΙΣΤΟΣ ΕΔΟΚΙΜΑΣΕΝ ΩΙ Ο ΗΛΙΟΣ ΕΔΩΚΕΝ ΤΗΝ ΝΙΚΗΝ, ΕΙΚΟΝΟΣ ΖΩΣΗΣ ΤΟΥ ΔΙΟΣ, ΥΙΟΥ ΤΟΥ ΗΛΙΟΥ, ΠΤΟΛΕΜΑΙΟΥ

4 ΑΙΩΝΟΒΙΟΥ, ΗΓΑΠΗΜΕΝΟΥ ΥΠΟ ΤΟΥ ΦΘΑ,
ΕΤΟΥΣ ΕΝΑΤΟΥ ΕΦ ΙΕΡΕΩΣ ΑΕΤΟΥ ΤΟΥ
ΑΕΤΟΥ ΑΛΕΞΑΝΔΡΟΥ ΚΑΙ ΘΕΩΝ ΣΩΤΗΡΩΝ
ΚΑΙ ΘΕΩΝ ΑΔΕΛΦΩΝ ΚΑΙ ΘΕΩΝ ΕΥΕΡΓΕΤΩΝ
ΚΑΙ ΘΕΩΝ ΦΙΛΟΠΑΤΟΡΩΝ ΚΑΙ

5 ΘΕΩΝ ΕΠΙΦΑΝΟΥΣ ΕΥΧΑΡΙΣΤΟΥ, ΑΘΛΟΦΟ-
ΡΟΥ ΒΕΡΕΝΙΚΗΣ ΕΥΕΡΓΕΤΙΔΟΣ ΠΥΡΡΑΣ
ΤΗΣ ΦΙΛΙΝΟΥ, ΚΑΝΗΦΟΡΟΥ ΑΡΣΙΝΟΗΣ
ΦΙΛΑΔΕΛΦΟΥ ΑΡΕΙΑΣ ΤΗΣ ΔΙΟΓΕΝΟΥΣ,
ΙΕΡΕΙΛΣ ΑΡΣΙΝΟΗΣ ΦΙΛΟΠΑΤΟΡΟΣ ΕΙΡΗ-
ΝΗΣ

6 ΤΗΣ ΠΤΟΛΕΜΑΙΟΥ, ΜΗΝΟΣ ΞΑΝΔΙΚΟΥ
ΤΕΤΡΑΔΙ, ΑΙΓΥΠΤΙΩΝ ΑΕ ΜΕΧΕΙΡ ΟΚΤΩΚΑΙ-
ΔΕΚΑΤΗΙ, ΨΗΦΙΣΜΑ· ΟΙ ΑΡΧΙΕΡΕΙΣ ΚΑΙ
ΠΡΟΦΗΤΑΙ ΚΑΙ ΟΙ ΕΙΣ ΤΟ ΑΔΥΤΟΝ
ΕΙ[Σ] ΠΟΡΕΥΟΜΕΝΟΙ ΠΡΟΣ ΤΟΝ ΣΤΟΛΙΣ-
ΜΟΝ ΤΩΝ

7 ΘΕΩΝ ΚΑΙ ΠΤΕΡΟΦΟΡΑΙ ΚΑΙ ΙΕΡΟΓΡΑΜΜΑ-
ΤΕΙΣ ΚΑΙ ΟΙ ΑΛΛΟΙ ΙΕΡΕΙΣ ΠΑΝΤΕΣ ΟΙ
ΑΠΑΝΤΗΣΑΝΤΕΣ ΕΚ ΤΩΝ ΚΑΤΑ ΤΗΝ
ΧΩΡΑΝ ΙΕΡΩΝ ΕΙΣ ΜΕΜΦΙΝ ΤΩΙ ΒΑΣΙΛΕΙ
ΠΡΟΣ ΤΗΝ ΠΑΝΗΓΥΡΙΝ ΤΗΣ ΠΑΡΑ-
ΛΗΨΕΩΣ ΤΗΣ

8 ΒΑΣΙΛΕΙΑΣ ΤΗΣ ΠΤΟΛΕΜΑΙΟΥ ΑΙΩΝΟΒΙΟΥ,
ΗΓΑΠΗΜΕΝΟΥ ΥΠΟ ΤΟΥ ΦΘΑ, ΘΕΟΥ
ΕΠΙΦΑΝΟΥΣ, ΕΥΧΑΡΙΣΤΟΥ, ΗΝ ΠΑΡΕΛΑΒΕΝ
ΠΑΡΑ ΤΟΥ ΠΑΤΡΟΣ ΑΥΤΟΥ, ΣΥΝΑΧΘΕΝΤΕΣ
ΕΝ ΤΩΙ ΕΝ ΜΕΜΦΕ[Ι] [Ι]ΕΡΩΙ ΤΗΙ ΗΜΕΡΑΙ
ΤΑΥΤΗΙ ΕΙΠΑΝ·

9 ΕΠΕΙΔΗ ΒΑΣΙΛΕΥΣ ΠΤΟΛΕΜΑΙΟΣ ΑΙΩΝ-
ΒΙΟΣ, ΗΓΑΠΗΜΕΝΟΣ ΥΠΟ ΤΟΥ ΦΘΑ, ΘΕΟΣ
ΕΠΙΦΑΝΗΣ ΕΥΧΑΡΙΣΤΟΣ, Ο ΕΓ ΒΑΣΙΛΕΩΣ
ΠΤΟΛΕΜΑΙΟΥ ΚΑΙ ΒΑΣΙΛΙΣΣΗΣ ΑΡΣΙΝΟΗΣ,
ΘΕΩΝ ΦΙΛΟΠΑΤΟΡΩΝ, ΚΑΤΑ ΠΟΛΛΑ ΕΥΕΡ-
ΓΕΤΗΚΕΝ ΤΑ Θ ΙΕΡΑ ΚΑΙ

10 ΤΟΥΣ ΕΝ ΑΥΤΟΙΣ ΟΝΤΑΣ ΚΑΙ ΤΟΥΣ ΥΠΟ
ΤΗΝ ΕΑΥΤΟΥ ΒΑΣΙΛΕΙΑΝ ΤΑΣΣΟΜΕΝΟΥΣ
ΑΠΑΝΤΑΣ, ΥΠΑΡΧΩΝ ΘΕΟΣ ΕΚ ΘΕΟΥ ΚΑΙ
ΘΕΑΣ ΚΑΘΑΠΕΡ ΩΡΟΣ Ο ΤΗΣ ΙΣΙΟΣ ΚΑΙ
ΟΣΙΡΙΟΣ ΥΙΟΣ, Ο ΕΠΑΜΥΝΑΣ ΤΩΙ ΠΑΤΡΙ
ΑΥΤΟΥ ΟΣΙΡΕΙ, ΤΑ ΠΡΟΣ ΘΕΟΥΣ

11 ΕΥΕΡΓΕΤΙΚΩΣ ΔΙΑΚΕΙΜΕΝΟΣ ΑΝΑΤΕΘΕΙΚΕΝ
ΕΙΣ ΤΑ ΙΕΡΑ ΑΡΓΥΡΙΚΑΣ ΤΕ ΚΑΙ ΣΙΤΙ[Κ]ΑΣ
ΠΡΟΣΟΔΟΥΣ, ΚΑΙ ΔΑΠΑΝΑΣ ΠΟΛΛΑΣ
ΥΠΟΜΕΜΕΝΗΚΕΝ ΕΝΕΚΑ ΤΟΥ ΤΗΝ ΑΙΓΥ-
ΠΤΟΝ ΕΙΣ ΕΥΔΙΑΝ ΑΓΑΓΕΙΝ ΚΑΙ ΤΑ ΙΕΡΑ
ΚΑΤΑΣΤΗΣΑΣΘΑΙ

12 ΤΑΙΣ ΤΕ ΕΑΥΤΟΥ ΔΥΝΑΜΕΣΙΝ ΠΕΦΙΛΑΝ-
ΘΡΩΠΗΚΕ ΠΑΣΑΙΣ ΚΑΙ ΑΠΟ ΤΩΝ ΥΠΑΡ-
ΧΟΥΣΩΝ ΕΝ ΑΙΓΥΠΤΩΙ ΠΡΟΣΟΔΩΝ ΚΑΙ
ΦΟΡΟΛΟΓΙΩΝ ΤΙΝΑΣ ΜΕΝ ΕΙΣ ΤΕΛΟΣ
ΑΦΗΚΕΝ, ΑΛΛΑΣ ΔΕ ΚΕΚΟΥΦΙΚΕΝ, ΟΠΩΣ
Ο ΤΕ ΛΑΟΣ ΚΑΙ ΟΙ ΑΛΛΟΙ ΠΑΝΤΕΣ ΕΝ

13 ΕΥΘΗΝΙΑΙ ΩΣΙΝ ΕΠΙ ΤΗΣ ΕΑΥΤΟΥ ΒΑΣΙ-
ΛΕΙΑΣ, ΤΑ ΤΕ ΒΑΣΙΛΙΚΑ ΟΦΕΙΛΗΜΑΤΑ,
Α ΠΡΟΣΩΦΕΙΛΟΝ ΟΙ ΕΝ ΑΙΓΥΠΤΩΙ ΚΑΙ ΟΙ
ΕΝ ΤΗΙ ΛΟΙΠΗΙ ΒΑΣΙΛΕΙΑΙ ΑΥΤΟΥ, ΟΝΤΑ
ΠΟΛΛΑ ΤΩΙ ΠΛΗΘΕΙ, ΑΦΗΚΕΝ, ΚΑΙ ΤΟΥΣ
ΕΝ ΤΑΙΣ ΦΥΛΑΚΑΙΣ

14 ΑΠΗΓΜΕΝΟΥΣ ΚΑΙ ΤΟΥΣ ΕΝ ΑΙΤΙΑΙΣ ΟΝ-
ΤΑΣ ΕΚ ΠΟΛΛΟΥ ΧΡΟΝΟΥ ΑΠΕΛΕΥΣΕ ΤΩΝ
ΕΝΚΕΚΛ[Η]ΜΕΝΩΝ· ΠΡΟΣΕΤΑΞΕ ΔΕ ΚΑΙ
ΤΑΣ ΠΡΟΣΟΔΟΥΣ ΤΩΝ ΙΕΡΩΝ ΚΑΙ ΤΑΣ
ΔΙΔΟΜΕΝΑΣ ΕΙΣ ΑΥΤΑ ΚΑΤ ΕΝΙΑΥΤΟΝ
ΣΥΝΤΑΞΕΙΣ ΣΙΤΙ—

15 ΚΑΣ ΤΕ ΚΑΙ ΑΡΓΥΡΙΚΑΣ, ΟΜΟΙΩΣ ΔΕ ΚΑΙ
ΤΑΣ ΚΑΘΗΚΟΥΣΑΣ ΑΠΟΜΟΙΡΑΣ ΤΟΙΣ
ΘΕΟΙΣ ΑΠΟ ΤΕ ΤΗΣ ΑΜΠΕΛΙΤΙΔΟΣ ΓΗΣ
ΚΑΙ ΤΩΝ ΠΑΡΑΔΕΙΣΩΝ ΚΑΙ ΤΩΝ ΑΛΛΩΝ

ΤΩΝ ΥΠΑΡΞΑΝΤΩΝ ΤΟΙΣ ΘΕΟΙΣ ΕΠΙ ΤΟΥ
ΠΑΤΡΟΣ ΑΥΤΟΥ
16 ΜΕΝΕΙΝ ΕΠΙ ΧΩΡΑΣ· ΠΡΟΣΕΤΑΞΕΝ ΔΕ ΚΑΙ
ΠΕΡΙ ΤΩΝ ΙΕΡΕΩΝ ΟΠΩΣ ΜΗΘΕΝ ΠΛΕΙΟΝ
ΔΙΔΩΣΙΝ ΕΙΣ ΤΟ ΤΕΛΕΣΤΙΚΟΝ ΟΥ ΕΤΑΣ-
ΣΟΝΤΟ ΕΩΣ ΤΟΥ ΠΡΩΤΟΥ ΕΤΟΥΣ ΕΠΙ
ΤΟΥ ΠΑΤΡΟΣ ΑΥΤΟΥ· ΑΠΕΛΥΣΕΝ ΔΕ ΚΑΙ
ΤΟΥΣ ΕΚ ΤΩΝ
17 ΙΕΡΩΝ ΕΘΝΩΝ ΤΟΥ ΚΑΤ ΕΝΙΑΥΤΟΝ ΕΙΣ
ΑΛΕΞΑΝΔΡΕΙΑΝ ΚΑΤΑΠΛΟΥ· ΠΡΟΣΕΤΑΞΕΝ
ΔΕ ΚΑΙ ΤΗΝ ΣΥΛΛΗΨΙΝ ΤΩΝ ΕΙΣ ΤΗΝ ΝΑΥ-
ΤΕΙΑΝ ΜΗ ΠΟΙΕΙΣΘΑΙ, ΤΩΝ Τ ΕΙΣ ΤΟ ΒΑ-
ΣΙΛΙΚΟΝ ΣΥΝΤΕΛΟΥΜΕΝΩΝ ΕΝ ΤΟΙΣ
ΙΕΡΟΙΣ ΒΥΣΣΙΝΩΝ
18 ΟΘΟΝΙΩΝ ΑΠΕΛΥΣΕΝ ΤΑ ΔΥΟ ΜΕΡΗ, ΤΑ
ΤΕ ΕΓΛΕΛΕΙΜΜΕΝΑ ΠΑΝΤΑ ΕΝ ΤΟΙΣ ΠΡΟ-
ΤΕΡΟΝ ΧΡΟΝΟΙΣ ΑΠΟΚΑΤΕΣΤΗΣΕΝ ΕΙΣ
ΤΗΝ ΚΑΘΗΚΟΥΣΑΝ ΤΑΞΙΝ, ΦΡΟΝΤΙΖΩΝ
ΟΠΩΣ ΤΑ ΕΙΘΙΣΜΕΝΑ ΣΥΝΤΕΛΗΤΑΙ ΤΟΙ(Σ)
ΘΕΟΙΣ ΚΑΤΑ ΤΟ
19 ΠΡΟΣΗΚΟΝ· ΟΜΟΙΩΣ ΔΕ ΚΑΙ ΤΟ ΔΙΚΑΙΟΝ
ΠΑΣΙΝ ΑΠΕΝΕΙΜΕΝ, ΚΑΘΑΠΕΡ ΕΡΜΗΣ Ο
ΜΕΓΑΣ ΚΑΙ ΜΕΓΑΣ· ΠΡ(Ο)ΣΕΤΑΞΕΝ ΔΕ ΚΑΙ
ΤΟΥΣ ΚΑΤΑΠΟΡΕΥΟΜΕΝΟΥΣ ΕΚ ΤΕ ΤΩΝ
ΜΑΧΙΜΩΝ ΚΑΙ ΤΩΝ ΑΛΛΩΝ ΤΩΝ ΑΛΛΟΤΡΙΑ
20 ΦΡΟΝΗΣΑΝΤΩΝ ΕΝ ΤΟΙΣ ΚΑΤΑ ΤΗΝ ΤΑΡΑ-
ΧΗΝ ΚΑΙΡΟΙΣ ΚΑΤΕΛΘΟΝΤΑΣ ΜΕΝΕΙΝ ΕΠΙ
ΤΩΝ ΙΔΙΩΝ ΚΤΗΣΕΩΝ· ΠΡΟΕΝΟΗΘΗ ΔΕ
ΚΑΙ ΟΠΩΣ ΕΞΑΠΟΣΤΑΛΩΣΙΝ ΔΥΝΑΜΕΙΣ
ΙΠΠΙΚΑΙ ΤΕ ΚΑΙ ΠΕΖΙΚΑΙ ΚΑΙ ΝΗΕΣ ΕΠΙ
ΤΟΥΣ ΕΠΕΛΘΟΝΤΑΣ
21 ΕΠΙ ΤΗΝ ΑΙΓΥΠΤΟΝ ΚΑΤΑ ΤΕ ΤΗΝ ΘΑ-
ΛΑΣΣΑΝ ΚΑΙ ΤΗΝ ΗΠΕΙΡΟΝ, ΥΠΟΜΕΙΝΑΣ
ΔΑΠΑΝΑΣ ΑΡΓΥΡΙΚΑΣ ΤΕ ΚΑΙ ΣΙΤΙΚΑΣ

ΜΕΓΑΛΑΣ, ΟΠΩΣ ΤΑ Θ ΙΕΡΑ ΚΑΙ ΟΙ ΕΝ
ΑΥΤΗΙ ΠΑΝΤ[Ε]Σ ΕΝ ΑΣΦΑΛΕΙΑΙ ΩΣΙΝ·
ΠΑΡΑΓΙΝΟΜΕ—
22 ΝΟΣ ΔΕ ΚΑΙ ΕΙΣ ΛΥΚΩΝ ΠΟΛΙΝ ΤΗΝ ΕΝ
ΤΩΙ ΒΟΥΣΙΡΙΤΗΙ, Η ΗΝ ΚΑΤΕΙΛΗΜΜΕΝΗ
ΚΑΙ ΩΧΥΡΩΜΕΝΗ ΠΡΟΣ ΠΟΛΙΟΡΚΙΑΝ
ΟΠΛΩΝ ΤΕ ΠΑΡΑΘΕΣΕΙ ΔΑΨΙΛΕΣΤΕΡΑΙ
ΚΑΙ ΤΗΙ ΑΛΛΗΙ ΧΟΡΗ(ΓΙ)ΑΙ ΠΑΣΗΙ, ΩΣ ΑΝ
ΕΚ ΠΟΛΛΟΥ
23 Χ(Ρ)ΟΝΟΥ ΣΥΝΕΣΤΗΚΥΙΑΣ ΤΗΣ ΑΛΛΟΤΡΙΟ-
ΤΗΤΟΣ ΤΟΙΣ ΕΠΙΣΥΝΑΧΘΕΙΣΙΝ ΕΙΣ ΑΥΤΗΝ
ΑΣΕΒΕΣΙΝ, ΟΙ ΗΣΑΝ ΕΙΣ ΤΕ ΤΑ ΙΕΡΑ ΚΑΙ
ΤΟΥΣ ΕΝ ΑΙΓΥΠΤΩΙ ΚΑΤΟΙΚΟΥΝΤΑΣ ΠΟΛ-
ΛΑ ΚΑΚΑ ΣΥΝΤΕΤΕΛΕΣΜΕΝΟΙ, ΚΑΙ ΑΝ—
24 ΤΙΚΑΘΙΣΑΣ ΧΩΜΑΣΙΝ ΤΕ ΚΑΙ ΤΑΦΡΟΙΣ ΚΑΙ
ΤΕΙΧΕΣΙΝ ΑΥΤΗΝ ΑΞΙΟΛΟΓΟΙΣ ΠΕΡΙΕΛΑ-
ΒΕΝ, ΤΟΥ ΤΕ ΝΕΙΛΟΥ ΤΗΝ ΑΝΑΒΑΣΙΝ
ΜΕΓΑΛΗΝ ΠΟΙΗΣΑΜΕΝΟΥ ΕΝ ΤΩΙ ΟΓΔΟΩΙ
ΕΤΕΙ ΚΑΙ ΕΙΘΙΣΜΕΝΟΥ ΚΑΤΑΚΛΥΖΕΙΝ ΤΑ
25 ΠΕΔΙΑ, ΚΑΤΕΣΧΕΝ ΕΚ ΠΟΛΛΩΝ ΤΟΠΩΝ
ΟΧΥΡΩΣΑΣ ΤΑ ΣΤΟΜΑΤΑ ΤΩΝ ΠΟΤΑΜΩΝ,
ΧΟΡΗΓΗΣΑΣ ΕΙΣ ΑΥΤΑ ΧΡΗΜΑΤΩΝ ΠΛΗ-
ΘΟΣ ΟΥΚ ΟΛΙΓΟΝ ΚΑΙ ΚΑΤΑΣΤΗΣΑΣ
ΙΠΠΕΙΣ ΤΕ ΚΑΙ ΠΕΖΟΥΣ ΠΡΟΣ ΤΗΙ
ΦΥΛΑΚΗΙ
26 ΑΥΤΩΝ, ΕΝ ΟΛΙΓΩΙ ΧΡΟΝΩΙ ΤΗΝ ΤΕ
ΠΟΛΙΝ ΚΑΤΑ ΚΡΑΤΟΣ ΕΙΛΕΝ ΚΑΙ ΤΟΥΣ ΕΝ
ΑΥΤΗΙ ΑΣΕΒΕΙΣ ΠΑΝΤΑΣ ΔΙΕΦΘΕΙΡΕΝ, ΚΑ-
ΘΑΠΕΡ [ΕΡΜ]ΗΣ ΚΑΙ ΩΡΟΣ Ο ΤΗΣ ΙΣΙΟΣ
ΚΑΙ ΟΣΙΡΙΟΣ ΥΙΟΣ ΕΧΕΙΡΩΣΑΝΤΟ ΤΟΥΣ ΕΝ
ΤΟΙΣ ΑΥΤΟΙΣ
27 ΤΟΠΟΙΣ ΑΠΟΣΤΑΝΤΑΣ ΠΡΟΤΕΡΟΝ, ΤΟΥΣ
(ΔΕ)ΑΦΗΓΗΣΑΜΕΝΟΥΣ ΤΩΝ ΑΠΟΣΤΑΝΤΩΝ
ΕΠΙ ΤΟΥ ΕΑΥΤΟΥ ΠΑΤΡΟΣ ΚΑΙ ΤΗΝ ΧΩΡΑΝ

Ε[ΝΟΧΛΗΣ]ΑΝΤΑΣ ΚΑΙ ΤΑ ΙΕΡΑ ΑΔΙΚΗΣ-
ΑΝΤΑΣ ΠΑΡΑΓΕΝΟΜΕΝΟΣ ΕΙΣ ΜΕΜΦΙΝ,
ΕΠΑΜΥΝΩΝ
28 ΤΩΙ ΠΑΤΡΙ ΚΑΙ ΤΗΙ ΕΑΥΤΟΥ ΒΑΣΙΛΕΙΑΙ,
ΠΑΝΤΑΣ ΕΚΟΛΑΣΕΝ ΚΑΘΗΚΟΝΤΩΣ ΚΑΘ
ΟΝ ΚΑΙΡΟΝ ΠΑΡΕΓΕΝΗΘΗ ΠΡΟΣ ΤΟ ΣΥΝ-
ΤΕΛΕΣΘΗ[ΝΑΙ ΑΥΤΩΙ ΤΑ] ΠΡΟΣΗΚΟΝΤΑ
ΝΟΜΙΜΑ ΤΗΙ ΠΑΡΑΛΗΨΕΙ ΤΗΣ ΒΑΣΙΛΕΙΑΣ.
ΑΦΗΚΕΝ ΔΕ ΚΑΙ ΤΑ Ε[Ν]
29 ΤΟΙΣ ΙΕΡΟΙΣ ΟΦΕΙΛΟΜΕΝΑ ΕΙΣ ΤΟ ΒΑΣΙ-
ΛΙΚΟΝ ΕΩΣ ΤΟΥ ΟΓΔΟΟΥ ΕΤΟΥΣ, ΟΝΤΑ
ΕΙΣ ΣΙΤΟΥ ΤΕ ΚΑΙ ΑΡΓΥΡΙΟΥ ΠΛΗΘΟΣ ΟΥΚ
ΟΛΙΓΟΝ· ΩΣΑΥ[ΤΩΣ ΔΕ] ΚΑΙ ΤΑΣ ΤΙΜΑΣ
ΤΩΝ ΜΗ ΣΥΝΤΕΤΕΛΕΣΜΕΝΩΝ ΕΙΣ ΤΟ
ΒΑΣΙΛΙΚΟΝ ΒΥΣΣΙΝΩΝ ΟΘ[ΟΝΙ]—
30 ΩΝ ΚΑΙ ΤΩΝ ΣΥΝΤΕΤΕΛΕΣΜΕΝΩΝ ΤΑ
ΠΡΟΣ ΤΟΝ ΔΕΙΓΜΑΤΙΣΜΟΝ ΔΙΑΦΟΡΑ ΕΩΣ
ΤΩΝ ΑΥΤΩΝ ΧΡΟΝΩΝ· ΑΠΕΛΥΣΕΝ ΑΕ ΤΑ
ΙΕΡΑ ΚΑΙ ΤΗΣ Α[ΠΟΤΕΤΑΓ]ΜΕΝΗΣ ΑΡΤΑ-
ΒΗΣ Τ(Η)Ι ΑΡΟΥΡΑΙ ΤΗΣ ΙΕΡΑΣ ΓΗΣ, ΚΑΙ
ΤΗΣ ΑΜΠΕΛΙΤΙΔΟΣ ΟΜΟΙΩ(Σ)
31 ΤΟ ΚΕΡΑΜΙΟΝ ΤΗΙ ΑΡΟΥΡΑΙ, ΤΩΙ ΤΕ ΑΠΕΙ
ΚΑΙ ΤΩΙ ΜΝΕΥΕΙ ΠΟΛΛΑ ΕΔΩΡΗΣΑΤΟ ΚΑΙ
ΤΟΙΣ ΑΛΛΟΙΣ ΙΕΡΟΙΣ ΖΩΙΟΙΣ ΤΟΙΣ ΕΝ
ΑΙΓΥΠΤΩΙ, ΠΟΛΥ ΧΡΕΙΣΣΟΝ ΤΩΝ ΠΡΟ
ΑΥΤΟΥ ΒΑΣΙΛΕΙΩΝ ΦΡΟΝΤΙΖΩΝ ΥΠΕΡ ΤΩΝ
ΑΝΗΚΟΝ[ΤΩΝ ΕΙΣ]
32 ΑΥΤΑ ΔΙΑ ΠΑΝΤΟΣ, ΤΑ Τ ΕΙΣ ΤΑΣ ΤΑΦΑΣ
ΑΥΤΩΝ ΚΑΘΗΚΟΝΤΑ ΔΙΔΟΥΣ ΔΑΨΙΛΩΣ
ΚΑΙ ΕΝΔΟΞΩΣ ΚΑΙ ΤΑ ΤΕΛΙΣΚΟΜΕΝΑ ΕΙΣ
ΤΑ ΙΔΙΑ ΙΕΡΑ ΜΕΤΑ ΘΥΣΙΩΝ ΚΑΙ ΠΑΝΗΓΥ
ΡΕΩΝ ΚΑΙ ΤΩΝ ΑΛΛΩΝ ΤΩΝ ΝΟΜΙ[ΖΟΜΕ-
ΝΩΝ,]

33 ΤΑ ΤΕ ΤΙΜΙΑ ΤΩΝ ΙΕΡΩΝ ΚΑΙ ΤΗΣ ΑΙΓΥΠ-
ΤΟΥ ΔΙΑΤΕΤΗΡΗΚΕΝ ΕΠΙ ΧΩΡΑΣ ΑΚΟΛΟΥ-
ΘΩΣ ΤΟΙΣ ΝΟΜΟΙΣ, ΚΑΙ ΤΟ ΑΠΙΕΙΟΝ
ΕΡΓΟΙΣ ΠΟΛΥΤΕΛΕΣΙΝ ΚΑΤΕΣΚΕΥΑΣΕΝ
ΧΟΡΗΓΗΣΑΣ ΕΙΣ ΑΥΤΟ ΧΡΥΣΙΟ(Υ) ΤΕ Κ[ΑΙ
ΑΡΓΥΡΙ]—

34 ΟΥ ΚΑΙ ΛΙΘΩΝ ΠΟΛΥΤΕΛΩΝ ΠΛΗΘΟΣ ΟΥΚ
ΟΛΙΓΟΝ, ΚΑΙ ΙΕΡΑ ΚΑΙ ΝΑΟΥΣ ΚΑΙ ΒΩΜΟΥΣ
ΙΔΡΥΣΑΤΟ ΤΑ ΤΕ ΠΡΟΣΔΕΟΜΕΝΑ ΕΠΙΣ-
ΚΕΥΗΣ ΠΡΟΣΔΙΩΡΘΩΣΑΤΟ ΕΧΩΝ ΘΕΟΥ
ΕΥΕΡΓΕΤΙΚΟΥ ΕΝ ΤΟΙΣ ΑΝΗΚΟΥ[ΣΙΝ ΕΙΣ
ΤΟ]

35 ΘΕΙΟΝ ΔΙΑΝΟΙΑΝ· ΠΡΟΣΠΥΝΘΑΝΟΜΕΝΟΣ
ΤΕ ΤΑ ΤΩΝ Ι(Ε)ΡΩΝ ΤΙΜΙΩΤΑΤΑ ΑΝΑΝΕ-
ΟΥΤΟ ΕΠΙ ΤΗΣ ΕΑΥΤΟΥ ΒΑΣΙΛΕΙΑΣ ΩΣ
ΚΑΘΗΚΑΙ· ΑΝΘ ΩΝ ΔΕΔΩΚΑΣΙΝ ΑΥΤΩΙ
ΟΙ ΘΕΟΙ ΥΓΙΕΙΑΝ, ΝΙΚΗΝ, ΚΡΑΤΟΣ ΚΑΙ
ΤΑΛΛ ΑΓΑΘ[Α ΠΑΝΤΑ,]

36 ΤΗΣ ΒΑΣΙΛΕΙΑΣ ΔΙΑΜΕΝΟΥΣΗΣ ΑΥΤΩΙ
ΚΑΙ ΤΟΙΣ ΤΕΚΝΟΙΣ ΕΙΣ ΤΟΝ ΑΠΑΝΤΑ
ΧΡΟΝΟΝ·

ΑΓΑΘΗΙ ΤΥΧΗΙ,

ΕΔΟΞΕΝ ΤΟΙΣ ΙΕΡΕΥΣΙ ΤΩΝ ΚΑΤΑ ΤΗΝ
ΧΩΡΑΝ ΙΕΡΩΝ ΠΑΝΤΩΝ, ΤΑ ΥΠΑΡΧΟΝΤΑ
Τ[ΙΜΙΑ ΠΑΝΤΑ]

37 ΤΩΙ ΑΙΩΝΟΒΙΩΙ ΒΑΣΙΛΕΙ ΠΤΟΛΕΜΑΙΩΙ,
ΗΓΑΠΗΜΕΝΩΙ ΥΠΟ ΤΟΥ ΦΘΑ, ΘΕΩΙ ΕΠΙΦΑ-
ΝΕΙ ΕΥΧΑΡΙΣΤΩΙ, ΟΜΟΙΩΣ ΔΕ ΚΑΙ ΤΑ ΤΩΝ
ΓΟΝΕΩΝ ΑΥΤΟΥ ΘΕΩΝ ΦΙΛ[Ο]ΠΑΤΟΡΩΝ
ΚΑΙ ΤΑ ΤΩΝ ΠΡΟΓΟΝΩΝ ΘΕΩΝ ΕΥΕΡΓ[ΕΤΩΝ
ΚΑΙ ΤΑ]

38 ΤΩΝ ΘΕΩΝ ΑΔΕΛΦΩΝ ΚΑΙ ΤΑ ΤΩΝ ΘΕΩΝ
ΣΩΤΗΡΩΝ ΕΠΑΥΞΕΙΝ ΜΕΓΑΛΩΣ· ΣΤΗΣΑΙ ΔΕ
ΤΟΥ ΑΙΩΝΟΒΙΟΥ ΒΑΣΙΛΕΩΣ ΠΤΟ(ΛΕ)ΜΑΙΟΥ

ΘΕΟΥ ΕΠΙΦΑΝΟΥΣ ΕΥΧΑΡΙΣΤΟΥ ΕΙΚΟΝΑ ΕΝ ΕΚΑΣΤΩΙ ΙΕΡΩΙ ΕΝ ΤΩΙ ΕΠΙΦΑ[ΝΕΣΤΑΤΩΝ ΤΟΠΩΙ,]

39 Η ΠΡΟΣΟΝΟΜΑΣΘΗΣΕΤΑΙ ΠΤΟΛΕΜΑΙΟΥ ΤΟΥ ΕΠΑΜΥΝΑΝΤΟΣ ΤΗΙ ΑΙΓΥΠΤΩΙ, ΗΙ ΠΑΡΕΣΤΗΞΕΤΑΙ Ο ΚΥΡΙΩΤΑΤΟΣ ΘΕΟΣ ΤΟΥ ΙΕΡΟΥ, ΔΙΔΟΥΣ ΑΥΤΩΙ ΟΠΛΟΝ ΝΙΚΗΤΙΚΟΝ, Α ΕΣΤΑΙ ΚΑΤΕΣΚΕΥΑΣΜΕΝ[Α ΤΟΝ ΤΩΝ ΑΙΓΥΠΤΙΩΝ]

40 ΤΡΟΠΟΝ, ΚΑΙ ΤΟΥΣ ΙΕΡΕΙΣ ΘΕΡΑΠΕΥΕΙΝ ΤΑΣ ΕΙΚΟΝΑΣ ΤΡΙΣ ΤΗΣ ΗΜΕΡΑΣ ΚΑΙ ΠΑΡΑΤΙΘΕΝΑΙ ΑΥΤΑΙΣ ΙΕΡΟΝ ΚΟΣΜΟΝ ΚΑΙ ΤΑΛΛΑ ΤΑ ΝΟΜΙΖΟΜΕΝΑ ΣΥΝΤΕΛΕΙΝ ΚΑΘΑ ΚΑΙ ΤΟΙΣ ΑΛΛΟΙΣ ΘΕΟΙΣ ΕΝ [ΤΑΙΣ ΚΑΤΑ ΤΗΝ ΧΩΡΑΝ ΠΑ-]

41 ΝΗΓΥΡΕΣΙΝ ΙΔΡΥΣΑΣΘΑΙ ΔΕ ΒΑΣΙΛΕΙ ΠΤΟΛΕΜΑΙΩΙ ΘΕΩΙ ΕΠΙΦΑΝΕΙ ΕΥΧΑΡΙΣΤΩΙ, ΤΩΙ ΕΓ ΒΑΣΙΛΕΩΣ ΠΤΟΛΕΜΑΙΟΥ ΚΑΙ ΒΑΣΙΛΙΣΣΗΣ ΑΡΣΙΝΟΗΣ ΘΕΩΝ ΦΙΛΟΠΑΤΟΡΩΝ, ΞΟΑΝΟΝ ΤΕ ΚΑΙ ΝΑΟΝ ΧΡ[ΥΣΟΥΝ ΕΝ ΕΚΑΣΤΩΙ ΤΩΝ]

42 ΙΕ[Ρ]ΩΝ ΚΑΙ ΚΑΘΙΔΡΥΣΑΙ ΕΝ ΤΟΙΣ ΑΔΥΤΟΙΣ ΜΕΤΑ ΤΩΝ ΑΛΛΩΝ ΝΑΩΝ, ΚΑΙ ΕΝ ΤΑΙΣ ΜΕΓΑΛΑΙΣ ΠΑΝΗΓΥΡΕΣΙΝ, ΕΝ ΑΙΣ ΕΞΟΔΕΙΑΙ ΤΩΝ ΝΑΩΝ ΓΙΝΟΝΤΑΙ, ΚΑΙ ΤΟΝ ΤΟΥ ΘΕΟΥ ΕΠΙΦΑΝΟΥΣ ΕΥ[ΧΑΡΙΣΤΟΥ ΝΑΟΝ ΣΥΝΕ—]

43 ΞΟΔΕΥΕΙΝ· ΟΠΩΣ Δ ΕΥΣΗΜΟΣ ΗΙ ΝΥΝ ΤΕ ΚΑΙ ΕΙΣ ΤΟΝ ΕΠΕΙΤΑ ΧΡΟΝΟΝ, ΕΠΙΚΕΙΣΘΑΙ ΤΩΙ ΝΑΩΙ ΤΑΣ ΤΟΥ ΒΑΣΙΛΕΩΣ ΧΡΥΣΑΣ ΒΑΣΙΛΕΙΑΣ ΔΕΚΑ ΑΙΣ ΠΡΟΣΚΕΙΣΕΤΑΙ ΑΣΠΙΣ, [ΚΑΘΑΠΕΡ ΚΑΙ ΕΠΙ ΠΑΣΩΝ]

44 ΤΩΝ ΑΣΠΙΔΟΕΙΔΩΝ ΒΑΣΙΛΕΙΩΝ ΤΩΝ ΕΠΙ ΤΩΝ ΑΛΛΩΝ ΝΑΩΝ· ΕΣΤΑΙ Δ ΑΥΤΩΝ ΕΝ

ΤΩΙ ΜΕΣΩΙ Η ΚΑΛΟΥΜΕΝΗ ΒΑΣΙΛΕΙΑ ΨΧΕΝΤ, ΗΝ ΠΕΡΙΘΕΜΕΝΟΣ ΕΙΣΗΛΘΕΝ ΕΙΣ ΤΟ ΕΝ ΜΕΜΦ[ΕΙ ΙΕΡΟΝ, ΟΠΩΣ ΕΝ ΑΥΤΩΙ ΣΥΝ-]

45 ΤΕΛΕΣΘΗΙ ΤΑ ΝΟΜΙΖΟΜΕΝΑ ΤΗΙ ΠΑΡΑΛΗ-ΨΕΙ ΤΗΣ ΒΑΣΙΛΕΙΑΣ. ΕΠΙΘΕΙΝΑΙ ΔΕ ΚΑΙ ΕΠΙ ΤΟΥ ΠΕΡΙ ΤΑΣ ΒΑΣΙΛΕΙΑΣ ΤΕΤΡΑΓΩΝΟΥ ΚΑΤΑ ΤΟ ΠΡΟΕΙΡΗΜΕΝΟΝ ΒΑΣΙΛΕΙΟΝ ΦΥΛΑΚΤΗΡΙΑ ΧΡΥ[ΣΑ ΔΥΟ, ΟΙΣ ΕΓΓΡΑΦΗ-ΣΕΤΑΙ Ο-]

46 ΤΙ ΕΣΤΙΝ ΤΟΥ ΒΑΣΙΛΕΩΣ ΤΟΥ ΕΠΙΦΑΝΗ ΠΟΙΗΣΑΝΤΑΣ ΤΗΝ ΤΕ ΑΝΩ ΧΩΡΑΝ ΚΑΙ ΤΗΝ ΚΑΤΩ ΚΑΙ ΕΠΕΙ ΤΗΝ ΤΡΙΑ[Κ]ΑΔΑ ΤΟΥ ΤΟΥ (*sic*) ΜΕΣΟΡΗ, ΕΝ ΗΙ ΤΑ ΓΕΝΕΘ-ΛΙΑ ΤΟΥ ΒΑΣΙΛΕΩΣ ΑΓΕΤΑΙ, ΟΜΟΙΩΣ ΔΕ ΚΑΙ [ΤΗΝ ΕΠΤΑΚΑΙΔΕΚΑΤΗΝ ΤΟΥ ΦΑΩΦΙ]

47 ΕΝ ΗΙ ΠΑΡΕΛΑΒΕΝ ΤΗΝ ΒΑΣΙΛΕΙΑΝ ΠΑΡ[Α] ΤΟΥ ΠΑΤΡΟΣ, ΕΠΩΝΥΜΟΥΣ ΝΕΝΟΜΙΚΑΣΙΝ ΕΝ ΤΟΙΣ ΙΕΡΟΙΣ, ΑΙ ΔΗ ΠΟΛΛΩΝ ΑΓΑΘΩΝ ΑΡΧΗΓΟΙ [Π]ΑΣΙΝ ΕΙΣΙΝ, ΑΓΕΙΝ ΤΑΣ ΗΜΕ-ΡΑΣ ΤΑΥΤΑΣ ΕΟΡ[ΤΑΣ ΚΑΙ ΠΑΝΗΓΥΡΕΙΣ ΕΝ ΤΟΙΣ ΚΑΤΑ ΤΗΝ ΑΙ-]

48 ΓΥΠΤΟΝ ΙΕΡΟΙΣ ΚΑΤΑ ΜΗΝΑ, ΚΑΙ ΣΥΝ-ΤΕΛΕΙΝ ΕΝ ΑΥΤΟΙΣ ΘΥΣΙΑΣ ΚΑΙ ΣΠΟΝΔΑΣ ΚΑΙ ΤΑΛΛΑ ΤΑ ΝΟΜΙΖΟΜΕΝΑ, ΚΑΘΑ ΚΑΙ ΕΝ ΤΑΙΣ ΑΛΛΑΙΣ ΠΑΝΕΗΓΥΡΕΣΙΝ ΤΑΣ ΤΕ ΓΙΝΟΜΕΝΑΣ ΠΡΟΘΕ[ΣΕΙΣ ΤΟΙΣ ΠΑ-]

49 ΡΕΧΟΜΕΝΟΙΣ ΕΝ ΤΟΙΣ ΙΕΡΟΙΣ. ΑΓΕΙΝ ΔΕ ΕΟΡΤΗΝ ΚΑΙ ΠΑΝΗΓΥΡΙΝ ΤΩΙ ΑΙΩΝΟΒΙΩΙ ΚΑΙ ΗΓΑΠΗΜΕΝΩΙ ΥΠΟ ΤΟΥ ΦΘΑ ΒΑΣΙΛΕΙ ΠΤΟΛΕΜΑΙΩΙ ΘΕΩΙ ΕΠΙΦΑΝΕΙ ΕΥΧΑΡΙΣΤΩΙ ΚΑΤ ΕΝΙ[ΑΥΤΟΝ ΕΝ ΤΟΙΣ ΙΕΡΟΙΣ ΤΟΙΣ ΚΑΤΑ ΤΗΝ]

50 ΧΩΡΑΝ ΑΠΟ ΤΗΣ ΝΟΥΜΗΝΙΑΣ ΤΟΥ ΘΩΥΘ
ΕΦ ΗΜΕΡΑΣ ΠΕΝΤΕ, ΕΝ ΑΙΣ ΚΑΙ ΣΤΕΦΑΝ-
ΗΦΟΡΗΣΟΥΣΙΝ ΣΥΝΤΕΛΟΥΝΤΕΣ ΘΥΣΙΑΣ
ΚΑΙ ΣΠΟΝΔΑΣ ΚΑΙ ΤΑΛΛΑ ΤΑ ΚΑΘΗΚΟΝΤΑ
ΠΡΟΣΑΓΟΡΕ[ΥΕΣΘΑΙ ΔΕ ΤΟΥΣ ΙΕΡΕΙΣ ΤΩΝ
ΑΛΛΩΝ ΘΕΩΝ]
51 ΚΑΙ ΤΟΥ ΘΕΟΥ ΕΠΙΦΑΝΟΥΣ ΕΥΧΑΡΙΣΤΟΥ
ΙΕΡΕΙΣ ΠΡΟΣ ΤΟΙΣ ΑΛΛΟΙΣ ΟΝΟΜΑΣΙΝ
ΤΩΝ ΘΕΩΝ ΩΝ ΙΕΡΑΤΕΥΟΥΣΙΝ, ΚΑΙ ΚΑΤΑ-
ΧΩΡΙΣΑΙ ΕΙΣ ΠΑΝΤΑΣ ΤΟΥΣ ΧΡΗΜΑΤΙΣ-
ΜΟΥΣ ΚΑΙ ΕΙΣ ΤΟΥΣ Δ[ΑΚΤΥΛΙΟΥΣ ΟΥΣ
ΦΟΡΟΥΣΙ ΠΡΟΣΕΓΚΟΛΑΠΕΣΘΑΙ ΤΗΝ]
52 ΙΕΡΑΤΕΙΑΝ ΑΥΤΟΥ. ΕΞΕΙΝΑΙ ΔΕ ΚΑΙ ΤΟΙΣ
ΑΛΛΟΙΣ ΙΔΙΩΤΑΙΣ ΑΓΕΙΝ ΤΗΝ ΕΟΡΤΗΝ
ΚΑΙ ΤΟΝ ΠΡΟΕΙΡΗΜΕΝΟΝ ΝΑΟΝ ΙΔΡΥΕΣΘΑΙ
ΚΑΙ ΕΧΕΙΝ ΠΑΡ ΑΥΤΟΙΣ ΣΥΝΤΕΛΟ[ΥΝΤΑΣ
ΤΑ ΝΟΜΙΜΑ ΕΝ ΕΟΡΤΑΙΣ ΤΑΙΣ ΤΕ ΚΑΤΑ
ΜΗΝΑ ΚΑΙ Τ-
53 ΑΙ]Σ ΚΑΤ ΕΝΙΑΥΤΟΝ, ΟΠΩΣ ΓΝΩΡΙΜΟΝ ΗΙ
ΔΙΟΤΙ ΟΙ ΕΝ ΑΙΓΥΠΤΩΙ ΑΥΞΟΥΣΙ ΚΑΙ ΤΙ-
ΜΩΣΙ ΤΟΝ ΘΕΟΝ ΕΠΙΦΑΝΗ ΕΥΧΑΡΙΣΤΟΝ
ΒΑΣΙΛΕΑ, ΚΑΘΑΠΕΡ ΝΟΜΙΜΟΝ ΕΣΤΙ[Ν
ΑΥΤΟΙΣ. ΤΟ ΔΕ ΨΗΦΙΣΜΑ ΤΟΥΤΟ ΑΝΑ-
ΓΡΑΨΑΙ ΕΙΣ ΣΤΗ-
54 ΛΑΣ Σ]ΤΕΡΕΟΥ ΛΙΘΟΥ ΤΟΙΣ ΤΕ ΙΕΡΟΙΣ ΚΑΙ
ΕΓΧΩΡΙΟΙΣ ΚΑΙ ΕΛΛΗΝΙΚΟΙΣ ΓΡΑΜΜΑΣΙΝ,
ΚΑΙ ΣΤΗΣΑΙ ΕΝ ΕΚΑΣΤΩΙ ΤΩΝ ΤΕ ΠΡΩΤΩΝ
ΚΑΙ ΔΕΥΤΕΡΩΝ [ΚΑΙ ΤΡΙΤΩΝ ΙΕΡΩΝ ΠΡΟΣ
ΤΗΙ ΤΟΥ ΑΙΩΝΟΒΙΟΥ ΒΑΣΙΛΕΩΣ ΕΙΚΟΝΙ]

CHAPTER III

I.—EARLY PUBLICATIONS OF THE DEMOTIC TRANSLATION OF THE GREEK TEXT ON THE ROSETTA STONE

The Demotic text on the ROSETTA STONE was first made available for study by the publication of the facsimiles of the Stone mentioned above (p. 30). In 1802 the famous Orientalist SILVESTRE DE SACY thought that he had identified the equivalents of certain Greek proper names (see his *Lettre au Citoyen Chaptal*, Paris: l'Imprimerie de la Rêpublique), and in the same year J. D. ÅKERBLAD published the statement that he had not only done the same thing, but that he had formulated a Demotic alphabet (see his *Lettre adressée au Citoyen de Sacy*, Paris: l'Imprimerie de la Rêpublique). In 1814 YOUNG read a complete translation of the Demotic text before the Society of Antiquaries of London, and published it in the *Museum Criticism*, Cambridge, 1815, Part VI, and in *Archaeologia*, London, 1817, vol. xviii. A grammatical analysis of the two Egyptian texts on the Stone by F. SALVOLINI appeared at Paris in 1836, and it was asserted by scholars at the time that he had derived much help in his interpretations from a perusal of the papers of CHAMPOLLION LE JEUNE. The *Analyse grammatical du*

Texte Demotique du Décret de Rosette, which was published by L. F. J. C. DE SAULCY in Paris in 1845, was a valuable work, and it had the effect of putting the study of Demotic upon a scientific footing among scholars.

But the first scholar who really understood the meaning of the Demotic text on the Stone was H. BRUGSCH, who, in his *Sammlung Demotischer Urkunden* (Berlin, 1850) gave a translation of it, with a running commentary, which showed that he had discovered the true principle of its interpretation. Five years later he published his *Grammaire Démotique,* wherein he explained the general principles of the language and " écriture populaire " of the ancient Egyptians. In 1880 E. RÉVILLONT published a *Chrestomathie Demotique,* in which the words of the Demotic text were separated, and side by side with each was given its equivalent in French, and its rendering in Greek on the Stone. Our knowledge of the Demotic text was greatly increased by Dr. J. J. HESS, who in 1902 published, at Freiburg, his valuable Dissertation entitled *Der Demotische Teil der Dreisprachigen Inscrift von Rosette.* This work, which is, unfortunately, out of print and very scarce, contains word-for-word and running translations, and a comparison of the Demotic with the Greek text, and with fragments of the hieroglyphic version. A careful copy of the Demotic text was published by J. KRALL in

Part I of his *Demotische Lesestücke*, Vienna, 1897–1903, and SETHE gave a transliteration of the Demotic text, together with the original Greek, arranged interlinearly under the hieroglyphic text found on the Stone and on the Stele from Annobairah in his *Hieroglyphische Urkunden der Graechisch-Römischen Zeit.*, III, p. 169, Leipzig, 1916. Finally, the eminent Demotologist W. SPIEGELBERG has given a critical edition of the Demotic text, with a transliteration, translation and notes in his *Der demotische Text . . . der Priesterdekret von Kanopus und Memphis* (*Rosettana*), Heidelberg, 1922.

II.—ENGLISH TRANSLATION OF THE DEMOTIC TRANSLATION

[THE DATE OF THE DECREE]

1 [In the 9th year, the fourth day of the month ḲSNṬḲS,] which makes (*i.e.* is equivalent to) the eighteenth day of the second month of the season PER-T, of the PHARAOH[1], the Young One, who as PHARAOH hath appeared upon the throne of his father, the lord of uraei-crown, whose renown is great, who hath stablished EGYPT, having beautified it, whose heart is disposed benevolently towards the

[1] The Demotic texts adds ā–u–s = *ānk hutcha senb*, 𓋹𓍑𓋴, *i.e.* "life, strength, health [be to him]," after the manner of the old Egyptian inscriptions.

gods, HORUS OF NUBTI, who hath beautified the lives of men and women, the lord of the Seṭ-festival,[1] like PTAH TEN (or Tenn), the king (Åti) like unto RĀ,

2 [the King of UPPER AND LOWER EGYPT], the son of the Father-Loving Gods, the chosen of PTAḤ, to whom the RĀ hath given victory, the living image of AMEN, the son of the RĀ, PTOLEMY, the everliving, the beloved of PTAḤ, the god who appeareth, whose goodness (or, beauty) is splendid, the son of PTOLEMY, and ARSINA (ARSINOË), the Father-Loving Gods, when

AIAṬUS, the son of AIAṬUS, was priest of ALEXANDER, and the SAVIOUR GODS, and

3 the [BROTHER-GODS and the] WELL-DOING GODS, and the FATHER-LOVING GODS, and PTOLEMY, the god who appeareth, whose benefits are splendid; and PRA (PYRRHA), the daughter of PILINS (PHILINOS) was the bearer of the gift of victory before BRNIGA (BERENICE), the Well-Doing [Goddess]; and ARIA (AREIA), the daughter of TIAGNS (DIOGENES), was the bearer of the

4 basket before ARSINA (ARSINOË), the Brother-Loving [Goddess]; and HRANA (IRENE), the daughter of PTOLEMY, was the priestess of ARSINA (ARSINOË), the Father-Loving [Goddess].

[1] Celebrated to renew the life of the king.

[The Introduction]

On this day the Decree :

The priests who direct the services, and the ministrants (prophets ?), and the priests, who enter into the sanctuaries to array the gods in their apparel, and the scribes of the Books of the God, and the scribes of the House of Life, and the other priests from the temples of Egypt,

5 who come [to Memphis] at the festival whereat the Pharaoh Ptolemy, the everliving, the beloved of Ptaḥ, the god who appeareth, whose good deeds are splendid, received the office (or, dignity) of sovereign, from the hand of his father, and had assembled in the house of the god in Men-Nefer (Memphis) spake [thus] :—

[Ptolemy V as benefactor of the temples of Egypt]

Inasmuch as the Pharaoh Ptolemy, the everliving, the god who appeareth, whose good deeds are splendid, the son of Pharaoh

6 and the Queen Arsina (Arsinoë), the Father-Loving Gods, hath been in the habit of conferring many benefits upon the temples of Egypt, and upon all those who are under his office as Pharaoh, since he was a god, the son of a god, [and] a goddess, being a similitude

PLATE V.

Ptolemy V Epiphanes, arrayed in the apparel of a high priest, offering incense to the gods.

Ptolemy V Epiphanes making offerings to the ram-headed god Khnemu, lord of Qebḥet and Senmut.

of the god HORUS, the son of ISIS, the son of OSIRIS, who saved his father OSIRIS, and his heart being well-disposed towards the gods, he hath given much silver and much grain for the temples of EGYPT (**Plate V**),

7 and hath [incurred] many expenses in order to bring peace again in EGYPT, and to replace order in the temples, and he hath bestowed benefactions upon the whole army which were under his office as PHARAOH.

[PTOLEMY V REDUCES SOME TAXES AND ABOLISHES OTHERS]

As concerning the taxes and contributions which remained [unpaid] in EGYPT, some of them he reduced, and some of them he remitted entirely, in order to bring it about that the soldiers and all the other people might enjoy prosperity during the time of his overlordship.

8 The taxes which were due to the PHARAOH from the people who lived in EGYPT, and all the other folk who [lived] under his beneficent rule as PHARAOH, and the arrears of payments, which amounted to a very large sum, he remitted entirely.

[The people who were in prison, and those who were suffering through long-standing suits, he set free.]

[PTOLEMY V CONFIRMS THE REVENUES OF THE TEMPLES AND RESTORES THEIR FORMER REVENUES]

Concerning the offerings made to the gods, and the silver and the grain for the maintenance of the priests
9 which should be given yearly to the temples, and the contributions to the gods which were made from the vineyards, and from the fruit and vegetable gardens, and all the other things which they possessed in the time of his father, he ordered that they should continue to remain their property. He commanded also in respect of the priests that they should not pay out of the property of the priests, contributions larger than those which they had paid in the time of his father, up to the first year of his own reign.

[ABOLITION OF THE PRIESTS' ANNUAL JOURNEY TO ALEXANDRIA, AND REDUCTION OF THE BYSSUS TAX]

He released the people
10 who were employed in the temples from the journey which they had hitherto made annually to the HOUSE OF ALEXANDER (*i.e.* ALEXANDRIA).

He commanded that sailors should not be seized [by the press gangs].

He remitted two-thirds of the cloths of byssus which the temples had been obliged to pay to the house of PHARAOH.

[THE RESTORATION OF PEACE IN THE COUNTRY AND THE GRANTING OF AN AMNESTY]

He restored to their former condition all the things which for a long time past had ceased to be observed (?).

11 And he took the greatest care that what it had been customary to do for the gods should be performed in a right and fitting manner. And he permitted men to enjoy justice, even as did THOTH, the Great Great.

And he commanded concerning those soldiers who had returned from the fighting, and also concerning the other men who, during the revolt which had taken place in EGYPT, had followed another course, that they

12 should betake themselves to their own homes, and should be allowed to resume possession of the properties which they had held formerly.

[PTOLEMY V PROTECTS EGYPT FROM ENEMIES FROM WITHOUT]

He took the greatest care to dispatch infantry, cavalry, and ships against those who had come by land and by sea to make war upon EGYPT. To effect this he expended very large sums in silver and grain in order that the temples and the inhabitants of EGYPT should enjoy peace.

[PTOLEMY V PUNISHES THE REBELS OF LYCOPOLIS]

He sent an expedition against the town of SHKAN, which the enemy
13 had fortified in every [possible] way, and its interior was filled with arms and every kind of munition of war. He surrounded the aforesaid town with walls and dams on its outer side against the enemy who were inside it, and who had done many harmful (or, wicked) things against EGYPT, for they had forsaken the way of PHARAOH'S commandments and the commands
14 of the gods. He blocked up the canals which carried water into the aforesaid town. The PHARAOHS his predecessors had never been able to do such a thing ; to carry this out he spent a very large sum of silver.

He stationed foot-soldiers and cavalry on the aforementioned canals, [both] to watch them and to make safe [the dams] against the inundations of the waters [of the NILE], which in the eighth year [of his reign] were very great,
15 when the aforementioned canals poured [their] waters over many of the very low-lying lands. The PHARAOH captured the town by assault in a very short time. He slaughtered the enemy who were in their innermost places,

and he handed them over to the block of justice, even as did the RĀ, and HORUS, the son of ISIS, had done in times of old those who had been their enemies in the self-same place.

[PUNISHMENT OF THE LEADERS OF THE REVOLT AGAINST PTOLEMY IV PHILOPATOR]

16 Now, the enemy had gathered together the soldiers, and had induced them to stir up riots and disorder in the [various] Nomes, and they had plundered the temples, and had forsaken the way of PHARAOH and his father. These the gods delivered over into his power in MEMPHIS at the festival of the reception of his exalted Office from the hand of his father, and he had them slain by means of the wood [*i.e.* he either crucified them or impaled them].

[REMISSION OF ARREARS OF TAXES AND CONTRIBUTIONS FROM THE TEMPLES]

17 He remitted the arrears of taxes which were due to PHARAOH up to the ninth year [of his reign], which amounted to a very large sum in silver, and large quantities of grain. [And he remitted also the value of the cloths of byssus, for which the temples were in debt, and they were liable to pay to the House of PHARAOH as a tax, as well as the balance (?) which was determined (?) upon, which they had [already] paid up to that time.

And he also commanded concerning the grain—now one *Artab* was levied upon every *arura* (*i.e.* acre) of the lands which were sacrosanct property,

18 and also one vessel of wine was levied upon every *arura* of the vineyard lands which were sacrosanct property—[PHARAOH] withdrew [his claim in each case].

[PTOLEMY V PROVIDES FOR THE SACRED ANIMALS, AND THE WORSHIP OF THE GODS; HIS REWARD FOR THE SAME]

He bestowed many benefactions upon APIS[1] and MNEVIS,[2] and the other sacred animals of the EGYPTIANS, far more than his predecessors had done, for his mind was at all times wholly occupied with plans for their benefit. He gave what was necessary for their embalmment and burials, which were performed in a splendid and honourable manner; and he supplied everything which was required for their temples (**Plate VI**).

19 whensoever a festival had to be celebrated, and he provided the burnt offerings which had to be set before them, and everything else which befitted their cult. The honours which appertained to the temples, and the other honours of EGYPT, he made to be observed (or,

[1] The Bull-god of Memphis.

[2] The Bull-god of Heliopolis.

paid) each in its own special manner according to the law which regulated the same. He gave large quantities of gold, and silver, and grain, and other things to the temple-towns (?) of Apis. He made new decorations and works to be carried out
20 whereof the workmanship was exceedingly beautiful.

He caused new temples, and sanctuaries, and altars, to be built for the gods, and he restored [all] their former arrangements; for he possessed the heart of a god who was benevolently disposed towards the gods, and he sought out (?) means for increasing the honour due to them so that they renew the period of his overlordship during his reign as Pharaoh in a suitable manner.

In return for these [efforts] the gods have given to him victory, [and] power, [and] might, [and] strength,
21 [and] health, [and] every [other] kind of good thing, and his Office as Pharaoh shall remain established for him and for his children for ever.

[The priests decree additional honours for Ptolemy V and his ancestors]

With good fortune!

It hath entered into the heart[s] of the priests of all the temples in Upper Egypt and in LOWER EGYPT, to multiply the honours which [are paid in] the temples to the PHARAOH PTOLEMY, the everliving, the god who appeareth, whose benefits are splendid,

22 and those of the FATHER-LOVING GODS who begot him, and those of the WELL-DOING GODS who begot those who begot him, and those of the BROTHER-LOVING GODS who begot those who begot them, and those of the SAVIOUR GODS, the fathers of his fathers.

[STATUES OF PTOLEMY V AND THE LOCAL CHIEF GODS ARE TO BE SET UP IN ALL THE TEMPLES]

And there shall be set up a statue of the PHARAOH PTOLEMY, the everliving, the god who appeareth, whose benefits are splendid, and they shall call it

23 " PTOLEMY, the PROTECTOR OF EGYPT," whereof the interpretation is, " PTOLEMY who protecteth EGYPT," together with a statue of the god of the city [in the act of] giving him a sword of victory, in the temple and in each and every temple ; [these shall be set up] in conspicuous places in the temples, and they shall be made after the fashion of the workmanship of the Egyptian handicraftsman.

And the priests shall minister to the statues in the temples, [that is to say] in each and every temple, three times daily,

24 and they shall set before them the implements (?) of the cult, and they shall perform for the other rites and ceremonies which it is right and proper to perform, even those which are performed for the other gods at the festivals and during the processions on the aforenamed days.

[A WOODEN STATUE OF PTOLEMY V IN A GOLDEN SHRINE TO BE SET UP IN THE TEMPLES]

And they shall set up a divine portrait-statue of the PHARAOH PTOLEMY, the god who appeareth, whose benefits are splendid, [the son of] PTOLEMY and the Queen (literally Pharaohess) ARSINOË, the FATHER-LOVING GODS, and a shrine of gold in the temples,
25 that is to say in each and every temple, and they shall place them in the most holy places in the sanctuaries side by side with the other shrines of gold.

When the great festivals are being celebrated, during which the gods are made to appear from out of their shrines, the shrine of the god who appeareth, whose benefits are splendid, shall also be made to appear with them.

Now in order that the shrine may be known to men both now and to the end of time, they shall set upon this shrine ten gold crowns of PHARAOH, with an uraeus attached to each one

of them, according to what is usually done in
26 the case of crowns of gold, and they shall be placed upon the shrine instead of the uraei which are on other shrines, and the double crown  shall be in the middle of them. For it was in that crown that the PHARAOH appeared in the temple of MEMPHIS when there was done to him what is prescribed by the Law at the reception of the Office of PHARAOH. And upon the upper side of the rectangle, which is away from the crown, in the middle
27 of the gold crowns described above, a papyrus and a reed shall be placed. And they shall set a vulture on a basket, with a reed below it, on the right-hand corner of the gold shrine, and they shall set an uraeus, with a basket beneath him, on a papyrus on the left-hand corner [of the shrine]. And the interpretation thereof is "The PHARAOH hath made bright UPPER and LOWER EGYPT."

[SPECIAL FESTIVALS ARE TO BE ESTABLISHED IN HONOUR OF PTOLEMY V]

Inasmuch as it hath already been established by law that the last day (the 30th) of the fourth month of the season of SHEMU (MESORE),
28 which is the Birthday of the PHARAOH, is to be celebrated in the temples as a festival and a day of rejoicing, and also the seventeenth

day of the second month of the season AKHET (PAOPHI), the day on which the ceremonies connected with his reception of the Office of PHARAOH are performed—now the birth of PHARAOH, and his reception of the Office of PHARAOH were the beginning of the happiness (or, prosperity) in which men have participated —therefore these days, that is to say the seventeenth and the thirtieth days of each month, shall be celebrated as festivals in all the temples of EGYPT.

29 And burnt offerings, and drink offerings, and every other kind of offering shall be brought every month, according to the regulations which apply to the other festivals, at both these festivals. And these things which the people bring shall be destined for the men who serve in the temples.

And moreover, the days from the first day of the first month of the season AKHET, to the fifth day of the same, shall be celebrated as a five-day festival and a period of rejoicing in the temples and throughout all EGYPT in honour of the PHARAOH PTOLEMY, the ever-living, the god who appeareth, whose benefits are splendid. And the people shall wear garlands

30 and shall bring burnt offerings, and drink offerings, and [all] the other things which it is right and proper [to bring].

[The priests of Ptolemy V shall assume a new title]

The priests who are in the temples of Egypt, that is to say, in each and every temple shall, in addition to the other priestly titles which they have, be called "Priests of the god who appeareth, whose benefits are splendid." And they shall write this title in all their official documents, and they shall write and engrave the title of the rank of "priest of the god who appeareth, whose benefits are splendid" upon their rings.

[Private individuals may participate in paying these honours to Ptolemy V]

31 Such private individuals as wish to make a model of the golden shrine of the god who appeareth, whose benefits are splendid, and to bring it forth when they are living in their houses, shall be permitted to do so. And they shall at the same time celebrate the above-mentioned festivals and days of rejoicing, every month and every year, so that it may be well known that those who dwell in Egypt pay honour to the god who appeareth, whose benefits are splendid, according to the law.

[The promulgation of the decree]

And the Decree shall be written upon a tablet of hard stone in the writing of the words of the god, in the writing of letters (or, books) and in the writing of the IONIANS, and they shall set it up in the first temples, [and] in the second temples, [and] in the third temples close to the gold statue of the everliving PHARAOH.

III.—TRANSLITERATION OF THE DEMOTIC TRANSLATION OF THE DECREE

1 [Ḥa-t-sp 9·t Ḳsnṭḳs ssu 4] ntī ȧr ȧbṭ n rmt (n) Kmī ȧbt 2-nu pr-t ssu 18 (n) Pr-āa ā.u.s. pa ḫal ȧ-ȧr ḫā (n) Pr-āa ā.u.s. (n) ta ȧs-t (n) paīf īt nb na āriu ntī na-āa taīf pḥ·t ȧ-ȧr smn Kmi ȧuf ṭī-t na-nfr-f ntī na-mnḫ ḥatī-f ȧ-ȧr na ntru ntī ḥr paīf tchtchi (djdji) ȧ-ȧr ṭī-t na-nfr pa ānḫ n na rmtu pa nb n na rnpu n ḥbs m-ḳṭi Ptḥ Tni ā.u.s. Pr-āa m-ḳṭi Pa-Rā

2 [Pr-āa ā.u.s. n na tshu ntī ḥrī] na tshu ntī hri pa shrī n na ntru mr ītu r stp Ptḥ r ṭī nf Pa-Rā pa tchra (djra) pa tut ānḫ (n) Åmn pa shrī (n) Pa-Rā Ptlumis ānḫ tcht (djt) Ptḥ mr pa ntr pr ntī na-ān taīf mṭ-nfrt Ptlumis ȧrm Arsina na ntru mr ītu ȧu uāb Algsanṭrs ȧrm na ntru ntī nḫm ȧrm

3 [na ntru snu ȧrm] na ntru mnḫu ȧrm na ntru mr ītu ȧrm Pr-āa ā.u.s. Ptlumias pa ntr pr ntī na-ān taīf

mṭ-nfrt Aiaṭus sa Aiaṭus r Pra sa·t n
Pilins (n) fi shp (n) pa ḳni m-baḥ Brniga
ta mnḫ-t (r) Aria sa-t n Ṭiagns (n) fi
4 [ṭn m-baḥ Arsi]na ta mr sn r Hrana
sa-t n Ptlumias n uāb Arsina ta mr īt-s
n hru ȧpn ut na mr-shn ȧrm na ntru
ḥm ȧrm na uābu ntī shm (r) pa ntī-uāb
r ȧr mnḫ n na ntru ȧrm na sẖu mdji-ntr
ȧrm na sẖu pr-ānḫ ȧrm na kīu uābu
ȧ-ȧr ȧaī n na ȧrpiu (n) Kmi
5 [r Mn-nfr n] pa ḥb n pa shp ta ȧau
(n) ḥrī r ȧr Pr-āa ā.u.s. Ptlumias ānḫ
tcht (djt) Ptḥ mr pa ntr pr ntī na-ān
taīf mṭ-nfrt (n) ṭt paīf īt ȧ-ȧr tut n
ḥ-t-ntr (n) Mn-nfr ȧ-ȧr tchṭ (djt)
n-ṭ-t ḫpr-f r ḫer ȧr Pr-āa ā.u.s.
Ptlumias ānḫ tcht (djt) pa ntr pr ntī
na-ān taīf mṭ-nfrt (sa) Pr-āa ā.u.s.
Ptlumias
6 [ȧrm ta Pr-āa·t] Arsina na ntru mr-ītu
mṭ-nfrt āshai n na ȧrpiu (n) Kmi ȧrm
na ntī ẖn taīf ȧaw (n) Pr-āa ā.u.s. ṭru
ȧuf n ntr shrī (n) ntr ntr-t ȧuf mḫi r
Ḥr sa 'Ȧst sa Usīr ȧ-ȧr nḫtī paīf īt Usīr
r ḥatī-f mnḫu ḥr na ntru r uaḥ-f ṭī-t
ḥṭ āshai pr-t āshai n na ȧrpiu (n) Kmi
7 āshai r tī-t ḫpr sgrḥ ẖn
Kmi r smn na ȧrpiu r uaḥ-f ṭī-t shp n
ta mtgtī ntī ẖn taīf ȧw (n) ḥrī ṭrs pa ḥti
pa shkr r un-nau āḥā n Kmi un-nau

Ḳsh-f ẖnu un-nau ui-f r-ru n tchatcha
(djadja) r ṭī-t ḫpr pa mshā ȧrm na kīu
rmt ṭru ȧuu nfr (n) paīf ha ntī
8 [Pr-āa ā.u.s. na] spu n Pr-āa ā.u.s. r
un-nau ā-ui na rmtu ntī n Kmi ȧrm na
ntī n taīf ȧau (n) Pr-āa ā.u.s. ṭru ȧuu
ȧr ȧpt āsha-t ui-f r ru na rmtu n un-nau
tchṭḥ (djṭḥ) ȧrm nau un-nau un luḥ
ā-uī-u n ssu āshai ui-f r-ru ḥn-f-s (r)-ṭb
na ḥtp-ntru n na ntru ȧrm na ḥṭ na
pr-tu ntī auu tī-t-st n sntgsi r naīu
9 [ȧrpiu] ẖr rnp·t ȧrm na ṭnīu ntī ḫpr n na
ntru n na aḥu arli na aḥu ṭgi pa sp nkt
ṭru r un-nau ȧuu mḥt n-ȧmu ȧ-ȧr-ḫr
paīf īt r ṭī-t mnu ẖr-ru ḥn-f-s ān (r)-ṭb
na uābu r tm ṭī·t ṭīu paīu ṭn n ȧr uāb
n ḥua pa un-nau ȧuu ṭī·t-s r hn ḥat-sp
I-t ȧ-ȧr-ḥr paīf īt ui-f r na rmtu
10 [ntī ẖn] na ȧauu n na ȧrpiu n pa aun r
un-nau ȧuu ȧr-f r pa ā (n) Algsanṭrs
ẖr rnp·t ḥn-f-s r tm kp rmt ẖn ui-f r ta
ṭnīt ⅔ n na shes-nsuu r un-nau ȧuu ȧru
n pr Pr-āa ā.u.s. n na ȧrpiu mṭ nb ȧ-ȧr
ẖaā paīu gi n ssu āshai āuf ȧn n-ȧmu
r paīu tchnf (djnf) n
11 [(?)mtr] ȧuf ȧr nbu nb r ṭī-t ȧru na ntī n
sntī n ȧru n na ntru n gi ȧuf mtru paīs
smṭ n ṭi-t ȧru pa hp n na rmtu r ẖ pa
ȧr Ṭḥutī pa āa pa āa ḥn-f-s ān (r) ṭba
na ntī ȧuu r ȧaī ẖn na rmtu ḳnḳn ȧrm

pa sp rmt ȧ-ȧr ḫpr ḥr kt-h̲-t mī-t (?) n
pa th̲th̲ ȧ-ȧr ḫpr (n) Kmi r tī-t
12 [stau] st (r) naīu maāu mtu naīu nktu
ḫpr h̲rru ȧr-f nbu nb r ṭi·t shm mshā
ḥtr biri ub na ȧ-ȧr ȧaī n pa āṭ pa īm
r ȧr aḥ ub Kmi ȧr-f hī āshai n ḥṭ pr-t
ub nai r ṭi-t ḫpr na ȧrpiu ȧrm na rmtu
ntī (n) Kmi auu sgrḥ shm-f r ta rsa·t (n)
Shkan
13 [r un] nau ȧnb (n) ṭ-t na sbau h̲r ka-t
nb r un sṭbḥ āshai sbṭi nb (n) paīs h̲n
arb-f ta rsa·t (n) rn-s n sbṭ un (n) pais
bnr (r) ṭba na sbau r un-nau (n) paīs
h̲n r un-nau uaḫu ȧr gmā āshai r Kmi
ȧuu ḫaā pa mit n pa āsh-sḥn n Pr-āa
ā.u.s. ȧrm pa āsh-sḥn
14 [n na] ntru ṭī-f ṭnu na īāru r un-nau
ṭī-t shm mu n ta rsa·t (n) rn-s r bn r̲ḫ
na Pr-āau ā.u.s. ḥatīu ȧr-s m-ḳṭ-s ȧru ḥṭ
āshai n hi ubu ȧp-f mshā rmt rṭui-f ḥtr
r ra (n) na īāru n rnu r ḥrḥ r-ru r-ṭī-t
utchau (udja) r ṭba na mḥu n pa mu r
un-nau āiu n ḥa-t-sp 8·t
15 r na īāru n rnu na ntī ṭī-t shm mu r
ȧtn āshai auu mṭiu m-shs thaī Pr-āa ā.u.s.
ta rsa·t n rn-s (n) tchra (djra) (n) ṭ-t n
ssu sbḳ ȧr-f ȧr sḫi (n) na sbau r un-nau
n paīs h̲n ȧr-f st n r
h̲ pa ȧr Pa-Rā ȧrm Ḥr-sa-Ȧs·t n na ȧ-ȧr
ȧr sba r-ru n na maāu n

16 rnu (n) ta ḥa-t na sbau ȧ-ȧr tutu mshā ȧuu ḫpr ḥa-tu r tẖtẖ na tshu ȧuu gmā r na ȧrpiu ȧuu ḫaā pa mit n Pr-āa ā.u.s. ȧrm paīf īt ṭī na ntru ȧr-f ȧr-sḫi n-ȧmu (n) Mn-nfr ẖn pa ḥb n pa shp ta ȧaw (n) ḥrī r ȧr-f (n)-ṭ-t paīf īt ṭī-f smau (?) st (n) pa ḫt ui-f r na spu (n)

17 Pr-āa ā.u.s. ntī āuī na ȧrpiu r hn (r) ḥa-tsp 9·t ȧuu ȧr ȧp-t n ḥṭ pr-t āshai paīs smṭ n sun na shs nsutu ntī āuī na ȧrpiu ẖn na ntī ȧuu ȧru r pr Pr-āa ā.u.s. ȧrm pa sta ntī mn (n) nau ȧru r hn (r) pa tīa (n) rn-f ḥn-f-s ān (r) ṭba pa (n) sut r I aḥ r un-nau-ȧru shṭi-f n na aḥu n pa ntr-ḥtp pāīs

18 smṭ n pa ȧrp r̲ I aḥ (n) na aḥu ȧrli n na ḫtp-ntru n na ntru ui-f r-ru ȧr-f mṭ-nfrt āshai (n) Ḥȧp Ur-mr ȧrm na kīu āuau ntī ḫuī (n) Kmi (n) ḥua nau un-nau nau un-nau ḥa-f ȧru (r) ḥatī-f ḥr paīu āsh-sḥn (n) tīa nb ȧu-f ṭī-t na ntī ȧuu uaḫu ub taīu ḳis-t ȧuu āi ȧuu shāsh ȧu-f thaī na ntī ȧuu

19 sḫniu r naīu ȧrpiu ȧuu ȧr ḥb ȧuu ȧr grl ḥa-tu ȧrm pa sp mṭ ntī pḥ (n) ȧru na mtu pḥ-tu ntī pḥ n na ȧrpiu ȧrm na kīu mṭ-pḥ-tu (n) Kmi ȧr-f smnu ḥr paīu gi r ẖ pa hp ṭī-f nb ḥṭ pr-ṭ āshai ȧrm kt-ẖ·t nkt ub ta as·t Hȧp ṭī-f mnnḳu ta īp-t (n) mai n īp-t ȧu.

20 na-ān-s m-shs ṭī-f mnnḳu ḥa-t-ntr knḥi
ḫau (n) mai (n) ntru tī-f ȧr kt-ẖt paīu
gi ȧuf n īr(*sic*)·t (*read* ḥatī) n ntr mnḫ
ḥr na ntru ȧuf shn na mṭ-pḥ-tu (n) na
ȧrpiu r tī-t ȧru (n) mai (n) paīf ha ntī
Pr-āa ā.u.s. (n) pa gi ntī pḥ ṭī nf na
ntru (n) ta shb-t (n) nai pa tchra (djra)
pa ḳni pa nāsh pa utcha (udja) pa
21 snbi ȧrm na kīu mṭ-nfru ṭru r ṭaī-f ȧau
(n) Pr-āa ā.u.s. smn ẖr-rf ȧrm naīf ẖrṭu
shā tcht (djt) ȧrm pa sḫni nfr pḥ-s n ḥatī
(n) na uābu (n) na ȧrpiu (n) Kmi ṭru
na mṭu-pḥ-tu ntī mtu Pr-āa ā.u.s. Ptlumias
ānkh tcht (djt) pa ntr pr ntī na-ān taīf
mṭ-nfrt ẖn na ȧrpiu
22 ȧrm na nti mtu na ntru mr ītu ȧ-ȧr ṭī-t
ḫpr-f ȧrm nti mtu na ntru mnḫu ȧ-ȧr ṭī-t
ḫpr na ȧ-ȧr ṭī-t ḫpr-f ȧrm na ntī mtu na
ntru snu ȧ-ȧr ṭī-t ḫpr na ȧ-ȧr ṭī-t ḫpru
ȧrm na ntī mtu na ntru ntī nḥm na ītu
(n) naīf ītu r ṭī-t āiu mtuu ṭī-t ȧāḥā uā
tutu (n) Pr-āa ā.u.s. Ptlumias ānḫ tcht
(djt) pa ntr pr ntī na-ān taīf mṭ-nfrt
23 mtuu tchṭ (djṭ) nf Ptlumias ntch (ndj) Bḳi
ntī ȧu paīf uhm Ptlumias ȧ-ȧr nḫtī Kmi
ȧrm uā tutu (n) pa ntr (n) ta nȧu-t ȧuf
ṭī-t nf ḫpsh ḳni n pa ȧrpi ȧrpi sp-2 (n)
pa maā ntī unḥ n pa ȧrpi ȧuu r r ẖ īp·t
rmt (n) Kmi mtu na uābu shms na tutuu
n pa ȧrpi ȧrpi sp-2 sp-3 ẖr hru

24 mtuu ḫaā ṭbḥ à-àr ḥru mtuu àr nu pa sp mṭ ntī (n) hp (n) àru (r) ẖ pa ntī àuu àrf (n) na kīu ntru (n) na ḥbu na ḫāu n na hruu (n) rnu mtuu ṭī-t ḫā sḫm ntr (n) Pr-āa ā.u.s. Ptlumias pa ntr pr ntī na-ān taīf mṭ-nfrt sa Ptlumias àrm ta Pr-āa·t Arsina na ntru mr Pr-āa (*read* ītu) àrm ta ga-t n nb pa àrpi

25 àrpi sp-2 mtuu ṭī-t htp-s (n) pa ntī uāb[u] àrm na kīu gau àu àr na ḥbu āaiu ntī àuu ṭī-t ḫā na ntru n-àmu ḫpr mtuu ṭī-t ḫā ta ga-(t) (n) pa ntr pr ntī na-ān taīf mṭ-nfrt àrmu r-ṭī-t ḫpr-f àuu sun ta ga-(t) n pa hru àrm pa sp tīa ntī àn-àu mtuu ṭī-t sḥn (n) nb 10 n Pr-āa ā.u.s. r uā-t ārāi n-àmu r uā r ẖ pa ntī

26 (n) hp n àrf r na sḥnu (n) nb r tchatcha (djadja) (n) ta ga-(t) n ta shb-t (n) na ārāiu ntī ḫpr ḥr tchatcha (djadja) (n) pa sp ga mtuu pa sḫnt ḫpr (n) ta mte-t (mti-t) (n) na sḥnu ḫpr mtu-f r ḫā Pr-āa ā.u.s. n-àm-f (n) ḥ-t ntr (n) Mn-nfr àuu àr nf n na ntī n hp n àru (n) pa shp ta àau (n) ḥrī mtuu ḫaā (n) ta r(-t) ḥrī-t (n) àfṭ ntī (n) pa bnr (n) na sḥnu (n) pa mtī (mte)

27 (n) pa sḥn (n) nb ntī sẖ ḥrī uā-t uatch-t (uadj-t) àrm uā shmā mtuu ḫaā na ārāiu ḥr uā-t nbu r uā shmā ẖrr-s ḥr pr-àmntī r pa ḳḥ (r) tchatcha (djadja) (n) ta ga-(t) (n) nb mtuu ḫaā uā-t ārāi r uā-t nbu

h̲rr-s ḥr uā uṭ r īabī ntī åu paīf uhm
Pr-āa ā.u.s. å-år sḥtch (shdj) shmāi mḥi
(n)-ṭ-t ḫpr-f åu 4nu shmu ārḳī ntī åuu år pa
28 hru ms Pr-āa ā.u.s. n-am-f ḫpr åuf smn
(n) ḥb ḫā (n) ma årpiu ta ḥa-t paīs smṭ
(n) 2-nu pr-t (*sic*) ssu 17 nti åuu år nf na
åru pa shp ta åau (n) ḫrī n-åmf (r ?) ta
ḥat-t na mt-nfru å-år ḫpr (n) rmt nb pa
ms Pr-āa ā.u.s. ānḫ tcht (djt) årm pa shp
ta åau (n) ḥrī (r) årf år nai hruu ssu 17
ārḳī (n) ḥb h̲r åbṭ nb ḫn na årpiu (n) Kmī
ṭru mtuu år
29 grl uṭn pa sp mṭ ntī n hp (n) åru (n)
na kīu ḥbu (n) pa ḥb 2 h̲r åbt na nti
åuu åru (n) ābi mtuu tshu . . . na rmtu
ntī shms (n) pa årpi mtuu år ḥb ḫā (n)
na årpiu årm Kmi ṭr-f (n) Pr-āa ā.u.s.
Ptlumias ānḫ tcht (djt) pa ntr pr ntī
na-ān taīf mṭ-nfrt h̲r rnp-t tpī a-ḫt ssu I
shaā hru 5 åuu tha-ī kl(m)
30 auu år grl uṭn årm pa sp mṭ ntī pḥ (n)
åru na uābu ntī n na årpiu (n) Kmi årpi
sp-2 mtuu tchṭ (djṭ) nu na uābu (n) pa
ntr pr ntī na-ān taīf mṭ-nfrt n uaḥ r na
kīu rn n uāb mtuu sh̲-f n gi n tchta (djlā)
mṭ nb mtuu sh̲ ta åau n uāb (n) pa ntr
pr ntī na-ān taīf mṭ-nfrt (n) naiu gltīu
mtuu shf-s ḥr
31 atu mtu-s ḫpr åus āuī ṭ-t na rmtu mshā
ān nti åuu uaḫ (r) ṭī-t ḫā pa smṭ (n)

ta ga-t (n) nb (n) pa ntr pr ntī na-ān taīf mṭ-nfrt ntī ḥrī r ṭī-t ḫpr-s (n) naīu maāu mtuu ȧr na ḥbu na ḫāu ntī sẖ ḥrī ẖr rnp-t mtuf ḫpr ȧus sun tchṭ (djṭ) na ntī n Kmi ṭī-t pḫ pa ntr pr ntī na-ān taīf mṭ-nfrt

32 r ẖ pa ntī n hp n ȧrf mtuu sẖ pa ut n uitī (n) ȧni tchri (djri) n sẖ mṭ-ntr sẖ shā-t sẖ Uinn mtuu ṭī-t ȧāḥā-f n na ȧrpiu mḥ-1 na ȧrpiu mḥ-2 na ȧrpiu mḥ-3 ȧ-ȧr ṭ-t pa tut n Pr-āa ā.u.s. ānḫ tcht(djt)

CHAPTER IV

I.—EARLY PUBLICATIONS OF THE HIEROGLYPHIC VERSION ON THE ROSETTA STONE

The oldest published copies of the hieroglyphic text on the ROSETTA STONE will be found in the facsimile published by the Society of Antiquaries of London in 1802–3; in the *Description de l'Égypte Antique*, tome v, plate 53; and in LEPSIUS, *Auswahl der wichtigsten Urkunden des aegyptischen Alterthums*, Leipzig, 1842, plate 18. The first to attempt to translate any part of the hieroglyphic text on the Stone was THOMAS YOUNG, who published his "interpretation of some parts of it" in *Archaeologia*, vol. xviii, London, 1817, p. 70. The text, with a Latin translation, was published by H. BRUGSCH in his *Inscriptio Rosettana hieroglyphica*, Berlin, 1851, and another Latin translation, with the text, was published by M. A. UHLEMANN (*Inscriptionis Rosettanae hieroglyphicae decretum* . . ., Leipzig, 1853). Further attempts to translate the text were made by F. CHABAS (*L'inscription hiéroglyphique de Rosette*, Chalon-sur-Saône, 1867); by S. SHARPE (*The Rosetta Stone in hieroglyphics and Greek,* London, 1871); and a facsimile of the Stone, together with transcripts of the Greek and hieroglyphic texts (printed in type), and English translations were published by BUDGE (*The Decrees of Memphis and Canopus,* London, 1904, 3 vols. (now out of print). The best facsimile of the Stone, though on a comparatively small scale, was published by the Trustees of the BRITISH MUSEUM (*The Rosetta Stone,* London, 1913, folio, with letterpress by BUDGE).

As soon as Egyptologists were able to translate the hieroglyphic text on the Stone, they realized that more than one-half of it had been broken away. It was known as far back as 1848 that a mutilated copy of the Decree of Memphis existed on the walls of the great temple of Philae, but from this only restorations of single words and very short passages of the missing text could be made. Early in the "eighties" of the last century a limestone stele inscribed with a copy of the hieroglyphic version of the Decree of Memphis was found at NUBAYRAH, near DAMANHUR in LOWER EGYPT. The stele is rounded at the top and is 4 ft. 2 in. high and 1 ft. 8 in. wide. See BOURIANT, "La stèle 5576 du Musée de Boulaq et l'inscription de Rosette," in the *Recueil de travaux,* Paris, 1885, vol. vi, pp. 1–20; BAILLET, *Le décret de Memphis et les inscriptions de Rosette et de Damanhour,* Paris, 1905; and AHMAD BEY

KAMAL, *Catalogue générale des antiquités égyptiennes*, No. 22188, with a photographic reproduction. The best and most complete transcripts of the hieroglyphic text are those of SETHE (*Urkunden*, iv, p. 169) and SPIEGELBERG (*Kanopus und Memphis* (*Rosettana*), Heidelberg, 1922).

II.—RUNNING TRANSLATION OF THE HIEROGLYPHIC TRANSLATION

[THE DATING OF THE DECREE]

N.B.—In this translation, **N** = Stele of Nubayrah and **R** = Stele of Rosetta.

N 1 The ninth year, the fourth day of the month of XANDIKOS, which is the equivalent of the eighteenth day of the second month[1] of the season PER-T (*i.e.* the season of "going forth"), according to the inhabitants of TA-MER-T (*i.e.* the LAND OF THE INUNDATION, OR EGYPT), under the Majesty of the HORUS-RĀ, the YOUTH, who hath ascended as king upon the throne of his father, Lord of the Crown of the South and of the Crown of the North, mighty one of strength (or, valour), the stablisher of the TWO LANDS (*i.e.* EGYPT), who is the benefactor (or, the beautifier) of TA-MER-T,

[1] The Coptic Mekhir, ⲙ̅ϣⲓⲣ.

N 2 whose heart is benevolently disposed towards the gods, the Horus who vanquished Set (Nubti) of Nub (*i.e.* Ombos),[1] who is vigorous of life for men, lord of the Set festivals[2] like Ptaḥ-Tenn, Prince, like Rā, King of the South (Upper Egypt) and the North (Lower Egypt), heir of the Father-Loving Gods (Philopatores, *i.e.* Ptolemy IV and his Queen), the chosen of Ptaḥ, Usr-ka-Rā,[3] the living image of Åmen, the son of the Sun (Rā), Ptolemy, the everliving, the beloved of Ptaḥ, the god who appeareth [like the sun ?], the lord of benefactions (or, beauties),

N 3 the son of Ptolemy and Arsinoë, the two Father-Loving Gods, when Aiatus, the son of Aiaṭus, was priest of Alexander, and of the two Saviour Gods (Soteres), and of the two Brother-Gods (Adelphoi) and of the two Well-Doing Gods (Eucharistoi),

[1] Greek *ἀντιπάλων ὑπερτέρου*; the Demotic has "he who [stands] upon his enemy." The old legend says that Osiris and Horus stood upon Set when they had defeated him. Erman has shown that  is an incorrect representation of a very ancient picture in which the Hawk of Horus is seen leading captive 6,000 men.

[2] The celebration of these festivals renewed, it was thought, the life of kings.

[3] This was the name of Ptolemy V as king of the South and North.

N 4 and of the two Father-Loving Gods, and the god who appeareth, the lord of benefits ; and

PYRRHA, daughter of PHILINUS, was the bearer of the prize of victory (athlophoros)

N 5 before BERENICE, the Well-Doing QUEEN ; and

AREIA, the daughter of DIOGENES, was the bearer of the basket (canephoros) before ARSINOË, the Brother-Lover ; and

N 6 EIRENE, the daughter of PTOLEMY, was priestess of ARSINOË, the Father-Lover.

[THE ASSEMBLING OF THE PRIESTHOODS OF ALL EGYPT AT MEMPHIS]

On this day DECREE : The directors of the services in the temples (high priests ?),

N 7 [and] the ministers of the gods (prophets ?), [and] the priests who presided over the Mysteries of the gods, [and] the priests who cleanse and who go into the holy place to array the gods in their [festal] apparel, [and] the scribes who copy the books of the gods, and the sages of the College of the House of Life, and

N 8 the other priests who came from the Two Regions of the South and the North to WHITE WALL (*i.e.* MEMPHIS) for the festival whereat his Majesty, the King of the South and of the North, the Lord of the Two Lands, PTOLEMY, the everliving, the beloved of PTAḤ, the god who appeareth, the lord of benefits, received the kingdom from his father. They went into the sanctuary of the

N 9 BALANCE OF THE TWO LANDS,[1] and behold they spake, [saying,] :—

[SUMMARY OF THE BENEFITS CONFERRED ON EGYPT BY PTOLEMY V]

Now the King of the South and the North, the heir of the two Father-Loving Gods, the chosen of PTAḤ, USR-KA-RĀ, the living image of ÅMEN, the son of RĀ, PTOLEMY, the ever-living, the beloved of PTAḤ, the god who appeareth, the lord of benefits, the son of the King of the South and of the North, PTOLEMY, and the Queen, the Lady of the Two Lands, ARSINOË, the two Father-Loving Gods, hath done many (or, great) and good deeds of all kinds for

N 10 the Horus Lands, and for those who dwell in them, and for every person who is under his beneficent rule, in every possible manner—he is like a god, the son of two gods, who hath been born upon earth by a goddess, being the similitude of HORUS, the son of ISIS, the son of OSIRIS, who avenged his father OSIRIS—

[1] A name of Memphis, which marked the place where Lower Egypt ended on the South, and Upper Egypt ended on the North.

N 11 Behold, His Majesty possesseth the heart of a beneficent (or, perfect) god towards the gods—he hath given large amounts of silver (*i.e.* money), and great quantities of grain, to the temples of EGYPT. [And] he hath given very many precious gifts in order to promote peace and good order in TA-MER-T, and to establish (or, endow) the sanctuaries of the South and the North.

[THE GIFTS OF PTOLEMY V TO HIS TROOPS]

His Majesty gave gifts to the soldiers who were under his august authority,
N 12 to every man according to his rank.

[PTOLEMY V REDUCES SOME TAXES AND ABOLISHES OTHERS]

[As concerning] the taxes on the people throughout EGYPT, and the dues from the nobles which remained [unpaid], those which were due to him he diminished, and others he abolished altogether, so that both the soldiers and the civilians might be comfortable during the period in which he was the one sovereign Lord.

[PTOLEMY V REMITS ARREARS OF TAXATION]

N 13 The arrears of taxes which were due from the people, and also from all the inhabitants of BAQ-T (EGYPT), who lived under his beneficent rule (or, authority) in every part of the country, he remitted entirely; the amount remitted was a vast sum, and it is impossible to say how great it was.

N 14 Those who had been arrested and had been thrown into prison, and every person therein who had been detained there for crimes committed a long time ago, he showed compassion upon.

[PTOLEMY V CONFIRMS THE REVENUES OF THE TEMPLES]

His Majesty promulgated a DECREE, saying:—

"As concerning the sacred gifts (*i.e.* offerings) made to the gods, and the [amounts of] the silver and the grain which are given to the temples annually, and the possessions of all kinds of the gods in the vineyards and in the plantations (or, gardens)

N 15 of the nome, and all the properties which were in their possession under the Majesty of his august father, shall continue to belong to them."

And he further commanded, [saying]:—

"The contributions made by the hands of the priests to the . . . shall not exceed in amount that which they were [in the habit of] contributing up to the first year of [the reign of] the Majesty of his august father."

[PTOLEMY V RELEASES THE PRIESTHOOD FROM TAXATION AND FROM THEIR ANNUAL JOURNEY TO ALEXANDRIA, AND ABOLISHES THE PRESS GANG, AND REMITS TWO-THIRDS OF THE TAX ON BYSSUS]

N 16 Moreover, His Majesty released the orders of priests who minister at prescribed hours in the temples from the journeys which they made to the WALL OF ALEXANDER (*i.e.* ALEXANDRIA) at a certain period of the year.

[And] His Majesty commanded, [saying] :—" Behold, men who are employed on ships shall not be seized [by press gangs ?]."

[And] His Majesty remitted two-thirds of the pieces of byssus which

N 17 were made in the temples for the king's house.

[PTOLEMY V RESTORES THE PEACE AND PROSPERITY OF EGYPT]

Likewise every thing which had been in a state of disorder for a long time past, His Majesty restored them to the excellent condition in which they had formerly been. He was exceedingly careful to ensure that everything which it had been customary to do

N 18 for the gods should be performed in the most exact and best possible manner. And moreover, he treated the people with the strictest justice, even as did THOTH the Great Great.

[Ptolemy V proclaims a general amnesty]

He commanded also *concerning certain men who came back among the warriors, and* [*concerning*] *the remainder who were on another road* (?) *during the revolt which took place in Egypt, that they should go back to their own places,*[1] and should remain in possession of their own property.

[Ptolemy V takes steps to protect Egypt against invaders]

[And] His Majesty took care to despatch infantry, and cavalry, and ships to repulse those who came

N 19 to attack Egypt from the sea-coast (?) as well as from the Great Green Sea (*i.e.* the Mediterranean), and he gave large sums of silver and vast quantities of grain in order that the Horus Lands and Ta-Mer-t might be maintained in a state of peace.

[Ptolemy V besieges Lycopolis]

His Majesty marched *against the town of Shekam, which the enemy had fortified with works* (*i.e.* defences) *of every kind, and in it were collected many weapons and everything necessary for fighting. He* (*i.e.* the King) *surrounded the aforesaid town with walls, and*

[1] The words in italics are added from the Demotic version (l. ii.)

he made dams outside of them because the[1] enemy who were inside it,

N 20 because they had committed many great atrocities in BAQ-T (EGYPT) [and] they had transgressed the way beloved of His Majesty and the ordinances of the gods.[2] He (*i.e.* the king) blocked

N 21 all the canals which flowed into this city, the like of which had never been done by any of the King's ancestors.[3] He expended a very large amount of money in effecting these works. His Majesty stationed his infantry, and [his] cavalry, at the mouths of these canals to keep guard over them, and to strengthen them (*i.e.* the dams), *because the inundations of the waters* [*of the Nile*] *which took place in the eighth year* [*of the*] *King's reign were very extensive, and the waters of the aforesaid canals flooded many low-lying lands,*[4] and were very deep. His Majesty took this town by assault (?) *in a very short time.*

1 The words in italics are supplied from the Demotic version (ll. 14 and 15).

2 There is no equivalent in the Greek for the passage beginning  and ending 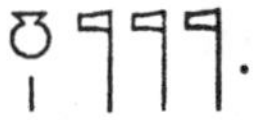.

3 There is no equivalent in the Greek for the passage beginning  and ending .

4 The words in italics are added from the Demotic version (ll. 12 and 13).

N 22 He crushed those of the enemy who were brought out from the interior of the town, [and] he made a great massacre of them, even like unto the massacre which RĀ, and HORUS, the son of ISIS, made of their enemies in that same place aforetime (?).

[PTOLEMY V PUNISHES THE LEADERS OF THE REBELLION AGAINST HIS FATHER PTOLEMY IV PHILOPATOR]

R 1 Behold,[1] the enemy had gathered together the soldiers, and they were at their head, and they led astray [the people] in the [other] nomes, and looted the Horus Lands (*i.e.* the temples and their estates). They transgressed the way of His Majesty and his august father. The gods bestowed victory upon him, and some of them were brought into ÀNEB ḤETCH-T (*i.e.* WHITE WALL or, MEMPHIS)

N 23 at the time of the celebration of the festival whereat he received the kingdom from his father. He slaughtered them by setting them up upon wood (*i.e.* he either crucified or impaled them).

[PTOLEMY V REMITS THE ARREARS OF TAXES AND CONTRIBUTIONS DUE TO THE KING FROM THE TEMPLES]

His Majesty remitted the arrears of taxes which were due to him from the temples up

[1] The ROSETTA text begins with the sign .

to the ninth year of [his reign]—very many large quantities of silver, and masses of grain,
R 2 and likewise the cloth of byssus which the temples were obliged to give to the King's house, and the balance (?), which was fixed (or, determined) upon for the quantity of the cloth which they, up to this day had already delivered. And as concerning the grain, he remitted the five bushels[1] which were levied on the *arura*[2] in the field of the gods, and likewise the measure
N 25 of wine which was [levied on the *arura*] in the vineyard lands [of the gods].

[The endowments of Apis, Mnevis, and the other sacred animals, made by Ptolemy V]

He provided great endowments for Apis[3] [and] Mnevis,[4] and
R 3 all the [other] sacred animals, such endowments being larger than those which his ancestors had made ; his heart occupied itself

[1] The Greek has ἀρτάβη (a word derived from the Persians) = 1 medimnus + 3 choenices. The Egyptians borrowed the word and it appears in Coptic under the forms **ⲉⲣⲧⲟⲃ**, **ⲣ̄ⲧⲟⲃ**, **ⲣ̄ⲧⲁⲃ**, etc. ; it is the *irdab* of the Arabs, and is in common use throughout the East to-day.

[2] Roughly "acre."

[3] The sacred bull of Memphis.

[4] The sacred bull of Heliopolis.

with plans (or, schemes for their welfare) at every moment. He provided everything which [their servants] required

N 26 for the embalmment of their bodies in great abundance and in an honourable fashion. He brought [also] the things which had to be provided in their temples for the celebration of the great festival, and made to be taken there animals to be slaughtered there for the burnt offerings, and the libations which were to be poured out, and everything which was necessary for the performance of the customary rites. Moreover, the gifts of honour which had [to be brought] in the temples, and all the great things of Egypt, His Majesty [provided] according to what was laid down in the regulations.

R 4 He gave gold, and silver, and grain in very large quantities, and all things, according to their number, for the house wherein the LIVING APIS dwelt, and His Majesty decorated anew with handsome work, which was exceedingly beautiful, and he made the LIVING HORUS to appear therein.

[THE DEVOTION OF PTOLEMY V TO THE SERVICE OF THE GODS AND HIS REWARD]

He set up (?) in new [work] the temples, and shrines, and altars of the gods, *and he permitted the other temples to resume their* [former]

customs.[1] Behold, His Majesty hath the heart of a well-doing god towards the gods and he concerneth himself with the . . . of the beautiful temples

R 5 so that they may renew during his [life-]time [his rule as] the Lord One (or one overlordship). As a reward for these things the gods and the goddesses have given unto him victory, and might, and life, and strength, and health, and every good things of every kind whatsoever and his great position is firmly established upon him and upon his children for ever.

[THE PRIESTS DECIDE TO AUGMENT THE HONOURS PAID TO PTOLEMY V AND HIS ANCESTORS]

WITH FORTUNATE HAPPENING! (*i.e.* may good luck attend this).

It hath entered into the heart of the priests of all the temples of the South (UPPER EGYPT) and the North (LOWER EGYPT) the strong words (*i.e.* honours) of the King of the South and of the North, PTOLEMY, the everliving, the beloved of PTAḤ, the god who appeareth (Epiphanes), the lord of benefit, in the Horus Lands to multiply; and the honours which

[1] The words in italics are supplied from the Demotic version, ti-f år ke-t ḥe-t paiu gai.

belong to the two Father-Loving Gods (PHILOPATORES) who begot him; and those which belong to the two Well-Doing Gods (EUERGETAI) who begot those who begot him;

R 6 and those of the two Brother Gods (ADELPHOI) who caused to come into being those who made them; and those of the two Saviour Gods (SOTERES), the fathers of those who begot them.

[THE PRIESTS DECIDE TO SET UP STATUES OF PTOLEMY V AND THE CHIEF LOCAL GOD IN EACH OF THE TEMPLES OF EGYPT]

And there shall be set up a statue of the King of the South and the North, PTOLEMY, the everliving, the beloved of PTAḤ, the god who appeareth, the lord of benefactions, and its name shall be called "PTOLEMY, the Avenger of Baq-t," whereof the interpretation (or, meaning) is, "Ptolemy, the Protector of KAM-T (EGYPT)," and (2) a statue of the god of the city, who shall be giving to him a royal sword of victory, [And these shall be set up] in every temple in UPPER and LOWER EGYPT, in the court of the temple to which the soldiers [have access], in the work of the sculptors of EGYPT.[1]

[1] *I.e.* the statues shall be of purely native workmanship, and not Greek.

R 7 And the priests who have the right of entry into the god-house (*i.e.* sanctuary) in every temple shall perform rites of worship before these statues three times daily, and they shall set before them the implements of the cult (?), and they shall perform with the greatest care every prescribed ceremony which will gratify their KAS (*i.e.* spirit doubles) in precisely the same way as they are performed for the gods of the Nomes on the festivals which are celebrated at the beginning of the seasons of the year, and on the days of festival, and on the aforesaid days.

[A WOODEN STATUE OF PTOLEMY V SHALL BE SET UP IN A SHRINE OF GOLD]

And there shall be fashioned a splendid statue of the King of the South and the North, PTOLEMY, the god who appeareth, the lord of benefits, the son of the King of the South and the North, PTOLEMY, and the Queen, the Lady of the Two Lands, ARSINOË, the two Father-Loving Gods,

R 8 and a magnificent [portable] shrine [made] of silver-gold, and inlaid with real precious stones of every kind, for every temple of the aforementioned regions, and they shall be set in the holy place, side by side with the shrines of the gods of the Nomes. Now therefore when the great festivals are celebrated, and the god in his august shrine cometh forth from his chamber (?), the holy shrine of the god who appeareth, the lord of benefits, shall make its appearance along with them.

[DESCRIPTION OF THE SHRINE]

In order to enable the people to recognize this shrinc from to day and for *ḥenti* periods of years (*i.e.* endless time), ten crowns of His Majesty, with an uracus in the front of each one of them,

R 9 as it is right and proper for every crown, shall be placed on this shrine, instead of the two uraei which are usually placed upon shrines, with the double crown  in the middle of them, because His Majesty shone therein in the HOUSE OF PTAḤ after he had performed every ceremony in connection with the introduction of the King into the House of the God when he received his great Office (or Rank). And there shall be placed on the upper side of the rectangle (?) which is on the outside of these crowns, [and] opposite to the double crown a cluster of rushes  and a cluster of papyrus . A vulture upon a basket, with a cluster of reeds  under her shall be

R 10 at the right corner (or, angle) of this shrine,

N 27 and an uraeus, likewise on a basket, with a cluster of papyrus under her  shall be on the left corner. The interpretation (or, meaning) of this is "The Lords of the Two Crowns illumine the Two Lands" (*i.e.* all Egypt).

[FESTIVALS ARE TO BE CELEBRATED ON THE BIRTHDAY OF PTOLEMY V, AND ON THE DAY OF HIS ACCESSION TO THE THRONE IN EACH MONTH]

Inasmuch as the last (*i.e.* the 30th) day of the fourth month of the season Shemu,[1]

N 28 the birthday of the beautiful and ever-living god, was established as a festival and a day of rejoicing in the Horus Lands (*i.e.* on the temple estates) in former times, and also the seventeenth day of the second month of the season AKHET,[2] the day whereon was performed for him the ceremony of the coronation of the King, when he received the kingdom from his father—now behold, the beginning (or, source) of all the many great

[1] The Mesōrē, ⲙⲉⲥⲱⲣⲏ of the Copts.

[2] The Paophi, or ⲡⲁⲁⲡⲉ of the Copts.

and beneficial things which those who dwell on these lands enjoy, is

R 11 the birthday of the great and everliving god, and the receiving by him.

N 29 of the kingdom—these days (viz.), the 17th day and the 30th day of every month shall be observed as festivals in all the temples of EGYPT, and a burnt offering shall be offered up, and a drink offering (or, libation) shall be poured out, and everything which it is right and proper to do at festivals shall be done on these days every month. Everything which is done on these festivals shall be carried on for [the benefit of] all those who perform their service (or, worship) in the house of the god.

[A FIVE-DAY FESTIVAL AT THE BEGINNING OF THE MONTH OF THOTH SHALL BE CELEBRATED ANNUALLY IN HONOUR OF PTOLEMY V]

There shall be celebrated a festival, and a day of rejoicing [observed] in the temples of

R 12 Egypt, all of them, [in honour] of the King of the South and North, PTOLEMY, the ever-living, the beloved of PTAḤ, the god who appeareth, the lord of benefits, each year, at the beginning of the first month of the season AKHET, and lasting from the first to the fifth day of the same, [during] which days the people shall [wear] garlands on their heads. The altars shall be provided with offerings and libations shall be poured out, and everything shall be done which it is right and proper to do [at festivals].

[THE PRIESTS OF PTOLEMY V SHALL ASSUME AN ADDITIONAL TITLE]

The priests of all the above-mentioned temples shall be called " priest (or, minister) of the god who appeareth, the lord of benefits," in addition to their usual titles as priests. They shall inscribe

R 13 it upon their official documents, and the title " priest of the god who appeareth, the lord of benefits," shall be engraved on the rings which they wear on their hands.

[PRIVATE PERSONS SHALL BE ALLOWED TO PAY THESE HONOURS TO PTOLEMY V]

Now behold, it is in the hands of those people who are wishful to do so to set up a copy of this shrine of " the god who appeareth, the lord of benefits," and to place it in their houses. And they shall celebrate these festivals and days of rejoicing every month and every year, so that it may be known that the dwellers in TA-MER-T (EGYPT) glorify

R 14 the "god who appeareth, the lord of benefits," as it is meet and right to do.

[THIS DECREE SHALL BE PUBLISHED]

This Decree shall be engraved upon a tablet of hard stone, in the writing of the words of the god (*i.e.* hieroglyphs), [and] in the writing of books (*i.e.* demotic), [and[in the writing of the Ḥaui-nebu (*i.e.* Greeks). And the tablet shall be set up in the sanctuaries, in each of the temples mentioned above, [of the] first, second ⌊and⌋ third ⌊class⌋, by the side of the statue of the King of the South and North, PTOLEMY, the everliving, the beloved of PTAḤ, the god who appeareth, the lord of benefits.

Characteristic portraits of **Ptolemy V,** and his father **Ptolemy IV Philopator,** and his grandfather **Ptolemy III, Euergetes I,** and their principal wives will be found on **Plates XII** and **XIII.** Portraits of the founder of the Ptolemaïc Dynasty, **Ptolemy I Soter,** and **Ptolemy IX** are also there given.

III.—THE HIEROGLYPHIC TRANSLATION OF THE DECREE WITH INTER-LINEAR TRANSLITERATION AND TRANSLATION

[The Dating of the Decree]

N 1 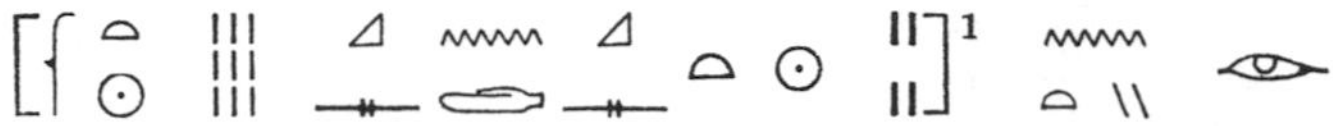

renp-t IX *Ḳsnṭḳs* *sesu IV* *enti* *àr*

Year 9, [month] Xandikos, day 4, which maketh

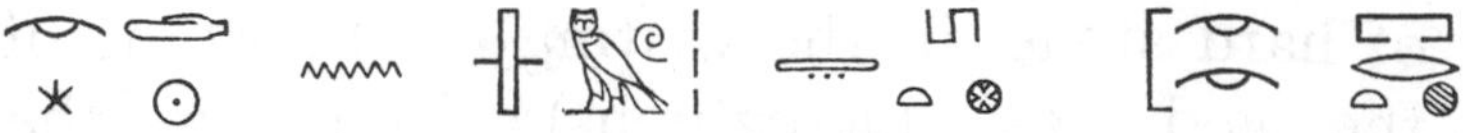

àbṭ *en* *àmiu* *Ta-Mer-t* *àbṭ II* *Per-t*

month of the dwellers in Ta-Mer (Egypt) {month two of the season Pert,}

sesu *XVIII* *kher* *ḥem* *en* *Ḥer-Rā* (?)

day 18, under the Majesty of the Horus-Rā

Ḥunnu *khā* *em* *nesu* *ḥer* *às-t*

the Youth, rising like a king upon the throne of

---

[1] The Nabayrah Stele has here 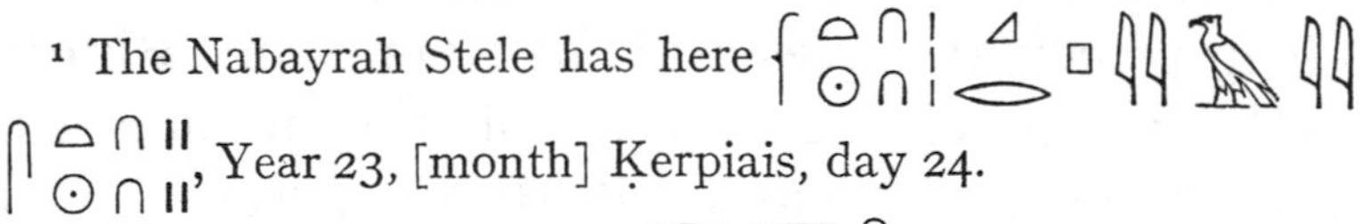, Year 23, [month] Ḳerpiais, day 24.

[2] The Nabayrah Stele has  IIII, Fourth month of Pert, day 24.

teb-f — *Nebtȧ* — *ur* — *peḥti*

his father, {lord of the Vulture crown and of the Uraeus crown,} mighty one of strength,

smen — *Taui* — *s-nefer* — *Ta-Mer-t*

{stablisher of the Two Lands, (*i.e.* of Egypt)} {benefactor of Ta-Mer (*i.e.* of Egypt),}

N 2 

menkh — *ȧb* — *kher* — *neteru* — *Ḥer Nub-ti*

benevolent of heart towards the gods, the Horus,

uatchi — *ānkh* — *en* — *hamemu* — *neb* — *ḥeb*

{making vigorous the life} of men and women, lord of the Seṭ-festivals

Ptaḥ-Tenn — *ma* — *ȧti* — *Rā* — *ma* — *nesu-bȧt*

Ptaḥ-Ten like, sovereign Rā like, {King of the South and North,}

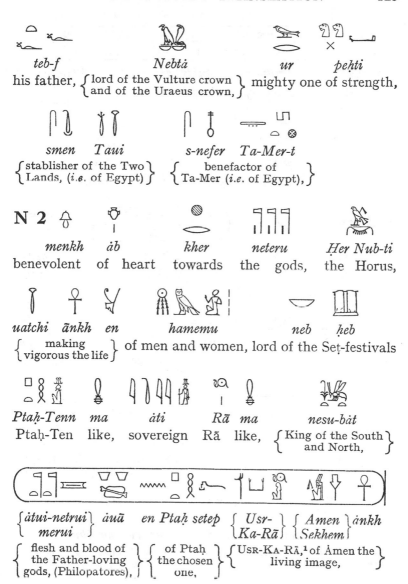

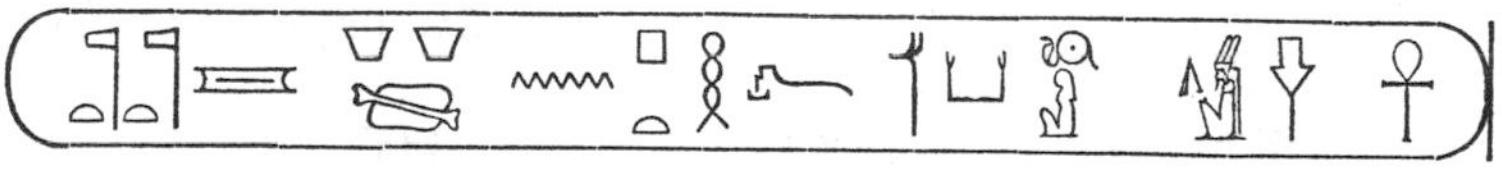

{*ȧtui-netrui merui*} — *ȧuā* — *en Ptaḥ setep* — {*Usr-Ka-Rā*} — {*Amen Sekhem*} *ȧnkh*

{flesh and blood of the Father-loving gods, (Philopatores),} {of Ptaḥ the chosen one,} {USR-KA-RĀ,[1] of Åmen the living image,}

---

[1] USRKARĀ is the Nesu-bȧt name of Ptolemy V.

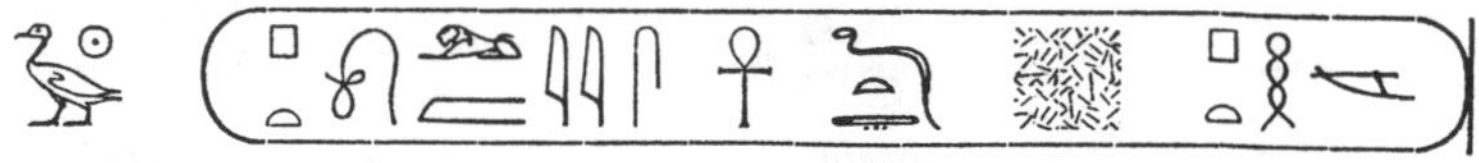

sa Rā *Ptulmis* *ānkh djet* . . . *Ptaḥ-mer*

Son of Rā, Ptolemy, the everliving { of Ptah beloved, }

neter *peri* *neb* *neferu*

the god appearing (Epiphanes) lord of benefactions,

N 3 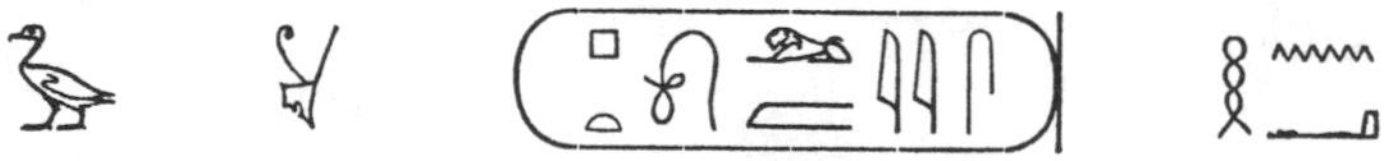

sa *en* *Ptulmis* *ḥenā*

son of Ptolemy and

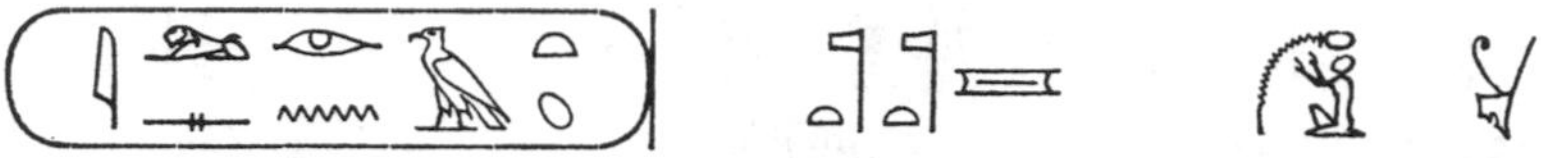

Ȧrsna *neterui ȧtui merui* *uāb* *en*

Arsinoë { of the Father-gods beloved, } priest of

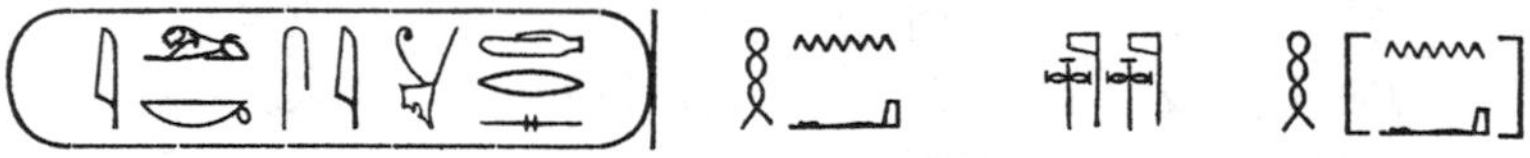

Ȧlksȧnṭrs *ḥenā* *neterui netchui* *ḥe[nā]*

Alexander { and the two gods who deliver, (Soteres), }

neterui senui *ḥenā* *neterui menkhui*

{ and the two gods [who are] brothers, (Adelphoi), } and { the two Well-doing gods, (Euergetai), }

---

[1] The Nabayrah Stele has .

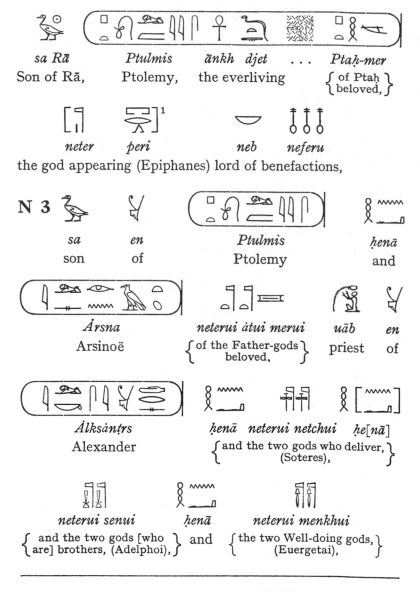

N 4 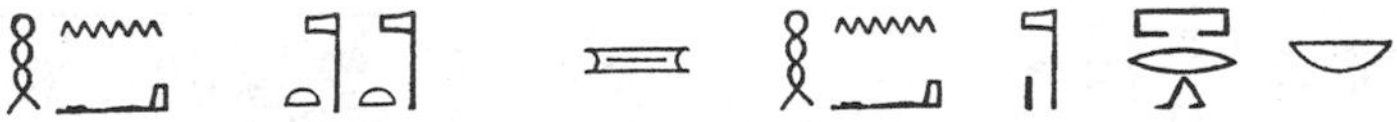

ḥenȧ	*neterui ȧtui*	*merui*	*ḥenȧ*	*neter*	*peri*	*neb*
and	{the two Father-loving gods, (Philopatores),}		and	{the god who appeareth, (Epiphanes),}		

neferu	*Aiaṭus*	*pa*
the lord of benefits,	Aiaṭus	the [son of]

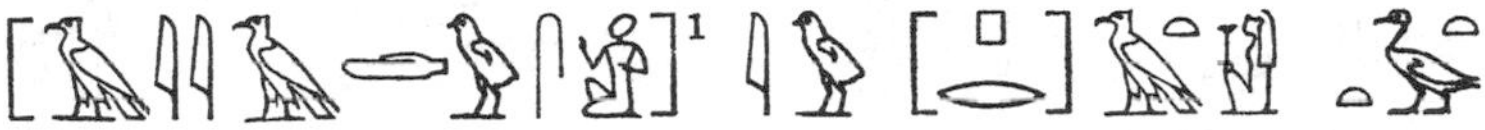

Aiaṭus	*ȧu*	*Pera*	*sa-tt*
Aiaṭus	being	Pyrrha,	daughter of

Pilins	*fai*
Philinus	the bearer of

---

[1] The Nabayrah Stele has the name of the priest of the 23rd year "Ptolemy, the [son of] Pyrrhides,"

Ptulmis *pa* *Perriṭs*

The name in brackets is suggested by Sethe as the original of 'Αέτου τοῦ 'Αέτου. Other suggestions of his follow.

[2] The Nabayrah Stele has "Demetria, daughter of Telemachus,"

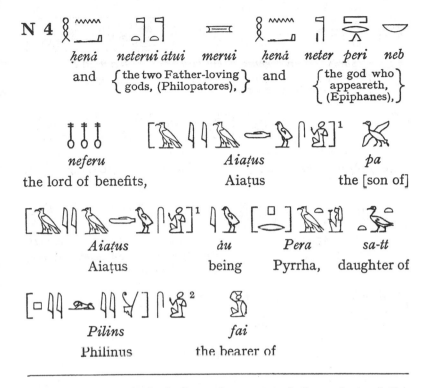

Ṭem *ṭrr* *sa-tt* *Talimkus*

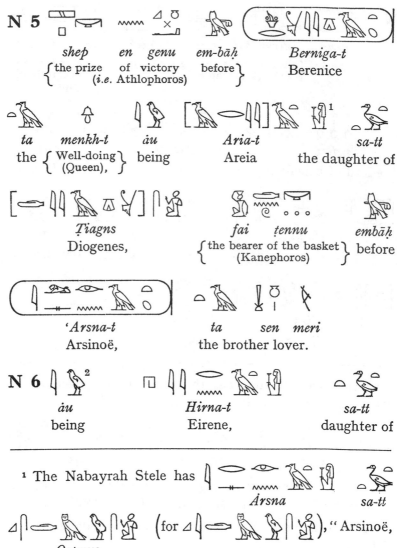

N 5 

shep *en* *genu* *em-bāḥ* *Berniga-t*
{the prize of victory before (*i.e.* Athlophoros)} Berenice

ta *menkh-t* *àu* *Aria-t* *sa-tt*
the {Well-doing (Queen),} being Areia the daughter of

Ṭiagns *fai* *ṭennu* *embāḥ*
Diogenes, {the bearer of the basket (Kanephoros)} before

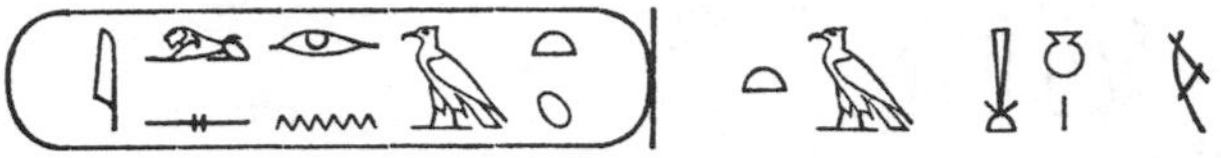

'Arsna-t *ta* *sen* *meri*
Arsinoë, the brother lover.

N 6 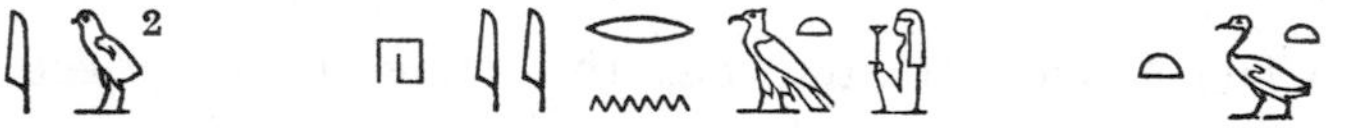

àu *Hirna-t* *sa-tt*
being Eirene, daughter of

---

[1] The Nabayrah Stele has  *Àrsna* *sa-tt*  *Qsṭmus* (for ), "Arsinoë, daughter of Cadmus."

[2] Nabayrah Stele, 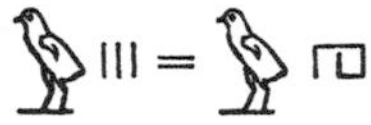.

Ptulmis *en* *uāb-t* *en* *Ȧrsna-t*
Ptolemy priestess of Arsinoë,

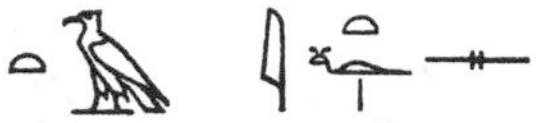

ta *ȧtf-s* *meri*
the lover of her father,

[The assembling of the priesthoods of all Egypt at Memphis]

hru *pen* *skhaui* *ȧu* *mer* *shenu*
day this Decree being the directors of services (?)

N 7

ḥem neteru *ḥeru sesheta* *neter*
[and] the prophets, {and those over the hidden things,} of the god of [and]

uābu *āqiu* *er* *bu* *tcheser* *smer*
the priests who go {into the place holy (*i.e.* the shrine)} [to] robe the gods

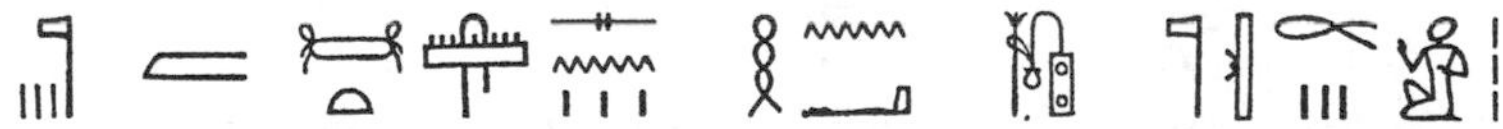

neteru *em* *sti* *-t-sen* *ḥenā* *saḥu* *madjaiu* *neter*
in their apparel, {and the scribes of the books of the gods,}

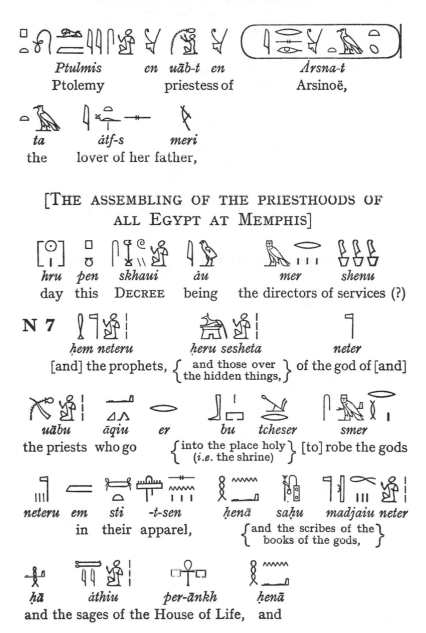

ḥā *ȧthiu* *per-ānkh* *ḥenā*
and the sages of the House of Life, and

N 8 

na ki uābu i em àterti-t

the other priests coming from the two regions of

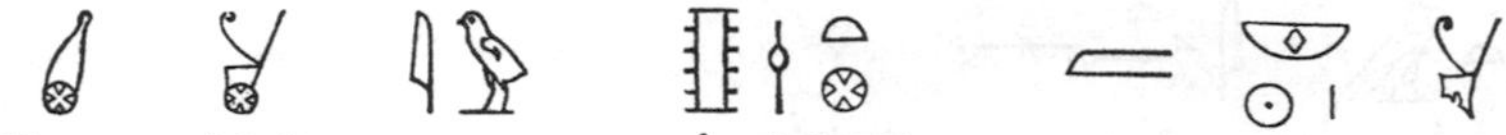

Res-t Meḥ-t àu Àneb-hedj em ḥeb en

{the South [and] the North} to {White Wall (*i.e.* Memphis)} on the festival of

seshep nesuit em tef-f àn ḥem Nesu-bat

receiving kingship from his father {Majesty, the King of the South and North,}

neb taui

lord of the Two Lands (*i.e.* Egypt),

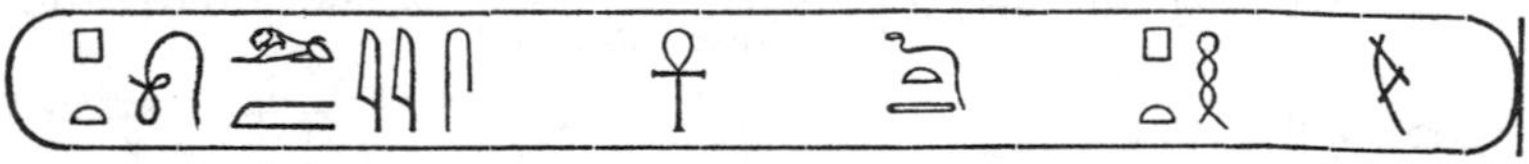

Ptulmis ānkh djet Ptaḥ meri

Ptolemy, the everliving, of Ptaḥ beloved,

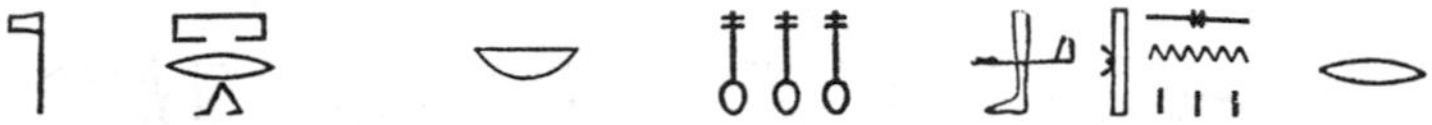

neter peri neb neferu āb-sen er

{the god appearing, (Epiphanes),} lord of benefactions they went into

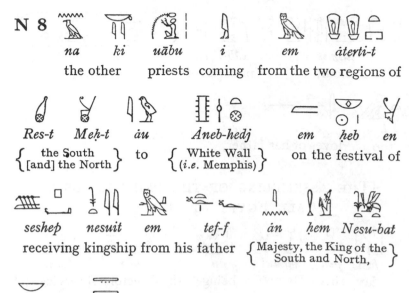

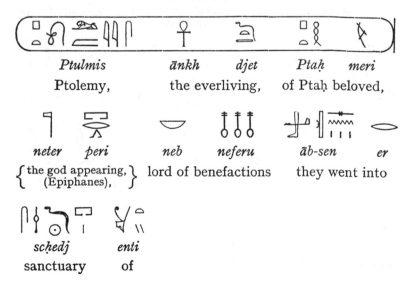

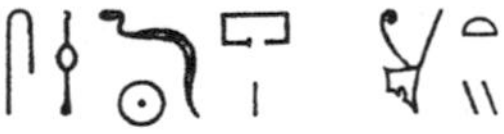

schedj enti

sanctuary of

N 9 

Makha-t Taui *àssu* *ka-sen*

{Balance of the Two Lands, (*i.e.* Memphis)} [and] behold (?) they spake [saying] :—

[SUMMARY OF THE BENEFITS CONFERRED ON EGYPT BY PTOLEMY V]

em enti *un*[1] *nesu-bat*

Since the King of the South and the North

Neterui àtui merui àtui àaū {*en-Ptaḥ-setep*} {*Usr-Ka-Rā Àmen-sekhem ānkh*}

{flesh and bone of the Father-loving gods,} {chosen of Ptaḥ,} {USR-KA-RĀ, of Àmen the living image,}

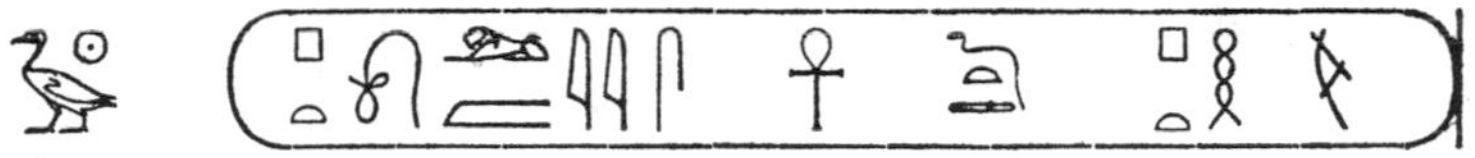

sa Rā *Ptulmis* *ānkh djet,* *Ptaḥ-meri*

son of Rā, Ptolemy, everliving, of Ptaḥ beloved,

neter peri *neb neferu* *sa en* *nesu bat*

{the god appearing,} {lord of benefactions,} son of {the King of the South and the North,}

---

[1] After  the Nabayrah Stele adds .

Ptulmis *ḥenā* *ḥeq-t* *neb-t* *taui*

Ptolemy, and the Queen, lady of the Two Lands,

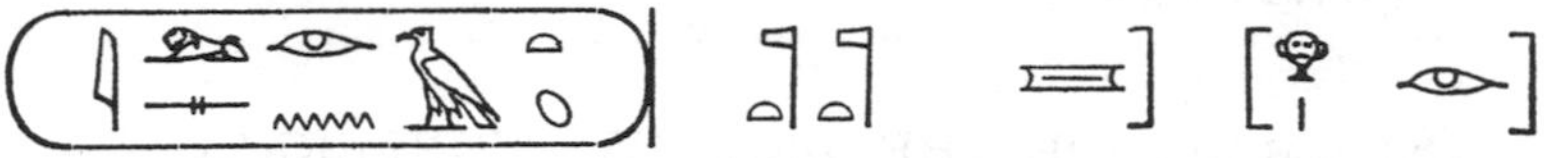

Ȧrsna *neterui ȧtui* *merui* *ḥer* *ȧri*

Arsinoë, {the two Father-loving gods,} hath done

khe-t *neb-t* *neferit* *uru* *em*

things of all kinds gracious, very many in

N 10

Ḥer *taiu* (?) *ḥā* *ȧmiu-sen* *nebu*

{the Horus Lands (*i.e.* the divine estates),} and {[for] the dwellers in them all,}

ḥer *sa* *neb* *un* *em* *khent* *ȧaui-f*

and person every [who] was under his rule

menkh-t *er* *āu-sen* *unen-f* *em* *neter* *sa*

beneficent, all of them, he being like a god, son of

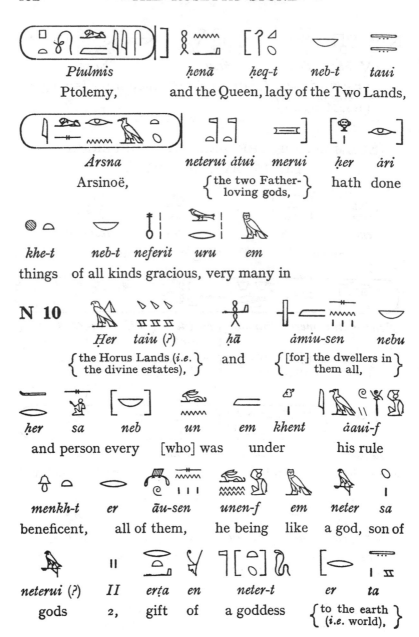

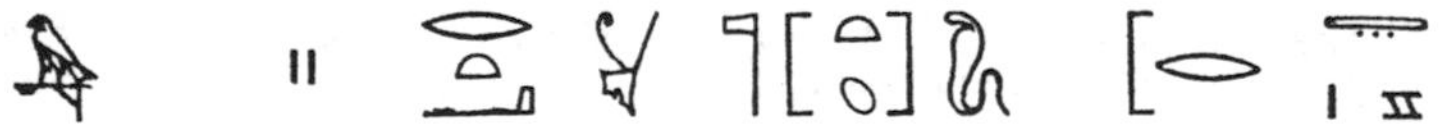

neterui (?) *II* *erṭa* *en* *neter-t* *er* *ta*

gods 2, gift of a goddess {to the earth (*i.e.* world),}

àuf — *em* — *s-tut* — *àu* — *Ḥer* — *sa*

he in the semblance of Horus, son of

As-t — *sa* — *Àsàr* — *ànedj* — *teb-f* — *Àsàr*

Isis, son of Osiris, the avenger of his father Osiris;

N 11

sesu — *ḥem-f* — *em* — *àb* — *en*

behold His Majesty with the heart of

neter menkh — *sher* — *neteru* — *erṭa-nef* — *ḥedj*

a beneficent god towards the gods, he gave silver

uru — *uaḥàu* — *genu* — *àu* — *erpiu* (?) — *nu Kam-t*

{in great quantities [and] grain} very much to the sanctuaries of Egypt,

erṭa-nef — *shepsu* — *uru* — *àu* — *gerḥ* — *Ta-Mer-t*

he gave precious objects {very many for the quieting of Ta-Mer-t (*i.e.* Egypt)}

er — *s-ṭeṭ* — *Qebḥui* (?)

[and] for the {stablishing of the sanctuaries of the South and the North;}

[THE GIFTS OF PTOLEMY V TO HIS TROOPS]

erṭa-f	*afṭ*	*en*	*mashāu* (?)	*unen*	*khent*	*àau-t-*
he gave	a gift	to	the soldiers	{who were under his authority}		

N 12 

f	*ur-t*	*mā*	*qeṭ-sen*
	august according to their ranks ;		

[PTOLEMY V REDUCES SOME TAXES AND ABOLISHES OTHERS]

ḥetr	*àru*	*ḥā*	*bak*	*en*	*àt*[*i*]
{the taxes of them (*i.e.* of the people) and}			dues	of	the noble

unu	*ṭi*	*āḥā*	*kher*	*Ta-mer-t*
which were		{standing (*i.e.* unsettled)}	from	Ta-Mer-t[1]

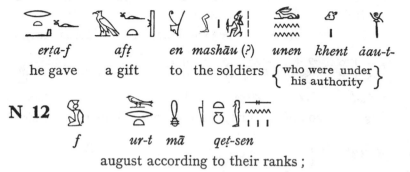

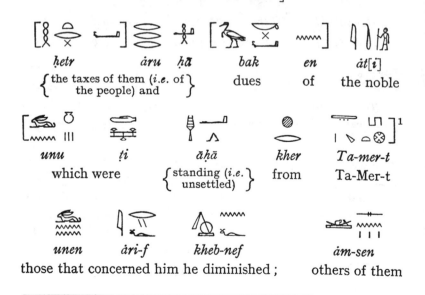

unen	*àri-f*	*kheb-nef*	*àm-sen*
those that concerned him he diminished ;			others of them

---

[1] Emendation by Sethe.

unen *erṭa-nef* *er* *ta* *àu- . . . . . . sen*

{he gave (*i.e.* remitted)} to the ground in their entirety;

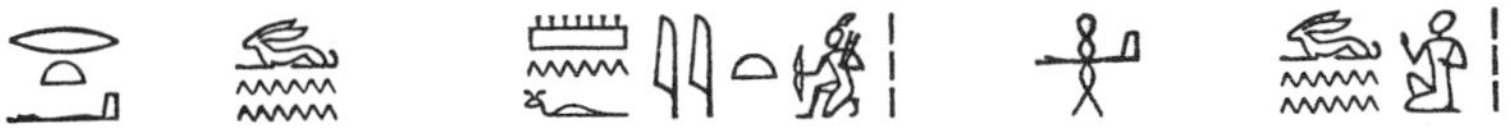

erṭa *unen* *menfitu* *ḥā* *uneniu*

he made to be the soldiers and the people

aq-tu *em* *rek-f* *en* *meṭ-neb-uā*

comfortable in his period of sole Kingship.

[Ptolemy V remits arrears of taxation]

N 13 

gerḥu *àru* *un* *kher* *hamemet*

{The arrears of taxes} of them which lay on the people

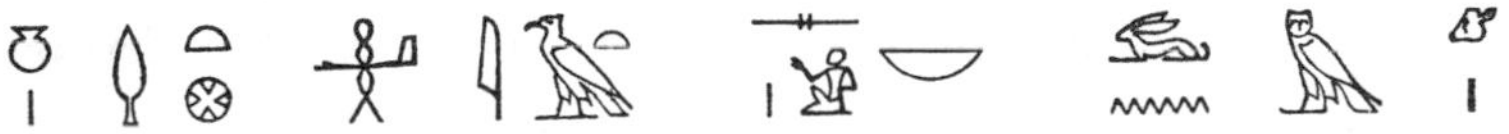

nu *Baq-t* *ḥā* . . . . *sa-neb* *un* *em* *khent*

of Egypt, and on . . . . {person every (foreigner ?)} being under

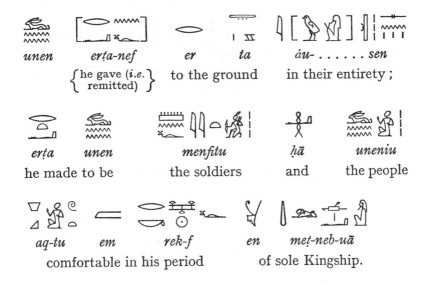

àaut-f *menkḥ-t* *er* - *āu-s* *erta-sen* *ḥem-f* *er* *ta*

his rule {gracious, all of them (?),} {laid them His Majesty on the earth (*i.e.* he remitted them)}

em åp-t ãa ån rekh tenu-sen khu-nef

an amount immense, not is known {how many they were.} He pardoned

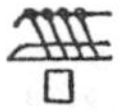

seshep

those who had been

N 14 

Seshep-iu unen ḥer-t ḥã ai sa-neb

arrested [and] who were in prison, and person every

. . . . enen em åri rer (?) ãu

{because (?) of [some]} crime committed time long [ago].

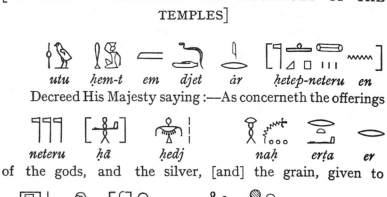

[Ptolemy V confirms the revenues of the temples]

utu ḥem-t em djet år ḥetep-neteru en

Decreed His Majesty saying :—As concerneth the offerings

neteru ḥã ḥedj naḥ erṭa er

of the gods, and the silver, [and] the grain, given to

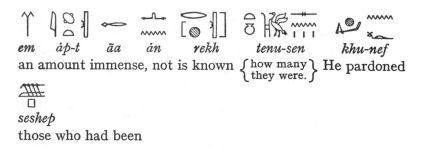

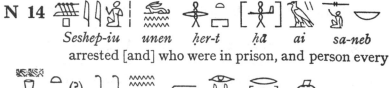

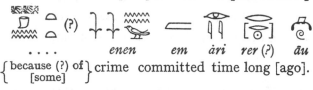

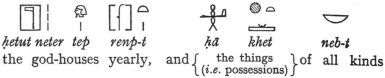

ḥetut neter tep renp-t ḥã khet neb-t

the god-houses yearly, and {the things (*i.e.* possessions)} of all kinds

neteru *aḥ-t* *nu* *àrr* ....

[for] the gods in the lands of {the vine [and] the plantation districts}

N 15 

nu *ḥesp* *ḥā* *khet* *neb* *unen*

of the nome, and the properties of all kinds [which]

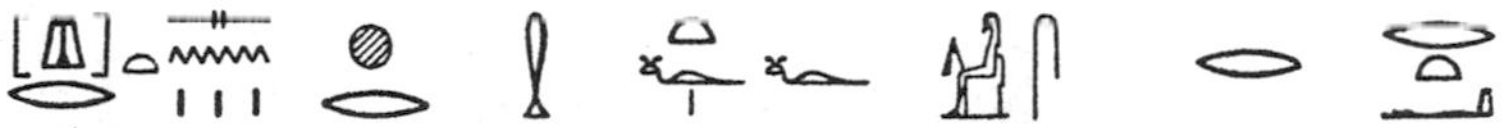

khert-sen *kher* *ḥem* *tef-f* *sheps* *er* *erṭa*

{were their possessions under the majesty} of his father august, shall be allowed

men-sen *kher-sen*

them to remain their properties.

[Ptolemy V releases the priesthood from taxation, and from their annual journey to Alexandria, abolishes the press gang, and remits two-thirds of the tax on byssus]

utu-net *às* *er* *tem* *erṭa* *meḥ-tu* *tennut*

He decreed:—Behold, shall not be made to be filled the ....

---

[1] Sethe would amend , *ṭena-t àru nu neteru em.*

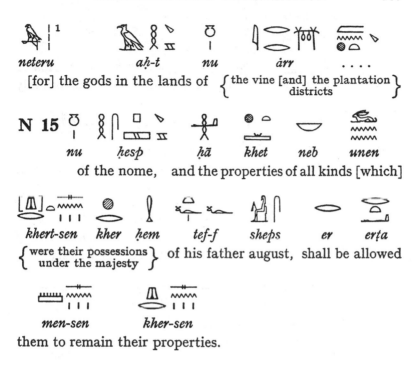

em *āāui* *uābu* *em* *ḥaui* *er* *unen* *erṭa* *ȧm*

by the hands of the priests by more than was given formerly

nefrit *er* *renp-t* *I* *ḥem* *tef-f* **16** *sheps*

up to year I of the Majesty of his father august.

N 16

er *ai* *ua* - *en* - *ḥem-f*

Moreover (?) released His Majesty

ȧu *uābu-unnut-ḥe-t-neter* *em* *utuit* *ȧri-sen*

{the priests of the hourly courses in the temple} from the journeys {[which] they made}

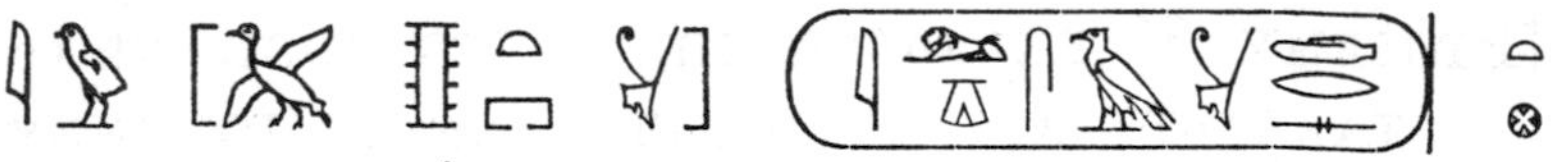

ȧu *pa* *Ȧneb* *en* *Ȧrgsanṭrs*

to the Wall of Alexander (*i.e.* Alexandria)

em *en* *renp-t*

at the prescribed periods of the year.

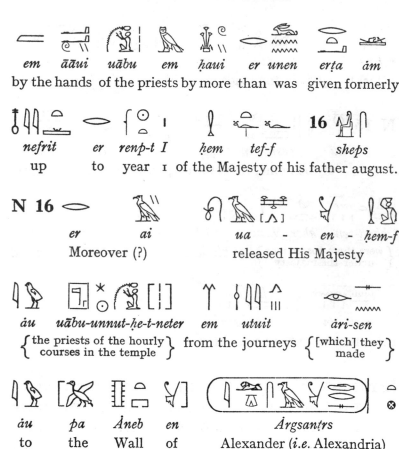

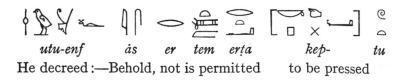

utu-enf *ȧs* *er* *tem* *erṭa* *kep-* *tu*

He decreed:—Behold, not is permitted to be pressed

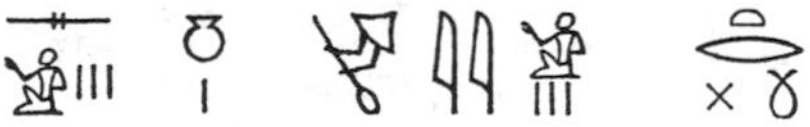

sau nu khenit ter

men of the sailors The cloths

N 17 

em peqt àri er per nesu

of byssus made for the King's house

em gesu peru āḥā-n-tu uaut en ḥem-f

in the temples. remitted His Majesty

⅔ sen

two-thirds of them.

[Ptolemy V restores the peace and prosperity of Egypt]

màtet àru khet neb un em senḥ-tu

Likewise thing every {[which] had been} in disorder (?)

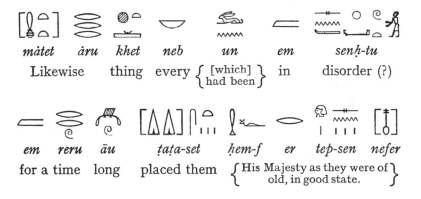

em reru āu ṭaṭa-set ḥem-f er tep-sen nefer

for a time long placed them {His Majesty as they were of old, in good state.}

unen-f ḥer meḥ àu āa ur ḥer àri

He had care great, very, to perform

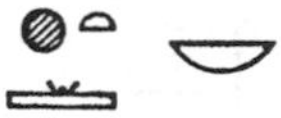

khet neb

thing every

N 18

tut en àru em meter

which was usually done according to the teaching

nu neteru mà enti er tep meter

of the gods, so that [it was performed] {in the best manner possible.}

màtet àru erṭa tep nefer en unniu mà

Likewise [he] gave {height of happiness (*i.e.* strict justice)} to men, as

àri en Ṭeḥuti āa āa

did Thoth, the Great Great.

---

[1] The words in brackets are added by Sethe from Phil. II, 5.

[Ptolemy V proclaims a general amnesty]

utu-nef *àsk* . . . .

He decreed behold . . . .

er *eṛta* *men* *khet-sen* *kher-sen*

to allow to remain their possessions under their own [hands].

[The engraver of the Nabayrah Stele has omitted a passage which corresponds to the Demotic:—ḥn-f-s ān (r) ṭba na ntī àuu r̠ àī h̠nu na rmtu ḳnḳn àrm pa sp rmt àȧr ḫpr ḥr kt-h̠-t mī·t(?) [Sethe has mh̠ru·t] n pa tḫtḫ àȧr ḫpr (n) Kmi r̠ ṭī·t [stau] st (r) naīu maāu (ll. 11 and 12). His Majesty decreed "concerning certain men who came back among the warriors, and [concerning] the remainder who were on another road (?) during the revolt which took place in Egypt, that they should go back to their own places," and should remain in possession of their own property.]

[Ptolemy V takes steps to protect Egypt against invaders]

rit-n ef *meḥ* *às* *ḥer* *eṛtā* *mshā*

He took care behold to make to go

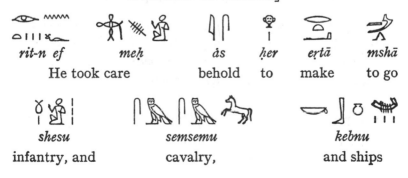

shesu *semsemu* *kebnu*

infantry, and cavalry, and ships

em *khesef* *en* *åaīu*

to drive back (or, against) those who came

N 19 

år *ḥu* *ḥer* *kam-t* *em* *ṭit* *måtet*

to fight against Egypt from the sea coast as well as

em *Uadj-ur* *ṭa nef* *ḥedj* *uaḥ* *uru*

{from the Great Green (*i.e.* Mediterranean).} He gave {silver and grain [in] great quantities}

er *sen* *er* *s-gerḥ* *Ḥer* *taiu* *ḥer*

to them to make quiet the Horus Lands and

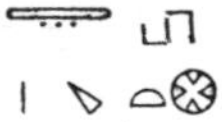

Ta-mer-t

{Ta-Mer-t (*i.e.* Egypt).}

[PTOLEMY V BESIEGES LYCOPOLIS]

shaås *hem-f* *åu* *Khenti* . . . .

Marched His Majesty against Khenti . . . .

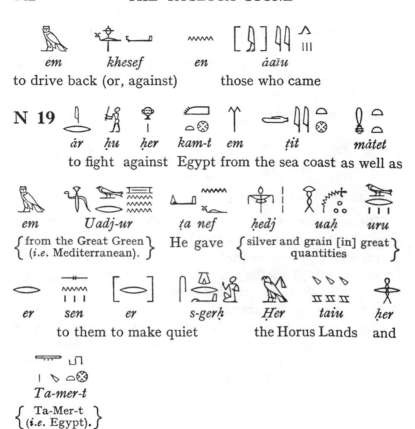

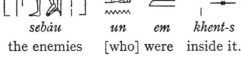

sebåu *un* *em* *khent-s*

the enemies [who] were inside it.

[The engraver of the Nabayrah Stele has omitted the passage which corresponds to the Demotic:—r ta rsat n Shkam [r un] nau ānb (n) ṭ-t na sbau ẖr ḳa-t nb r un sṭbḥ āshai sbṭi nb (n) paīs ẖn arb-f ta rsat (n) rn-s n sbṭ un (n) paīs bnr (r) ṭba na (ll. 12 and 13). His Majesty marched "against the town of Shekam, which the enemy had fortified with works (*i.e.* defences) of every kind, and in it were [collected] many weapons, and everything necessary for fighting. He (the King) surrounded the aforesaid town with walls and made dams outside of them, because] the" enemy who were inside it, etc.]

N 20 

djerenti *ȧri-sen* *tep* *khebsu*

because they had committed the greatest atrocities

uru *em* *Baq-t* *teh-sen* *meten* *mer*

very many in Egypt. They had transgressed the way beloved

nu *ḥem-f* *ḥa* *sekher* *nu* *neteru*[1]

of His Majesty and the ordinances of the gods.

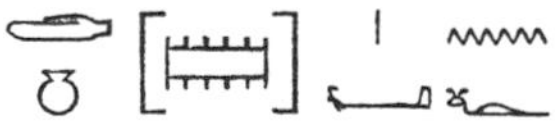

ṭen-nef

He blocked up

---

[1] There is no equivalent in the Greek text for the words 

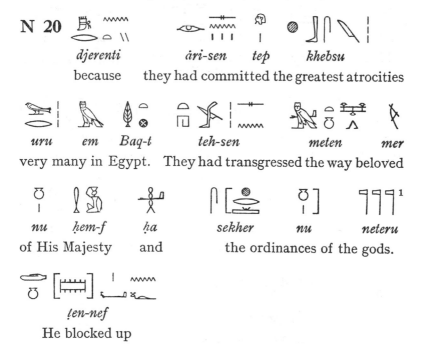

N 21 

àtru *neb* *enti* *sta* *er* *resit*

canal every which flowed into town

then *Àn* *ari* *matet* *àn* *nesiu* *tep-āu*

this; never had done the like the King's predecessors [his].[1]

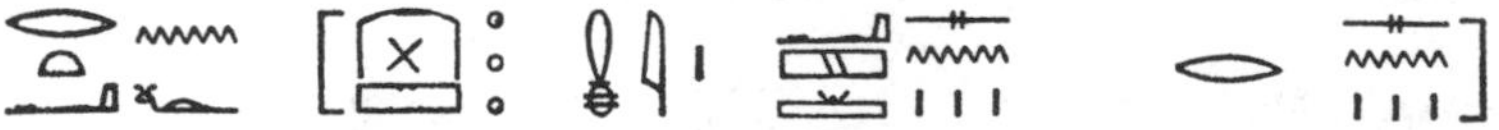

erṭa-nef *ḥedj* (?) *mà* *āsh-sen* *er* *sen*

He spent moneys {as many as were necessary} on their account.

erṭa *àn* *ḥem-f* *remt-reṭiu* (?)*-f* *semsemu*

Placed His Majesty his infantry [and] cavalry

er *re* *en* *aturu* *àpen* *er* *sau-sen*

at the mouth[s] of canals these to watch them

er *s-udja-sen*

to keep them in a strong state,

---

[1] There is no equivalent in the Greek text for the words .

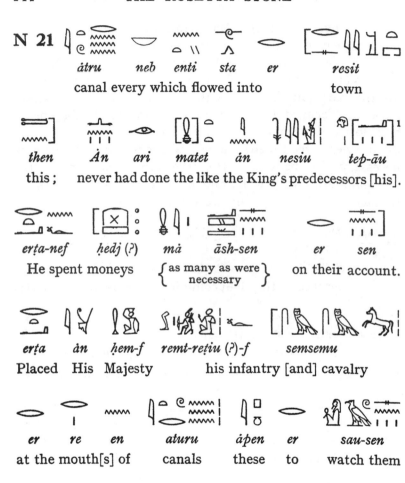

[The engraver of the Nabayrah Stele has omitted a passage corresponding to the Demotic :—(r̲) ṭba na mḥu n pa mu r un nau āiu n ḥa-t sp 8-t r̲ na īāru n rnu na ntī ṭī-t shm mu r ȧtn āshai (ll. 14 and 15), " because of the inundations of the water (*i.e.* the river Nile) which took place in the 8th year were great, and the waters of the aforesaid canals flooded many very low-lying fields " (?).]

medj-tu *em-shes* *maāt* *ḥeq* *en* *ḥem-f*

[and were] deep very. Captured His Majesty

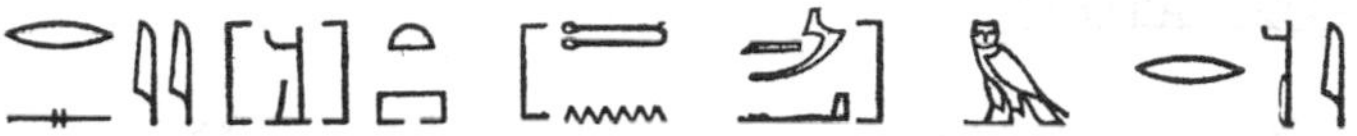 (*sic*)

resit *then* *maā* *em* [*djkȧ ?*]

town this .... with strength

N 22 

.... *uru* *kheb-nef* *ȧn*

.... great, he conquered [it]. [Those] brought in

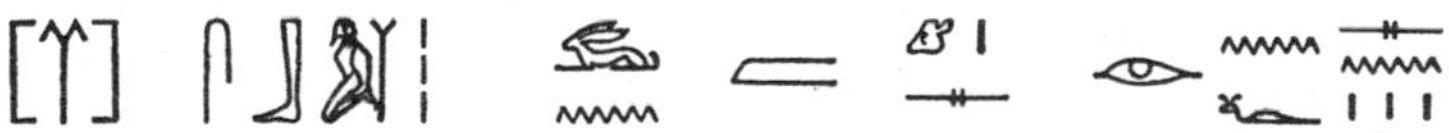

em *sebȧu* *unu* *em* *khents* *ȧri-nef-sen*

from among the enemy {who were in its interior,} he made them [of]

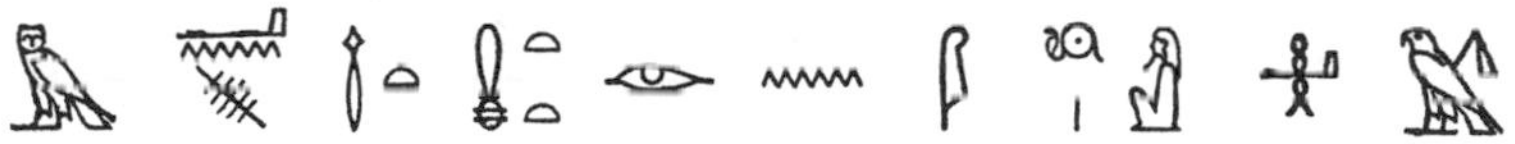

em *ān* *āa-t* *mȧtet* *ȧri* *en* *Shu* *Ra* (?) *ḥā* *Ḥer*

a massacre great as did Shu Rā (?) and Horus

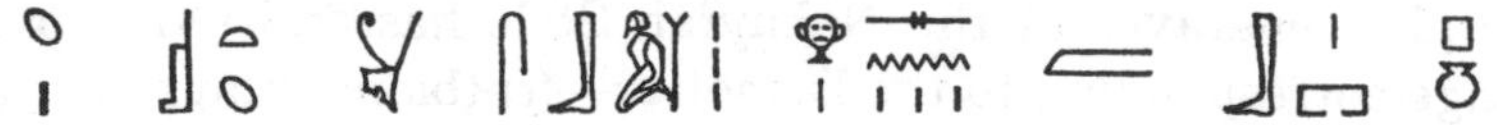

sa *As-t* *en* *sebâu* *ḥer-sen* *em* *bu* *pen*

the son of Isis, of the enemies to them in place that

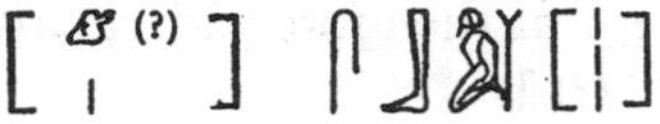

khent (?) *sebâu*

aforetime. The enemy

[PTOLEMY V PUNISHES THE LEADERS OF THE REBELLION AGAINST HIS FATHER PTOLEMY IV PHILOPATOR]

R 1 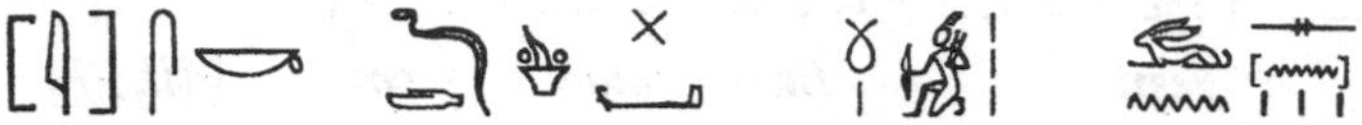

âsk *djeṭeb* *meshāu* *un-sen*

behold had gathered together the soldiers, they were

em *tep-sen* *seṭeman-sen* *teshu*

at their head, they led astray the nomes,

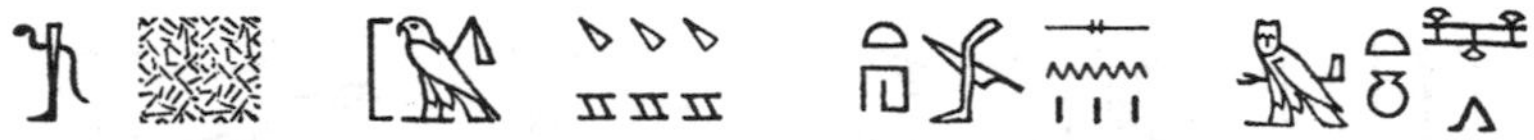

tcheb . . . . *Ḥer* *taiu* *tch-sen* *mten*

they pillaged {the Horus Lands, (*i.e.* the temple properties),} they transgressed the way

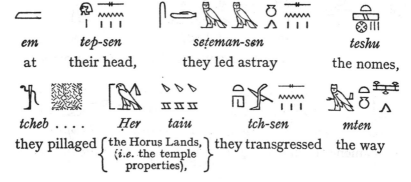

nu *ḥem-f* *ḥā* *tef-f* *sheps*

of His Majesty and his father august

erṭa en neteru kheb-f ȧn ȧm-sen

{granted the gods that he should conquer.} Were brought some of them

em Ȧneb Ḥetch-t

into White Wall (*i.e.* Memphis)

N 23 

em ḥeb seshep sek nesuit em tef-f

{at the festival of the receiving} behold {of the kingdom from his father,}

smam em erṭa tepu khe-t

slaying by placing [them] upon stake[s].

[PTOLEMY V REMITS THE ARREARS OF TAXES AND CONTRIBUTIONS DUE TO THE KING FROM THE TEMPLES]

gesḥ nu ḥem-f un kher gesu peru

{The arrears of taxes} of His Majesty, which were with the temples,

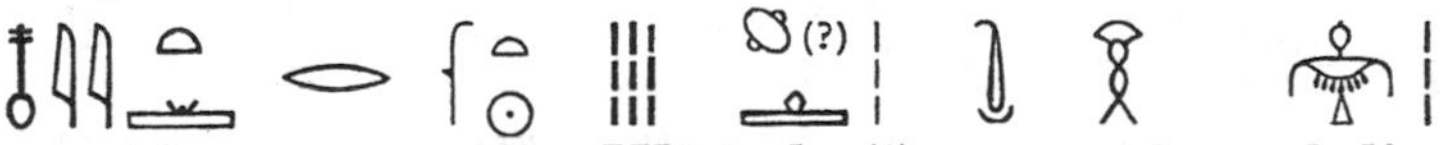

nefrit er renp-t IX ḥesbn (?) smen uaḥ ḥedj

up to year 9, {amounts heavy,} many, {of silver (*i.e.* money)}

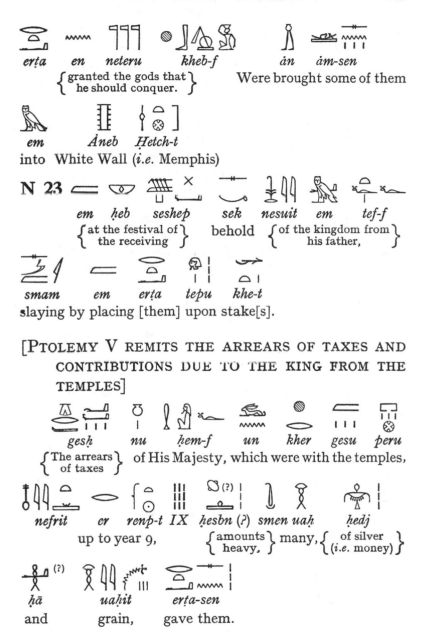

ḥā uaḥit erṭa-sen

and grain, gave them.

R 2 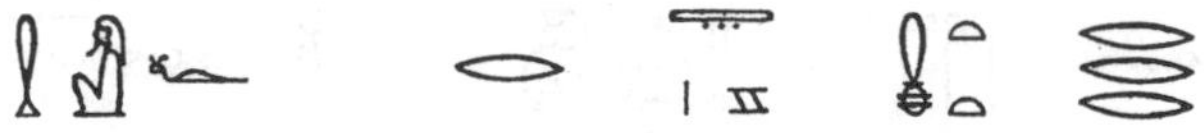

ḥem-f *er* *ta* *mȧtet* *ȧru*

His Majesty {to the ground, (*i.e.* he remitted them).} Likewise

N 24 

em *ṭer* *en* *peg* *erṭa* *er* *per nesu*

{as concerning the cloth of} {byssus to be given} {to the house of the King,}

un *kher* *gesu* *peru* *ḥā* *sta*

which was with the temples, and the balance (?)

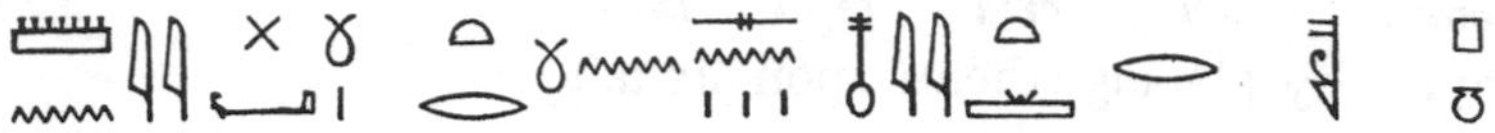

meni *ṭer* *ter-en-sen* *neferit* *er* *gen* *pen*

fixed of the cloth {which they should have delivered} up to period this.

āḥā *en* *ua* *uaḥit* *ḥeḳa* *V* *sheṭ-tu*

[He] remitted of the grain bushels 5 which were taken

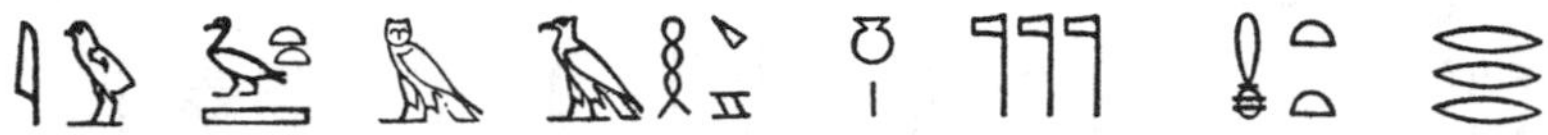

ȧu *satt-ta* *em* *aḥ-t* *nu* *neteru* *mȧtet* *ȧru*

on the arura in the field of the gods, and likewise

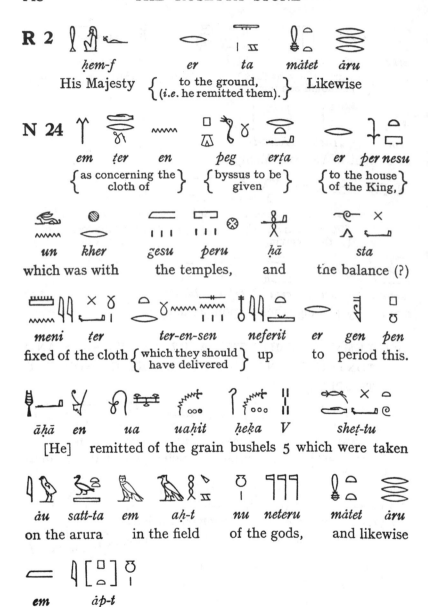

em *ȧp-t*

the measure

N 25 

em *àrp-sen* *em* *aḥ-t* *nu* *àrr*

of {their wine [which was taken on the arura] in the vineyard.}

[The Endowments of Apis, Mnevis, and the other sacred animals made by Ptolemy V]

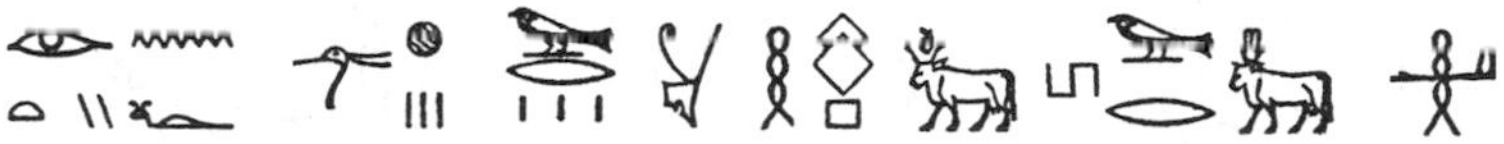

àritu-nef *àakhu* *uru* *en* *Ḥap* *Merur* *ḥā*

He made {endowments} great of Apis [and] Mnevis and

R 3 

āuiu *neb* *àaḳhu* *em* *heru* *er*

sacred animal every, endowments more than

àri-sen *en* *tep-āu* *àb-f* *āq* *ḥer*

had made they [his] ancestors. {His heart (*i.e.* mind)} {went (*i.e.* occupying itself)} with

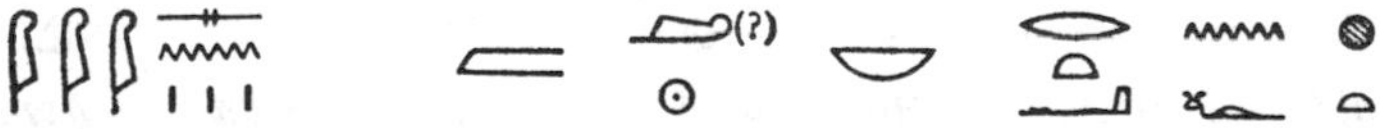

sekheru(?)-sen *em* *at (?)* *neb* *erṭa* *nef* *khet*

their plans (or, affairs) at moment every. He gave thing

nebt *djār-sen*

every [which] they needed

N 26 

er *āb* *dje-t-sen* *urtu* *djesertu*

for the embalmment of their bodies abundantly, lavishly.

athi-nef *sekhen* *àm-sen* *àu* *neter-ḥetu-sen*

He brought providing in them for their temples

em *ḥeb* *āa* *uaḥ* *ākh* *seqer*

at the festival great burnt offerings, [animals for] slaughter,

uṭen *ḥā* *khet* *nebt* *tut* *en* *àr*

drink offerings, and thing every usually made (*i.e.* offered),

s-maā *tep* *em* *peru* *ḥā* *khe-t*

{arranging in the correct manner,} {in the very best way,} in the temples, and things

nebt *uru* *nu* *Baq-t* . . . . *-sen* *ḥem-f*

all {in great quantities} of Egypt [provided] them His Majesty

. . . . *mà* *enti* *er* *hepu*

[maintaining] according to what [is] in the laws.

R 4 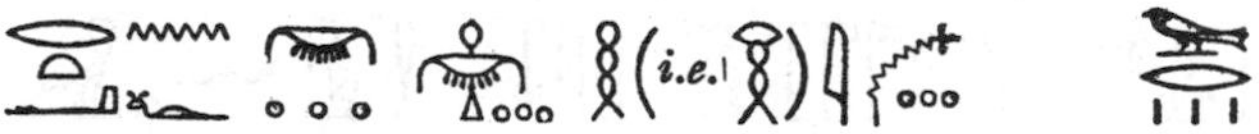

erṭa-nef *nubu* *ḥedjh-t* *naḥit* *uru*

He gave gold [and] silver [and] grain large quantities

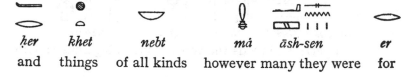

ḥer *khet* *nebt* *må* *āsh-sen* *er*

and things of all kinds however many they were for

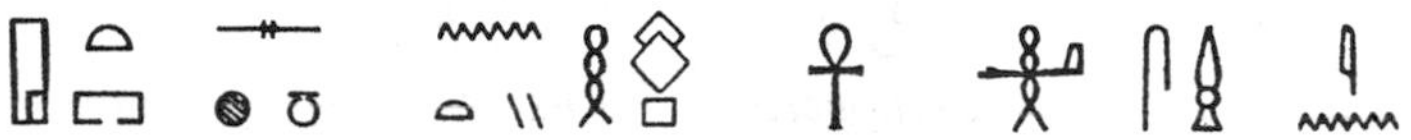

ḥe-t *sekhen* *enti* *Ḥap* *ånkhi* *ḥå* *s-khaker* *åm*

the temple of dwelling of Apis the living, and decorated [it]

ḥem-f *em* *ka-t* *menkh-t* *nema* *nefruis*

His Majesty with work perfect new, it was beautiful

em *shes* *maāt* *s-khā-nef* *Ḥap* *ånkhi* *eres*

exceedingly, he made to rise Ḥapi, the living one, in it.

[The devotion of Ptolemy V to the service of the gods and his reward]

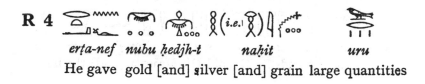

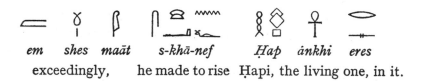

āsh . . . . -nef *neter ḥetu* *khemu* *khau*

He set up temples, and chapels, and altars

em ma en neteru ssu ḥem-f em áb

anew for the gods. Behold His Majesty [had] the heart

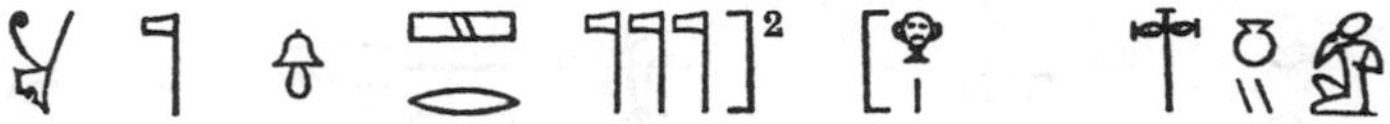

en neter menkh sher neteru ḥer nedji

of a god perfect towards the gods, concerning himself with

. . . . . *gesu peru neferu*

the affairs (?) of the temples beautiful,

R 5 

áu smau-sen em rek-f

so that they might renew in his time

en meṭ-neb-uā ásui enen erṭa-nef

the sole rule [of himself]. As a reward for {these things have given him}

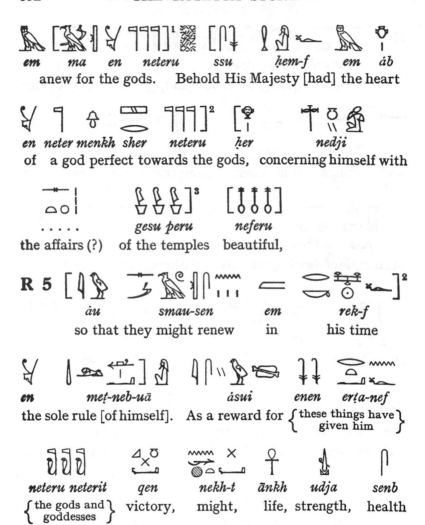

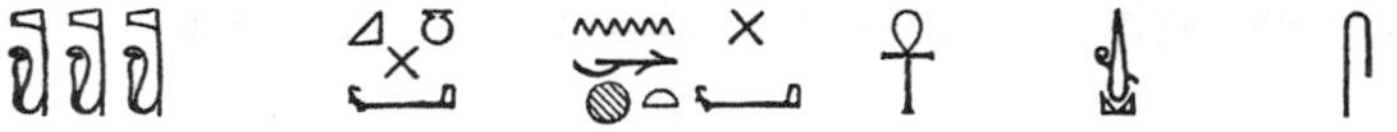

neteru neterit qen nekh-t ānkh udja senb

{the gods and goddesses} victory, might, life, strength, health

---

[1] Some words, the equivalent of the Greek τά τε προσδεόμενα ἐπισκευῆς προσδιωρθώσατο, are omitted here.

[2] The words in brackets are supplied from **N 11.**

[3] The words in brackets are supplied from Phil. II, 7.

ḥer *khe-t* *neb-t* *nefer* *er* *au-sen*

and everything good to the fullest possible extent of them;

er *àau-t-f* *ur-t* *ṭeṭ-tu* *kher-f* *ḥā*

is his rank great established for him and

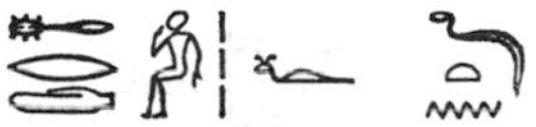

kharṭu-f *en djet*

his children for ever.

[The priests decide to augment the honours paid to Ptolemy V and his ancestors]

ḥā *sekhen* *nefer*

And a happening good [may there be]!

āq-s *em* *àb* *en* *uābu* *nu* *àterti*

It entered into the heart of the priests of temples

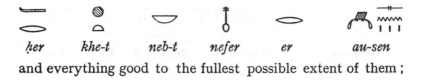

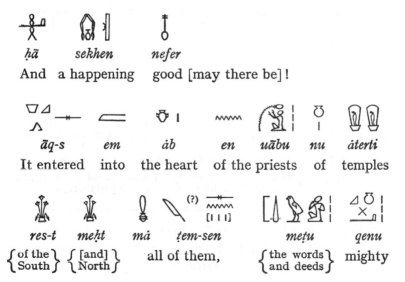

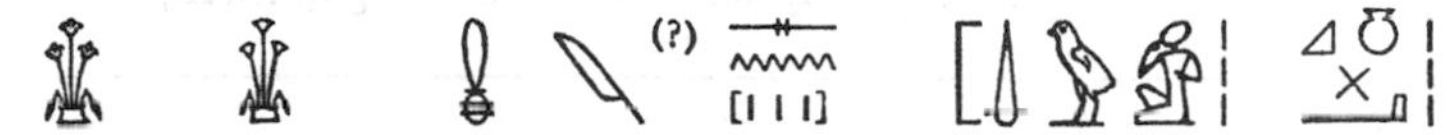

res-t *meḥt* *mà* *ṭem-sen* *meṭu* *qenu*

{of the South} {[and] North} all of them, {the words and deeds} mighty

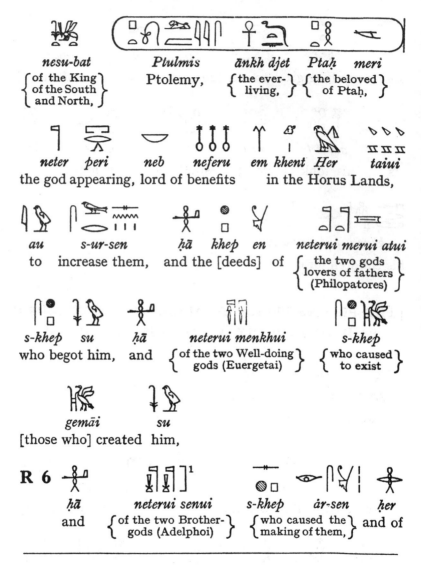

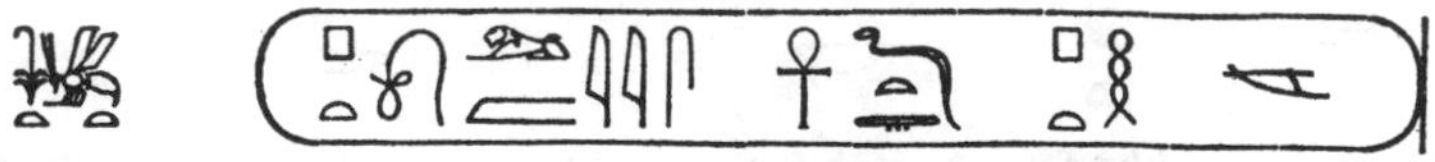

nesu-bat *Ptulmis* *ānkh djet* *Ptaḥ* *meri*

{of the King of the South and North,} Ptolemy, {the ever-living,} {the beloved of Ptaḥ,}

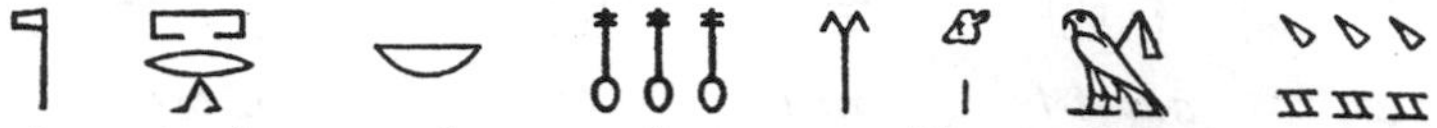

neter *peri* *neb* *neferu* *em* *khent* *Ḥer* *taiui*

the god appearing, lord of benefits in the Horus Lands,

au *s-ur-sen* *ḥā* *khep* *en* *neterui* *merui* *atui*

to increase them, and the [deeds] of {the two gods lovers of fathers (Philopatores)}

s-khep *su* *ḥā* *neterui menkhui* *s-khep*

who begot him, and {of the two Well-doing gods (Euergetai)} {who caused to exist}

gemāi *su*

[those who] created him,

R 6 

ḥā *neterui senui* *s-khep* *ār-sen* *ḥer*

and {of the two Brother-gods (Adelphoi)} {who caused the making of them,} and of

[1] The passage in brackets has been restored from the texts of the two Decrees found on the walls of the temple at Philae; for the details see Sethe, *op. cit.*, p. 188.

neterui nedjui	*djenfu*	*en*	*tut-sen*
the two gods who save (Soteres),	the fathers (?)	of	begetter their.

[THE PRIESTS DECIDE TO SET UP STATUES OF PTOLEMY V AND THE CHIEF LOCAL GOD IN EACH OF THE TEMPLES OF EGYPT]

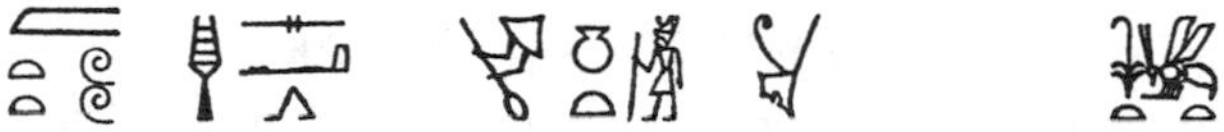

mtutu s-āḥā	*khent*	*en*	*nesu-bat*
Shall be set up a	statue	of	the King of the South and North,

Ptulmis	*ānkh djet*	*Ptaḥ meri*
Ptolemy,	the everliving,	beloved of Ptaḥ,

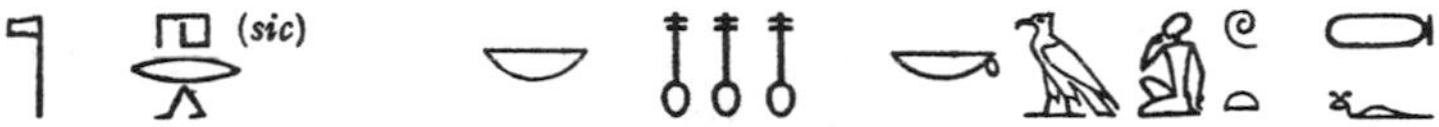

neter peri	*neb neferu*	*ka-tu*	*ren-f*
the god appearing,	lord of benefits,	shall be called	his name

Ptulmis	*nedji*	*Baq-t*	*uḥā-f*
"Ptolemy,	the Avenger	of Baq-t"	the interpretation whereof

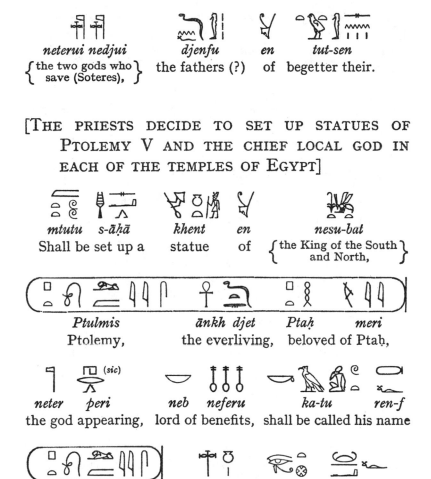

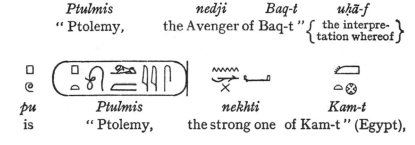

pu	*Ptulmis*	*nekhti*	*Kam-t*
is	"Ptolemy,	the strong one	of Kam-t" (Egypt),

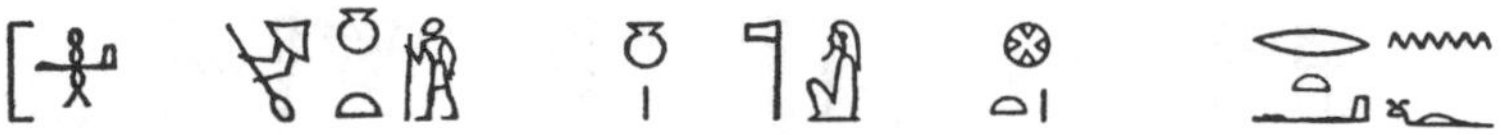

ḥā	*khent*	*nu*	*neter*	*nu-t*	*erṭa-nef*
and	a statue	of the	god	of the city	giving to him

khepesh	*nesu*	*en*	*qen*	*em*	*Qebhui*	*en*	*khem-t*
a sword	royal	of	victory,	in the	two Qebḥ	in	sanctuary

neb	*ḥer*	*ren-f*	*em*	*usekh-t*	*mashāu*	*enth*	*ḥe-t neter*
every	by	its name,	in	the court	of the soldiers	of	god-house (*i.e.* temple),

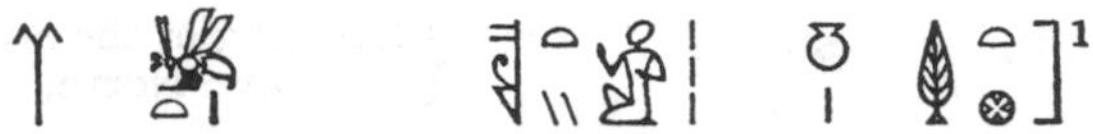

em	*ba-t*	*mesentiu*	*nu*	*Baq-t*
of the	workmanship	of all artisans	of	Egypt.

R 7 

emtu	*s-āqu*	*nu*	*ḥe-t neter*	*em*
Moreover	the priests who have the entry into the sanctuary	of the	house of the god	in

erpi	*neb*	*ḥer*	*ren-f*	*shems*	*khenui*	*āpen*
temple	every	by	its name	shall serve	two statues	these

em	*sep*	*III*	*em*	*kher*	*hru*	*ḥer*
	times	3	in	the course of	the day,	[and]

[1] The words in brackets are supplied from the texts found at Philae.

ȧr *erṭa* *ṭebḥ* *em-baḥ-sen* *ariti-sen*

{shall cause to set forth} {the sacred implements of the cult} before them, {they shall perform}

tep-reṭ *neb* *tut* *en* *ka-sen*

{prescribed ceremony} every {in correct fashion} for {their double[s]}

nia *ȧr* *en* *neteru* *ḥespu* *em* *ḥebu*

{as if it were being performed} for the gods of the nomes on the festivals

tep *genu* (?) *ḥer* *her* *en* *khā* *ḥā* (?) . . . .

{at the beginning of the seasons of the year,} and {on the day of the enthronement} and

hru *em* *ren-f*

[each] day by its name.

[A WOODEN STATUE OF PTOLEMY V, IN A SHRINE OF GOLD, SHALL BE SET UP]

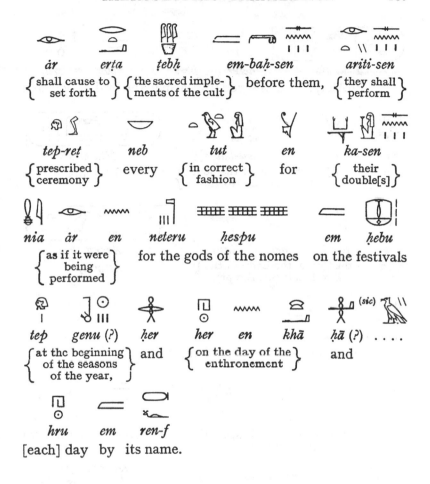

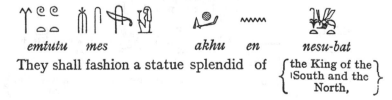

emtutu *mes* *akhu* *en* *nesu-bat*

They shall fashion a statue splendid of {the King of the South and the North,}

Ptulmis *neter* *peri* *neb* *neferu*

Ptolemy, the god appearing, the lord of benefits,

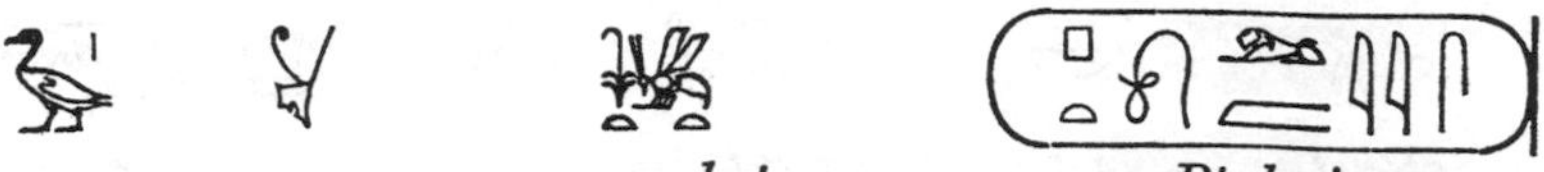

sa *en* *nesu-bat* *Ptulmis*

son of {the King of the South and the North,} Ptolemy

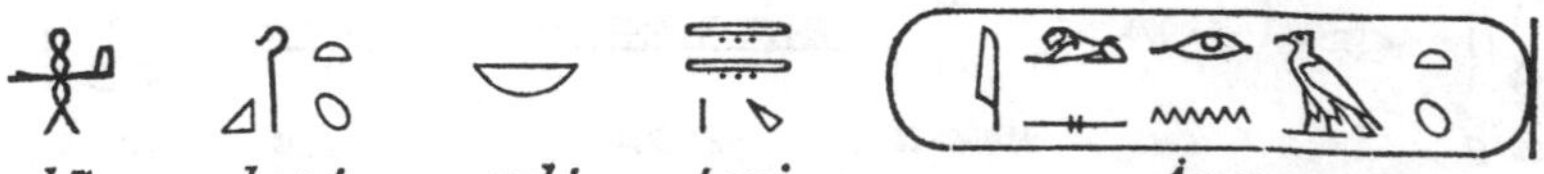

ḥā *ḥeq-t* *nebt* *taui* *Ȧrsna*

and {the Queen, the Lady of the Two Lands (*i.e.* Egypt),} Arsinoë,

neterui *merui atui*

the two gods loving fathers (Philopatores),

R 8 

ḥā *ga* (?) *sheps* *em* *djām* *meḥ* *em*

and {a shrine. (portable)} splendid of silver-gold inlaid with

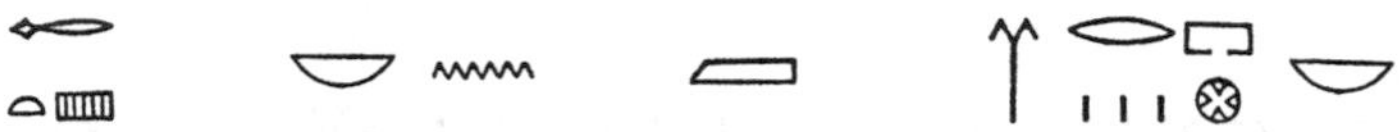

ȧa-t *neb* *en* *maā-t* *em* *erpin* *neb*

stone (precious) every of {genuineness (*i.e.* real gems, not paste)} in temple every

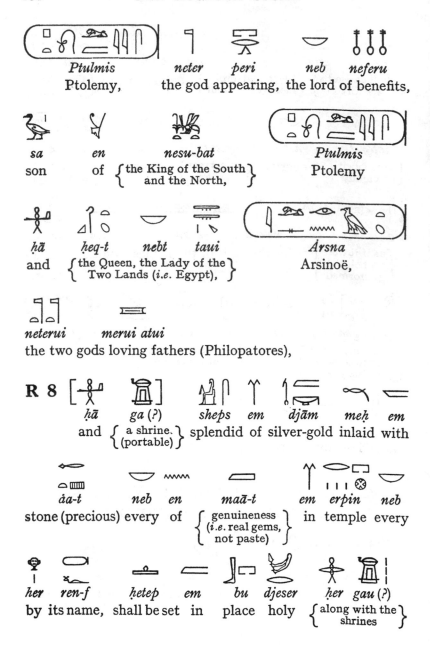

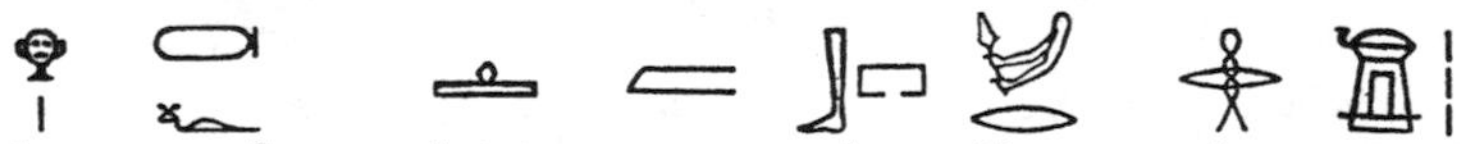

her *ren-f* *ḥetep* *em* *bu* *djeser* *ḥer* *gau* (?)

by its name, shall be set in place holy {along with the shrines}

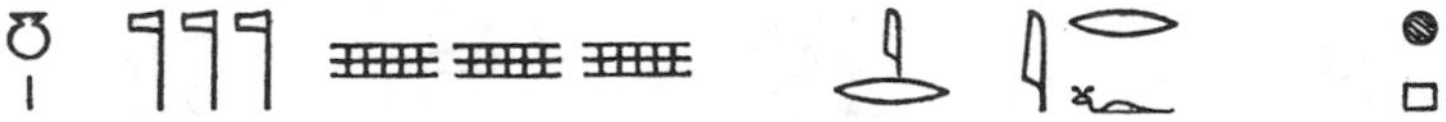

nu neteru ḥespu ȧr ȧref khep

of the gods of the nomes. Now therefore when take place

ḥebu uru per neter em qebḥ-t sheps er sa

the festivals great, {and cometh forth [each] god from his retreat (?)} holy with

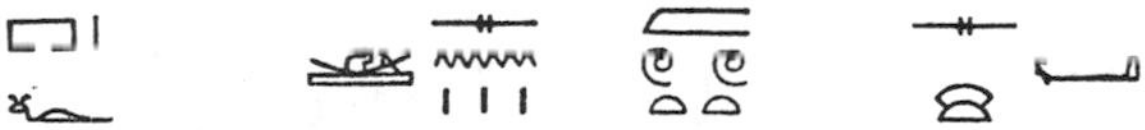

per-f ȧm-sen emtutu s-khā

{his house (*i.e* shrine)} among them, {shall rise up (in the processions)}

N 26 *ga (?) sheps en neter peri*

the shrine holy of the god who appeareth,

N 27 *neb neferu ḥer-sen*

the lord of benefits, along with them.

[Description of the shrine]

er erṭa saa-tu ga (?) then em

In order to make [men] to recognize shrine this, from

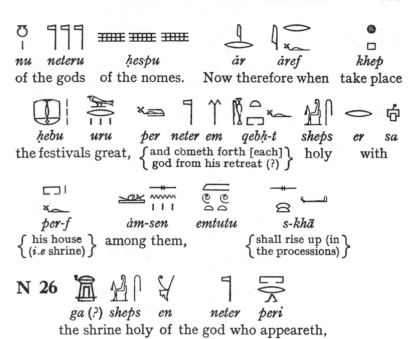

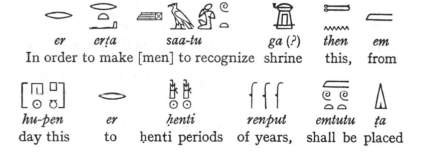

hu-pen er ḥenti renput emtutu ṭa

day this to ḥenti periods of years, shall be placed

seḥen *X* *nu* *ḥem-f* *er* *neter-t* (?)

crowns 10 of His Majesty with {an uraeus (*i.e.* cobra)}

tep-ā-sen *em* *uā* *neb* *ȧm*

on their fronts, on one every among [them].

R 9

mȧ *ȧr* *tep* *nefer* *em* *seḥen* *neb*

As is done {properly (or, rightly)} in respect of crown every,

ḥer tep *ga* (?) *then* *em* *ȧsui* *en* *urti* *un*

upon shrine this, instead of {the two uraei [which] are [usually]}

ḥer *tep* *ga* (?) *ȧu* *sekhem-ti* *em* *ḥer-ȧb* *ȧru*

on the tops of shrines, the double crown in the middle of them ;

djerenti *pesṭ* *ḥem-f* *ȧm-f* *em* *ḥe-t* *Ptaḥ*

because shone His Majesty in it in the house of Ptaḥ

em-khet *ȧr-nef* *ȧru* *neb* *bes* *nesu*

after {he had performed ceremony every [at the]} introduction of the King

er *ḥe-t* *neter* *kheft* *seshep-nef* *àaut-f* *ur-t*

into the temple when he received his rank great,

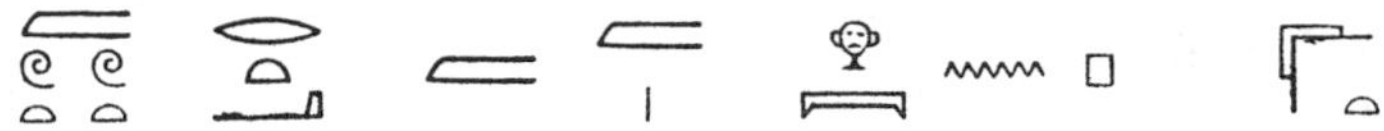

emtutu *erṭa* *em* *ges* *ḥeri* *en* *p-* *aft*

and shall be placed on the side upper of the rectangle (?)

enti *em* *sa* *seḥenu* *àpen* *em* *āqa* *en*

which is on the outside of crowns this, opposite to

sekhem-ti *pen* *shemā* *ḥā* *uadj-t*

double crown this, a cluster of rushes and a papyrus cluster.

ḥer *neb-t* *shemā* *kher-s* *ḥer*

{[There shall be] a vulture on a basket [and]} {a cluster of reeds} under her on

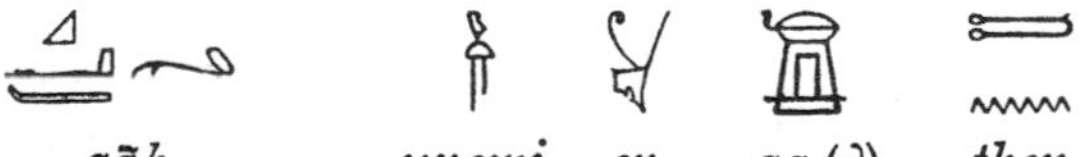

qāḥ *unemi* *en* *ga* (?) *then*

the angle (or corner) right of shrine this, [and]

R 10

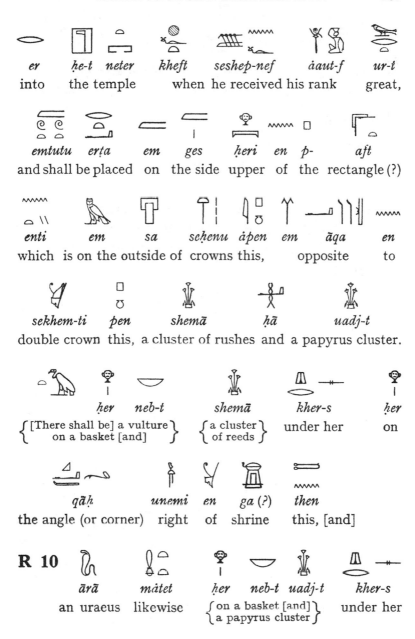

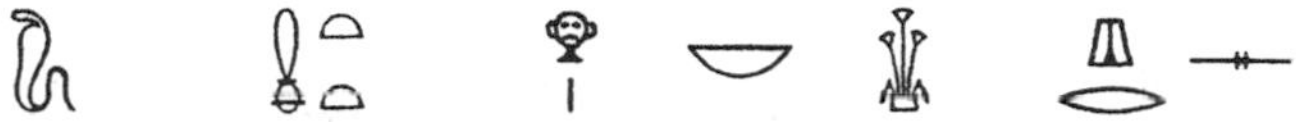

ārā *màtet* *ḥer* *neb-t* *uadj-t* *kher-s*

an uraeus likewise {on a basket [and] a papyrus cluster} under her

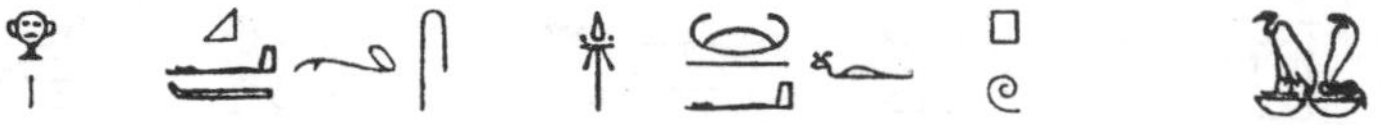

ḥer *qăḥ-s* *àbti* *uḥă-f* *pu* *Nebti*

on {her angle (or, corner)} {left, the meaning whereof is,} {the Lord of the Two Crowns}

schedj *Taui*

illumineth the Two Lands (*i.e.* Egypt).

[FESTIVALS ARE TO BE CELEBRATED ON THE BIRTHDAY OF PTOLEMY V AND ON THE DAY OF HIS ACCESSION TO THE THRONE IN EACH MONTH]

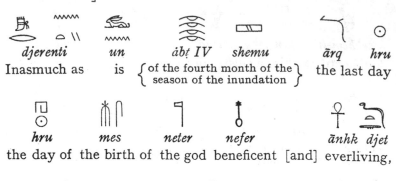

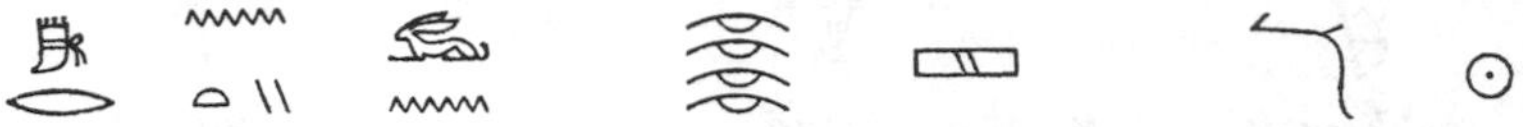

djerenti *un* *àbṭ IV* *shemu* *ărq* *hru*

Inasmuch as is {of the fourth month of the season of the inundation} the last day

hru *mes* *neter* *nefer* *ănhk* *djet*

the day of the birth of the god beneficent [and] everliving,

ṭeṭ-t *em* *ḥeb* *khă* *em* *Ḥer-taui*

was established as {a festival [and] day of rejoicing} in {the Horus Lands (*i.e.* on temple estates)}

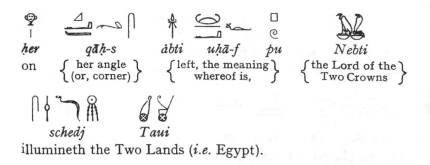

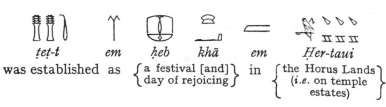

kher *ḥa-t* *màtt* *aru* *en* *àbṭ-II* *Akhet* *sesu* *XVII*

in former times, likewise {of the second month of the season Akhet} day 17

ȧri-nef *ȧru* *n* *nesu* *khā* *em* *seshep-nef*

{[whereon] he performed the ceremony of the coronation of the King} when he received

nesuit *em* *tef-f* *is* *eref* *khent*

the kingdom from his father. Behold now {the beginning (or source)}

em *khe-t* *neb-t* *ȧakhu* *uru* *un*

of things all splendid [and] great [that] are

tepu *taiu*

to those who are on the Lands

R 11

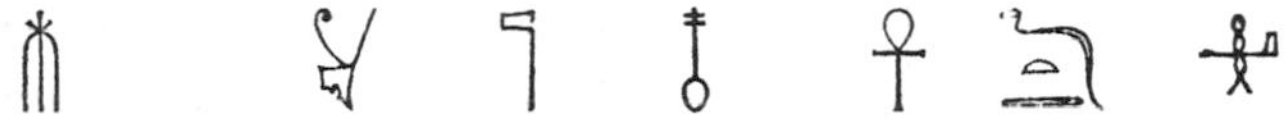

mes *en* *neter* *nefer* *ānkh* *djet* *ḥā*

is the birth of the god beneficent, living forever, and

seshep *ȧaui-f* *menkh-t* *ȧu* *mi* *ȧritu* *sesu*

{[his] reception of} {rank exalted (or, perfect).} Let be made days

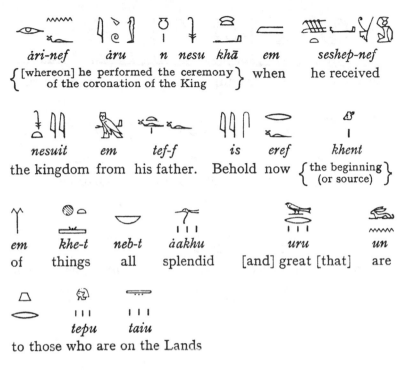

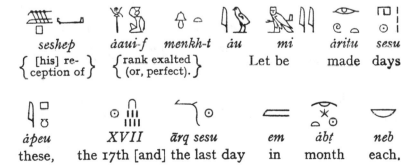

ȧpeu *XVII* *ārq sesu* *em* *ȧbṭ* *neb*

these, the 17th [and] the last day in month each.

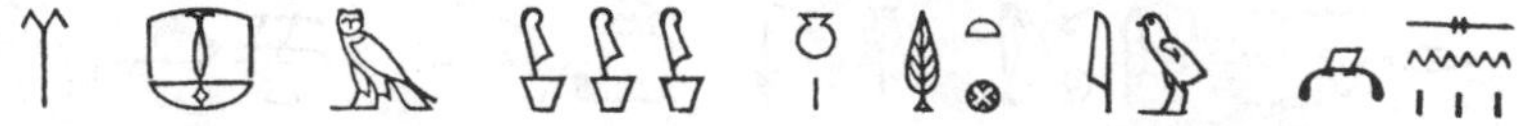

em ḥeb em gesu peru nu Baq-t àu au-sen

into a festival in the temples of Egypt all of them.

emtutu uaḥ ākh seger uṭenu ḥà

{Shall be offered a burnt offering,} shall be poured out libations, and

àri khe-t neb-t tut en àri em ḥebu

{shall be performed} {everything [which] it is right} to do {during the festivals}

em ḥeb àpen tep àbt neb khe-t neb-t àritu em

in festival[s] these month every. {Everything which is done on}

ḥebu àpen seshem àu sa neb àri ṭua-t-sen

{festivals these shall be conducted} for {men all who perform their service}

em he-t neter

in the temple.

[A FIVE-DAY FESTIVAL AT THE BEGINNING OF THE MONTH OF THOTH SHALL BE CELEBRATED ANNUALLY IN HONOUR OF PTOLEMY V]

emtutu *ȧr* *ḥeb* *khā* *en* *gesu peru* *nu*

{There shall be celebrated} {a festival [and]} {a day of rejoicing} in the temples of

R 12 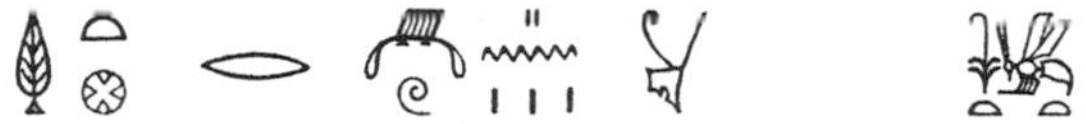

Baq-t *er* *ȧu-sen* *en* *nesu-bat*

Egypt, all of them, of {the King of the South and the North.}

Ptulmis *ānkh* *djet* *Ptaḥ* *meri*

Ptolemy, the everliving, of Ptaḥ beloved,

neter *peri* *neb* *neferu* *tep* *renp-t* *shā*

the god appearing, lord of benefits, yearly, beginning

em *tep* *akh-t* *sesu* *I* *nefrit* *er* *hu*

in {the first month} {of the season Akh-t} day I up to day

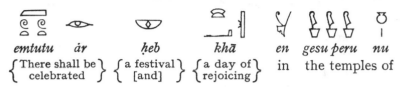

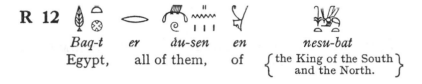

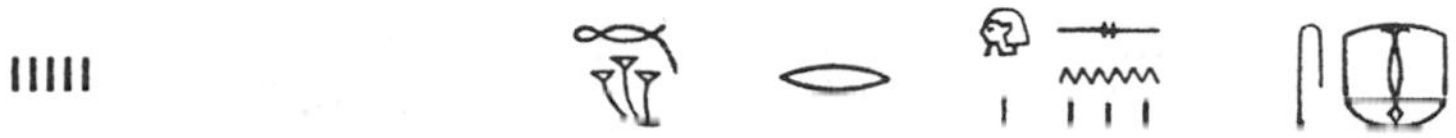

V *meḥ* *er* *djadja-sen* *s-ḥeb*

5. {[The people shall wear]} garland[s] on their heads, {shall be made festal}

khau	*s-qer*	*uṭenu*	*ḥā*	*khe-t*	*neb-t*	*tut*
the altars,	{shall be poured out libations,}		and	thing	every	{which it is proper}

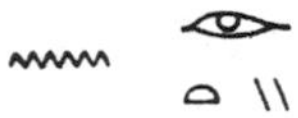

en	*ȧr-ti*
to do	[shall be done].

[The priests of Ptolemy V shall assume an additional title]

uābu	*nu*	*gesu peru*	*em*	*erpi* (*sic*)
The priests	of	the temples	in	temple

neb	*ḥer*	*ren-f*	*ka-tu-sen*	*ḥem neter peri* (*sic*)
every	by its name,		shall be called	{"priest of the god appearing,}

neb	*neferu*	*em*	*heru*	*ȧu*	*ȧaut*	*uābu*
lord of benefits"		in addition to			the ranks of priests	

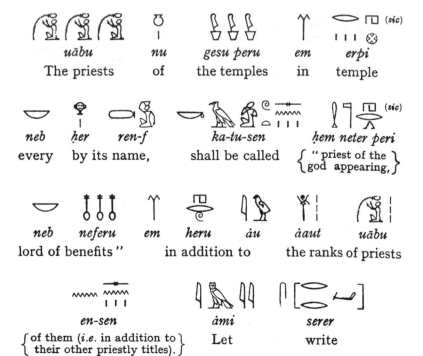

en-sen	*ȧmi*	*serer*
{of them (*i.e.* in addition to their other priestly titles).}	Let	write

R 13 

sen su ḥer tep-ta- ret-sen khet-tu

them it upon documents their, {and let be engraved}

àaut uāb en neter peri (sic) neb neferu

the rank "Priest of the god appearing, lord of benefits"

ḥer khetemu àri tet-sen

upon the ring[s] [worn on] their hand[s].

[PRIVATE PERSONS SHALL BE ALLOWED TO PAY THESE HONOURS TO PTOLEMY V]

às àret su un-s em āāui

Behold therefore it is in the hands

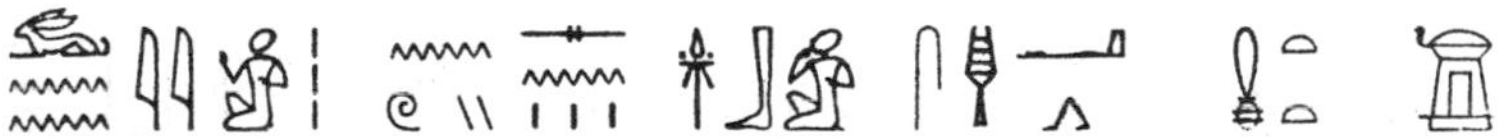

uneniu en-sen àlu s-āhā màtet ga

of [those] people who are wishful to set up a copy of shrine

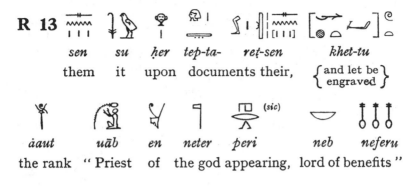

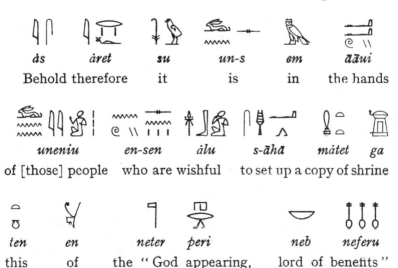

ten en neter peri neb neferu

this of the "God appearing, lord of benefits"

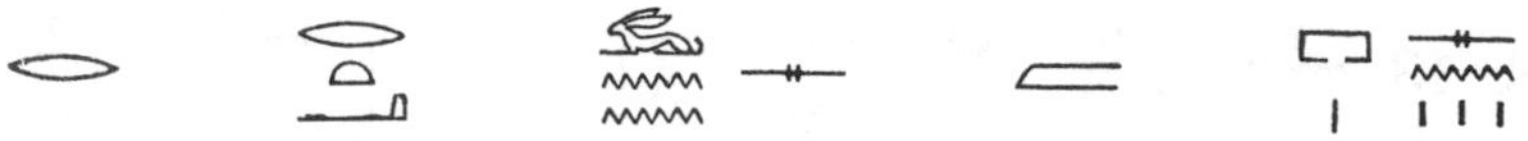

er *erṭa* *unen-s* *em* *per-sen*
to arrange for it to be in their houses.

emtutu *sen* *år* *ḥebu* *khāu* *åpen*
They shall celebrate festivals [and] {days of rejoicing} these

tep *åbṭ* *tep* *remp-t* *er* *erṭa* *såau-tu* *unen*
each month [and] each year {to make it be understood [that] are,}

åmiu *Ta-Mer-t* *ḥer* *djeser*
the dwellers in Egypt glorifying

R 14 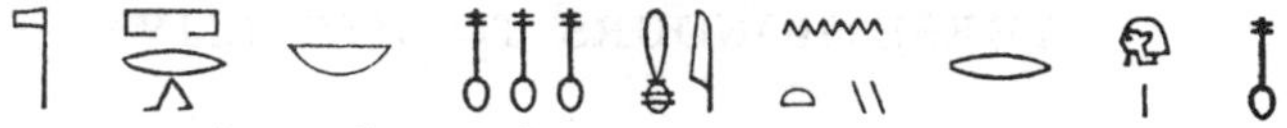

neter *peri* *neb* *neferu* *må* *enti* *er* *tep* *nefer*
{the "God appearing,} {lord of benefits,"} {even as is most right and proper.}

[THIS DECREE SHALL BE PUBLISHED]

khet-tu *skhau* *pen* *ḥer* *ākåit* *enti*
Shall be engraved decree this upon a tablet of

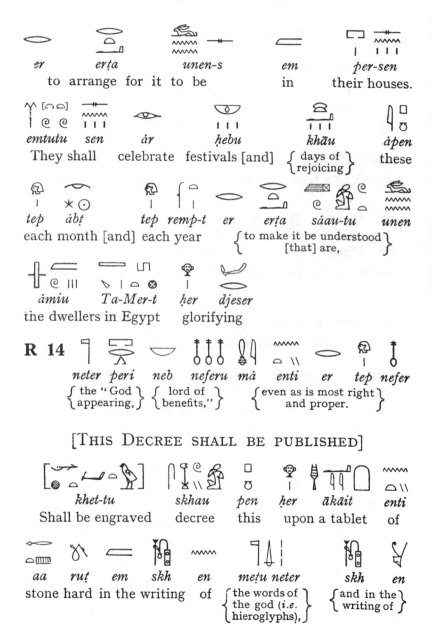

aa *ruṭ* *em* *skh* *en* *meṭu neter* *skh* *en*
stone hard in the writing of {the words of the god (*i.e.* hieroglyphs),} {and in the writing of}

shāc-t *skhi* *en* *Ḥau-nebu*

books (*i.e.* demotic) [and in] the writing of the Greeks.

erṭa *āḥā-f* *em* *gesu peru* *em* *erpi* *neb*

{Shall be made to stand it} in the sanctuaries in temples all

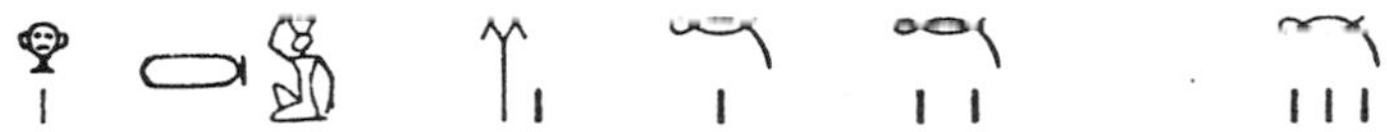

ḥer *ren-f* *em* *meḥ I* *meḥ II* *meḥ III*

by its name of the first, second [and] third [orders]

er *ges* *khent* *en* *Nesu-bat*

by the side of the statue of {the King of the South and North,}

Ptulmis *ānkh* *djet* *Ptaḥ* *meri*

Ptolemy, everliving, of Ptaḥ beloved,

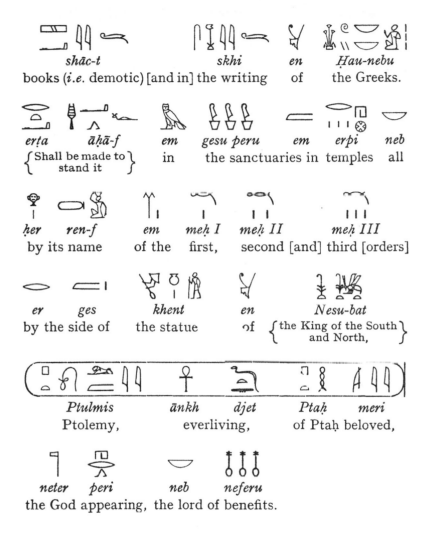

neter *peri* *neb* *neferu*

the God appearing, the lord of benefits.

A SHORT ACCOUNT OF THE DECIPHERMENT OF EGYPTIAN HIEROGLYPHS

CHAPTER V

I.—HIEROGLYPHIC, HIERATIC AND DEMOTIC (ENCHORIAL) WRITING

The GREEKS called HIEROGLYPHIC WRITING ἱερογλυφικὰ or, ἱερὰ γράμματα, and seem to have regarded it as a system of religious symbols of a mystical character, each of which possessed an esoteric meaning, which the Egyptian priests employed in engraving inscriptions on stone monuments. The GREEKS also knew that the priests used a cursive or simplified form of hieroglyphic writing when transcribing books, and to this they gave the name of HIERATIC (ἱερατικά); a still more simplified form was used in writing letters and business documents, and this was called DEMOTIC (δημοτικά), or ENCHORIAL. Hieroglyphs had no specially sacred character, though they were used to write the "words of the god," and there was nothing mystical or magical about them, for they are merely figures or pictures of objects, animate and inanimate, which stood for a word, a syllable, or a simple letter. The word "hieroglyphs" is used to describe the figures used in Mexican and other picture-writings, *e.g.* the Chinese, as well as those found in the Egyptian inscriptions.

The EGYPTIANS believed that hieroglyphic writing was invented by the god THOTH, and there is evidence that it, and the cursive form of it (Hieratic), were used in EGYPT throughout the dynastic period, and, for purely official purposes, until the second or third century A.D. It is doubtful when exactly the Demotic script came into general use, but it is probable that it superseded the Hieratic script under the XXVIth Dynasty, say about B.C. 600. Accurate knowledge of hieroglyphic writing was confined to the priests, who established schools in their colleges and temples, where the young men who were needed to keep the accounts and manage the business of the temples were educated. In these too were trained the scribes who made the copies of the various BOOKS OF THE DEAD which were sold to the public, and probably also the scribes who were employed by the Government in the fiscal and other Departments of State. There was no system of general education in EGYPT, and very few members of the public could read the inscriptions on the temples and obelisks and other monuments that were set up by the PHARAOHS. And it is doubtful if any adequate knowledge of hieroglyphic writing existed among the peoples who raided or conquered EGYPT. PIĀNKHI, the Nubian, and some of his successors at NAPATA set up stelae covered with hieroglyphic inscriptions, but the drafts of the texts were undoubtedly the work of native Egyptian scribes, and the sculptors who carved the reliefs on them, and the masons who cut the inscriptions, were native Egyptians. Both reliefs and texts betray the hand of the skilled and experienced workman. And no king of this Nubian Dynasty added a translation of his Egyptian text into any of the dialects of LOWER NUBIA (KENSET) or KASH (KÛSH), for the Meroïtic script which we find on several of the buildings of the PTOLEMIES was not invented in the VIIIth century B.C. The Meroïtic script appears to have been developed out of the Demotic, and it was much used in writing commemorative and funerary inscriptions in the first two or three centuries of the Christian Era.

II.—THE USE OF EGYPTIAN HIEROGLYPHS BY THE PERSIAN CONQUERORS OF EGYPT

The first conqueror of EGYPT to set up stelae engraved with hieroglyphic inscriptions, accompanied by translations in the language or languages of his native country, was DARIUS I, the Great, who arrived in Egypt about B.C. 517. To commemorate one of the greatest works which he did in EGYPT, *i.e.* the digging of a canal to join the NILE and the RED SEA, he set up large stelae at several places along the line of the canal, and the remains of several of them have been found.[1] These quadrilingual stelae were inscribed in hieroglyphs on one side, and in three kinds of cuneiform writing on the other, the languages represented by the cuneiform scripts being PERSIAN, ELAMITE (or, SUSIAN) and BABYLONIAN. On the remains of the stelae found at TALL AL-MASKHÛTAH, and at SARÂBYÛM (the SERAPEUM), and at SHALÛF and at SUWÊS (SUEZ), a figure of the king was sculptured on each side, and below were the inscriptions in the four languages giving the name of DARIUS and his titles as king of the whole world. (For the texts see WEISSBACH and BANG, *Die altpersischen Keilinschriften*, Leipzig, 1893.) DARIUS built a large temple in honour of ÅMEN-RĀ in the OASIS OF KHÂRGAH, and endowed a college at SAÏS for the education of the priests, and it is probable that he intended PERSIANS to be taught therein the Egyptian language and the art of writing in Egyptian hieroglyphs. Though DARIUS did so much for Egypt, and made handsome gifts to the temples, and did all he could to develop native institutions and commerce, he failed to make the language of Persia general in EGYPT, and the traces of Persian influence in the country were soon obliterated.

[1] The canal ran, from a place near BUBASTIS, through the modern WÂDÎ TÛMÎLÂṬ, and passing PA-TEM (PITHOM) made its way directly to the RED SEA. For the literature, see WIEDEMANN, *Aeg. Geschichte*, p. 680.

III.—THE USE OF EGYPTIAN HIEROGLYPHS BY THE PTOLEMIES AND CAESARS

Through the advent of the Greek mercenary, and the Greek trader, the knowledge of the Greek language spread rapidly throughout EGYPT, and after the peaceful annexation of the country by ALEXANDER THE GREAT, the study and use of hieroglyphic writing began to decline. The Egyptian scribes learned Greek, and the cultured Greeks who settled in ALEXANDRIA, DAPHNAE (TALL-DAFANNAH), ASWÂN and NAUCRATIS, and other large towns in EGYPT, learned Egyptian. Copies of the whole or parts of the Saïte Recension of the BOOK OF THE DEAD were no longer written in hieroglyphs, but in Hieratic, and even in the Demotic script. And although Egyptians in the Ptolemaïc period continued to have hieroglyphic texts written on coffins and funerary stelae and other tomb-furniture, it is tolerably certain that they were not understanded of the people. The PTOLEMIES, as Kings of EGYPT, adopted the ancient titles of the PHARAOHS, and caused the inscriptions on the temples and other buildings which they restored, or rebuilt, to be cut in hieroglyphic characters; but the language used at their Court was Greek, and the Greek language became predominant in the country. Legal and commercial documents were frequently written in Demotic and Greek, and the priests began to forget how to read and write the old picture-language of the country. The importance of Greek in the Ptolemaïc period is proved by the fact that the Decree which the priests promulgated at CANOPUS in honour of PTOLEMY III, EUERGETES I, and the Decrees which the priests promulgated at MEMPHIS in honour of PTOLEMY IV PHILOPATOR, and PTOLEMY V EPIPHANES, were first drafted in Greek and not in the Egyptian language. The Demotic version follows the Greek fairly closely, but the hieroglyphic versions show that their writers did not always know how to translate the Greek accurately. In some cases without the Greek original and the Demotic translation it would be impossible to translate the hieroglyphs.

The CAESARS, who followed the example of the Persian conquerors of Egypt, and the PTOLEMIES, adopted the principal titles of the PHARAOHS, and permitted, or perhaps ordered, their benefactions to the priesthoods of EGYPT to be recorded on the walls of the temples which they repaired, or rebuilt, in inscriptions written in hieroglyphs. But neither the PTOLEMIES nor the CAESARS took steps to prevent the knowledge of hieroglyphic writing from dying out. PTOLEMY II instructed MANETHO, a priest of SEBENNYTUS, to write a HISTORY OF EGYPT for him in Greek, but it was the information contained in the Egyptian texts that he wanted, and not the preservation of the original language.

IV.—GREEK WRITERS ON EGYPTIAN HIEROGLYPHS

Though there are passages in the works of Greek writers like HECATAEUS, HERODOTUS, and DIODORUS, which mention the hieroglyphs and the various kinds of Egyptian writing, they contain no evidence that their authors understood the true principles which underlay hieroglyphic writing. That there were among the learned Greeks who lived in Egypt men who had a real knowledge of the meaning and manner of use of some of the Egyptian hieroglyphs is proved by the extract given by JOHN TZETZES (A.D. 1110–80) in his "Exegesis" of HOMER'S ILIAD. He derived his facts from the work on HIEROGLYPHS[1] which was compiled by CHAEREMON[2] of NAUCRATIS, who lived in the first half of the first century after Christ. CHAEREMON was an official in the great Alexandrian Library, and it is clear that, as a sacred scribe, he had access to such native literature as the Library contained. The extract given by TZETZES is too long to quote here, but it is given in full by Birch (*Transactions of the Royal Society of Literature*, vol. iii, 2nd series, 1850, pp. 385–96; and by myself in *The Mummy*, 2nd ed., Cambridge, 1925, p. 129 f.). The general evidence of the extract suggests that CHAEREMON could read and translate ancient Egyptian texts.

[1] Περὶ τῶν ἱερῶν γραμμάτων. This work is no longer extant.

[2] He is called Χαιρήμων ὁ ἱερογραμματεύς by EUSEBIUS.

A passage in the "Stromateis" of CLEMENT OF ALEXANDRIA (born at ATHENS about A.D. 150, died about 220) shows that this learned churchman knew that the Egyptians used THREE kinds of writing, viz., EPISTOLOGRAPHIC (*i.e.* DEMOTIC or ENCHORIAL), HIERATIC and HIEROGLYPHIC. Hieratic he describes as the writing of the priests. The Hieroglyphic characters he divided into CYRIOLOGICAL and SYMBOLICAL, and in the latter the characters were classified as CYRIOLOGICAL by imitation, or TROPICAL, or ENIGMATICAL. But evidence that CLEMENT could read hieroglyphic writing is wanting.

Another interesting work on Egyptian Hieroglyphs (ΙΕΡΟΓΛΥΦΙΚΑ), somewhat similar in character to that of CHAEREMON, was compiled by the grammarian HORAPOLLON, who flourished in the reign of THEODOSIUS I. He was a native of PHAENEBYTHIS in the nome of PANOPOLIS in UPPER EGYPT, and as the town of PANOPOLIS was at that time a great centre of literary activity, it is probable that he had access to a number of ancient Egyptian papyri. Two books which are said to have formed part of his treatise "Hieroglyphika" are extant. In the introductory passage we are told that they were translated from the Egyptian language into Greek by a certain PHILIPPUS of whom, however, nothing is known. This seems to suggest that the Greek text which we now have is at best only a recension of the original work of HORAPOLLON. The first book contains evidence that the writer had a good knowledge of the meanings and uses of Egyptian hieroglyphs, and that he was familiar with inscriptions of the Ptolemaïc and Graeco-Roman periods. In the second book there are many absurd and fanciful statements about the meanings and significations of Egyptian hieroglyphs, and these are probably the work of the unknown PHILIPPUS, who like CHAEREMON, was ignorant of the phonetic values of the characters he described. In spite of this the book, as a whole, has a considerable value even to-day. For the Greek text see Conrad LEEMANS, *Horapollinis Niloi Hieroglyphica*, Amsterdam, 1835; and A. T. CORY, *The Hieroglyphics of Horapollo Nilous*, with an English translation and notes by S. SHARPE and S. BIRCH, London, 1840.

As long as the principal temples of Egypt were protected by the Roman Government, and the prefects took care that their revenues were not interfered with, there must have existed during the first two or three centuries of our Era priests who studied the ancient literature of the country, and could read, more or less correctly, the inscriptions on the monuments. TACITUS tells us (ii, 59) that when GERMANICUS CAESAR visited THEBES, an aged priest when called upon to read the inscriptions to him proceeded to read to him from the monuments the narrative of the conquests of RAMESES II, and the lists of tribute which the various conquered peoples paid to EGYPT. And in his "History" AMMIAN MARCELLIN quotes (xvii, 4, §17) the Greek translation of six lines of the hieroglyphic inscription on the obelisk of RAMESES II which was brought to ROME by AUGUSTUS, and set up in the CIRCUS MAXIMUS. The author of the translation was one HERMAPION, of whom unfortunately nothing is known.

V.—THE INTRODUCTION OF CHRISTIANITY INTO EGYPT, AND THE INVENTION OF THE COPTIC ALPHABET

Many of the principal Greek officials who died in Egypt were mummified, and their coffins, sarcophagi, funerary coffers and stelae, and even their mummy bandages, were inscribed in Greek. But during the whole of the period of Roman rule in EGYPT, the natives continued to mummify their dead, and the inscriptions upon their mummies were written sometimes in Demotic, and sometimes in hieroglyphs, to many of which new phonetic values had been given. Many of these inscriptions are untranslatable. The event which brought the use of hieroglyphic writing to an end for funerary purposes was the adoption of CHRISTIANITY by the EGYPTIANS as the result of the alleged preaching of ST. MARK at ALEXANDRIA in the second half of the Ist century A.D. The

EGYPTIAN CHRISTIANS loathed and abominated the religion and gods of their pagan ancestors, and wholly refused to employ either the hieroglyphic or demotic writing in their funerary inscriptions. Some time during the Ist century B.C. or the Ist century A.D. some persons thought they they would like to write the Egyptian language in Greek letters, probably because they found it very difficult to learn to read and write the demotic script. But, when they came to do so, they found that there were certain sounds in Egyptian for which the Greek alphabet contained no letters. Thereupon they added to the Greek alphabet seven letters,[1] which were formed of modifications of the hieratic and demotic symbols of certain hieroglyphs, and by degrees this composite alphabet came into use in the country. Whether the EGYPTIAN CHRISTIANS ever tried to write the translations of the Books of the Old and New Testaments in Demotic cannot be said, but it is improbable, for their one aim was to free themselves from contact with everything that appertained to the religion of their pagan ancestors, whom they regarded as besotted idolators.

The name usually given to the Egyptian Christians, " Ḳubbî " or " Gubbî," *i.e.* " man of Egypt," " Ḳubt," or " Gubt," *i.e.* EGYPT, is thought to be derived from the Greek name of EGYPT, Αἴγυπτος, which, in turn, seems to be

[1] These are ϣ, ϥ, ϧ, ϩ, ϫ, ϭ, ϯ.

derived from Ḥekaptaḥ, a name of Memphis. Another view is that the original Egyptian word for Egypt was Ageb, , and that it meant "the land of the flood," *i.e.* inundation, , which was poured out from the great World-Ocean by the Flood-god Ageb, . Others again would derive " Ḳubtî " or " Gubtî " from the name of the town of Qebti, 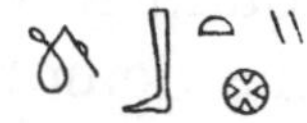, *i.e.* Coptos in Upper Egypt, whither the Egyptian Christians fled in large numbers during the Roman persecutions.

Be this as it may, the Christian Egyptians are now, and have for centuries been, known as " Copts," and the Egyptian language written in Greek letters is called " Coptic." How important this form of the Egyptian language was for the early decipherers of the Egyptian hieroglyphic inscriptions will be seen later on. In the course of time the use of Coptic superseded that of demotic in legal and many commercial documents, and many Books of the Bible, and the works of many of the Fathers of the Jacobite Church were translated into Coptic in the IVth century. For a century and a-half after the conquest of Egypt by 'Amr ibn al-Âṣi, the commander-in-chief of the Khalîfah 'Omar in 641, the Coptic language was employed by the Arab conquerors in their official documents, but, as the hold of the Arabs on the country increased Arabic took its place. The COPTS were expelled from Government offices in the VIIIth century, and then severely persecuted by the ARABS ; large numbers of them in EGYPT, NUBIA and the SÛDÂN apostatized, embraced ISLÂM, and adopted the Arabic language. Coptic fell into disuse rapidly, and though the COPTS continued to write the Liturgy in Coptic in their Service-Books, the priests read the Offices from the Arabic translations of them which were written, (and they still are) side by side with the Coptic texts. We may say then that all knowledge of hieroglyphic writing was lost by the end of the IIIrd century A.D. and that the Egyptian language, *i.e.* Coptic, was dead by the end of the XIIth century.

CHAPTER VI

I.—THE ATTEMPTS MADE TO DECIPHER THE EGYPTIAN HIEROGLYPHS IN EUROPE IN THE SIXTEENTH AND SEVENTEENTH CENTURIES

The study of the Egyptian hieroglyphs and hieroglyphic writing in what we may call modern times began with **Giovanni Pierio Valeriano Bolzani,** who, under the title of *Hieroglyphica*, published a treatise on the sacred writing of the Egyptians and other nations, in seven Books, at Basle in 1556. In an appendix he printed the two Books of HORAPOLLO (see p. 181), and added many learned notes, but with the exception of the material which he collected his work has no value, because he did not realize the nature of the problem which he was attempting to solve. His *Hieroglyphica* went through numerous editions, and stirred up interest in the Egyptian hieroglyphic inscriptions among the learned, especially in the royal inscriptions engraved on the Egyptian obelisks in Rome.

Soon after the publication of the *Hieroglyphica*, the question of the re-erection of some of the fallen obelisks in ROME began to occupy the minds of the Papal authorities. Eventually

Pope Sixtus V commissioned Fontana, the famous architect (1543–1607), to dig out the two largest obelisks, which were buried under the ruins of the Circus Maximus, and to re-erect them. The largest obelisk, that of Thothmes III, which was broken into three pieces, was re-erected by Fontana in the Piazza of St. John Lateran in 1588, and the smaller, that of Seti I, commonly known as the "Flaminian Obelisk," was re-erected by Fontana in the Piazza del Popolo in 1589. The demand in Rome at this time for information about the obelisks was so great that **Mercati M.** was obliged to issue the work on them which was entitled *Degli Obelischi di Rome,* Rome, 1589. In the following year he published a supplement, in which he attempted to give the meanings of the inscriptions on the obelisks, but his explanations are worthless.

The next scholar who tried to decipher the Egyptian hieroglyphs was **Athanasius Kircher** (born at Geisa in 1601, died 1680), a German Professor of Mathematics in the Collegio Romano (1635–43). He was a man of untiring energy and vast learning, but many of his writings suggest that he printed the contents of his notebooks without taking the trouble to digest them. He has been called "charlatan" and "impostor" by many writers, but a careful perusal of even what now seem to be his most ridiculous and impossible pronouncements, makes it difficult to believe that he was not sincere. Of course he was an enthusiast, and he held his erroneous views and beliefs with great tenacity. In the matter of Egyptian hieroglyphs it is clear that he thought that every character represented an *idea*. One example will be sufficient to show how this view affected his so-called translations. On the obelisk of DOMITIAN, commonly known as the "Pamphylian Obelisk," he saw the cartouche 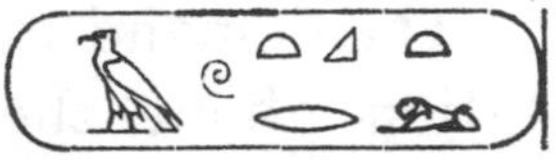. Now the seven characters in this cartouche represent the transcription into hieroglyphs of the Greek title "Autocrator," but KIRCHER'S translation of them may be rendered in English, "The author of fruitfulness and of all vegetation is OSIRIS, whose productive force was produced in his kingdom out of heaven through the holy Mophta." All his "translations" are equally nonsensical, but those who believed that he could read the Egyptian hieroglyphs expected him to produce from them mystical and magical information, and, like other blind leaders of the blind, he did what he was wanted to do. He lived in an age of credulity and superstition, and was a product of it. In spite of this he was a learned man, and there is much interesting information in the six principal works by which he is best known, viz., *Prodromus Coptus*, Rome, 1636; *Lingua Aegyptiaca restituta*, Rome, 1643;

Obeliscus Pamphilius, Rome, 1650; *Obelisci Aegyptiaci*, Rome, 1666; *Sphinx Mystagoga*, Amsterdam, 1676; and *Oedipus Aegyptiacus*, Amsterdam, 1680. During the whole of the XVIIth century KIRCHER was regarded as a great Egyptologist, and **Sir J. Marshall** made use of his writings in his *Canon Chronicus*, published at Frankfort in 1696.

There seems to be no doubt that KIRCHER'S writings gave an impetus to the study of the language and antiquities of ancient EGYPT, and a great many books on these subjects appeared during the XVIIIth century. Men of learning who travelled in Egypt during that century made copies of the inscriptions which they came across, and among them may be mentioned **P. Lucas** (*Voyage au Levant*, La Haye, 1705); **R. Pococke** (*Description of the East*, London, 1743–5); **C. Niebuhr** (*Reise durch Aegypten und Arabien*, Bern, 1779); and **F. L. Norden** (*Antiquities of Egypt, Nubia and Thebes*, London, 1791). But of the copies of inscriptions published in these works only those of NIEBUHR can lay any claim to general accuracy.

Throughout the century many attempts to decipher the Egyptian hieroglyphs were made in ENGLAND, FRANCE and GERMANY, and among the publications of such attempts may be mentioned those of **A. Gordon**, who published an *Essay* (London, 1737) which was really the work of

GOUGH, the antiquary; **N. Fréret** (*Essai sur les Hiéroglyphes*, Paris, 1744); **P. A. L. D'Origny** (*L'Égypte Ancienne*, Paris, 1762); **C. de Gebelin** (*Monde Primitif*, Paris, 1775); **J. H. Schumacher** (*Versuch der dunkeln und versteckten Geheimnisse näher aufzuklären*, Leipzig, 1754); **J. G. Koch** (*Tentamen enucleationis hieroglyphicorum*, Petropolis, 1788); **T. Ch. Tychsen** (*Ueber die Buchstabeninschrift der alten Aegypter*, 1790); and **P. E. Jablonski,** whose *Opuscula* were not published in a complete form until 1804. Some scholars published pictures of Egyptian monuments, with comments (see **A. C. P. De Caylus,** *Dissertation sur le Papyrus*, Paris, 1758), but the "explanations" of the hieroglyphs which they gave were merely the fruits of their imaginations and guesses.

Among the Egyptological books published during the XVIIIth century there are a few in which their authors showed that they really had some idea of the nature and character of Egyptian hieroglyphs. **Bishop Warburton** (1698–1779), in his *Divine Legation of Moses* (London, 1737–8), proved by quotations from ancient authorities that the hieroglyphs were not only employed to conceal the religious dogmas of the Egyptians, as KIRCHER had declared, and that they really *did* represent the Egyptian language, and were used by the Egyptians to record "their laws, policies, public morals, history and, in a word, all kinds of civil matters" (*Essai sur les Hiéroglyphes*, Paris, 1741). **C. L. J. de Guignes** analysed a number of groups of hieroglyphic characters, and came to the conclusion that some of the signs were determinatives, which resembled the "keys" or "radicals" in Chinese (*Essai sur le moyen de parvenir à la lecture et à l'intelligence des Hiéroglyphes Égyptiens*, Paris, 1770). **G. Zoega** wrote a history of the obelisks in Rome, and added to it extracts from ancient writers concerning them, and a series of learned dissertations as to their origin and signification (*De origine et usu Obeliscorum*, Rome, 1797). In the course of his study of them he came to the conclusion that the oval ring, with a bar at one end of it, , which we now call a "cartouche," contained symbols which represented either a name or a religious formula.[1] Zoega was not the first to suggest that the cartouches on the obelisks contained [royal] names, for J. J. Barthélemy had done so (see his "Explication d'un Bas-Relief Égyptien" in *Mémoires de l'Académie des Inscriptions*, tom xxxii (1761), p. 725; and in his "Réflexions générales" in the *Mémoires* for 1763). But it is possible that it was Zoega's suggestion which

[1] Zoega's words are: "Conspiciuntur autem passim in Aegyptiis monumentis schemata quaedam ovata sive elliptica planae basi insidentia, quae emphatica ratione includunt certa notarum syntagmata, sive ad propria personarum nomina exprimenda sive ad sacratiores formulas designandas."

induced the early students of the hieroglyphs to attempt to identify the names of PTOLEMY, CLEOPATRA and BERENICE before any other words.

II.—THE ATTEMPTS MADE TO DECIPHER THE EGYPTIAN HIEROGLYPHS IN THE NINETEENTH CENTURY

During the first quarter of the XIXth century many works on the Egyptian hieroglyphs appeared, and of these the following are of interest: **N. G. De Pahlin,** *Lettres sur les hiéroglyphes*, Weimar, 1802, and his *Essai*, Weimar, 1804; **J. von Hammer-Purgstall,** *Alphabets and Hieroglyphic Characters Explained*, London, 1806; **A. Lenoir,** *Nouvelle Explication*, 4 vols., Paris, 1809–21; and **P. Lacour,** *Essai sur les Hiéroglyphes*, Bordeaux, 1821. A certain interest in Egyptology generally was stirred up by the prize Essay of **J. Bailey,** *Hieroglyphicorum origo et natura*, Cambridge, 1816, but he only repeated several of the old theories about hieroglyphs which were made in the XVIIIth century, and left the subject of the decipherment of them untouched. The writers of these books were men of learning who spared themselves no trouble in their endeavours to wrest the secrets of the hieroglyphs from the inscriptions, but they all failed to do so because they did not understand their character and use. As they did not know the phonetic values of the hieroglyphs, they could not identify the language which they expressed. Moreover, they were unable even to identify all the objects represented by the hieroglyphs, for the simple reason that many of them are conventionalized pictures of beings and things animate and inanimate, of the nature and character of which they were, naturally, ignorant. Even to-day the objects which are represented by some of the hieroglyphs are unknown to us. The difficulty that confronted the students of Egyptian hieroglyphs in the XVIIth and XVIIIth centuries confronts Oriental archaeologists at the present time, in respect of the so-called HITTITE inscriptions which have been brought from CARCHEMISH and neighbouring sites to great European Museums. These inscriptions are written with characters resembling the hieroglyphs of EGYPT, and in spite of all the efforts made by distinguished scholars cannot, in my opinion, be read and translated at the present time. What the Hittitologists are waiting for is the discovery of a **bilingual inscription** in which one-half of it will be written in some known language, say, Assyrian, or Phoenician, or Hebrew. I am not forgetting that it has often been asserted that an object with a bilingual inscription in Hittite and cuneiform characters upon it has been discovered, and that the cuneiform inscription upon it has been satisfactorily read. But whatever clues it may have supplied, they have been insufficient to enable scholars to read and translate the " Hittite " hieroglyphic inscriptions from CARCHEMISH, and HAMATH, and ALEPPO.[1]

III.—EARLY ATTEMPTS TO DECIPHER THE EGYPTIAN TEXT ON THE ROSETTA STONE

Curiously enough at the very time when ZOEGA was writing and printing his book on Egyptian obelisks, and was actually stating his

[1] The object on which the bilingual " Hittite " and cuneiform inscription was found is described as a " boss " made of silver. It was offered by a dealer for purchase to the keeper

of the Departments of Antiquities in the British Museum some time before 1860, and was examined by Sir HENRY RAWLINSON and Dr. BIRCH. Neither scholar believed in the genuineness of the " boss," and the British Museum declined to buy it ; RAWLINSON believed the inscription to be a forgery, and BIRCH regarded the object as a cast made from a hard stone original. With characteristic foresight Mr. ROBERT READY made an electrotype copy of the inscription, and took several

belief that the ovals, *i.e.* cartouches, on them contained proper names, which, however, he was unable to read because they were not accompanied by transcriptions of them in Greek, the discovery of the ROSETTA STONE took place. We have already seen how NAPOLEON caused lithographers to make copies of the inscriptions on it, how " Citoyen " DU THEIL translated the Greek

---

wax impressions of it. The object was seen by Dr. A. D. MORDTMANN, who published accounts of it in *Münzstudien*, iii, 7, 8, 9, Leipzig, 1863, and in the *Zeitschrift* of the German Oriental Society, vol. xxvi, 3, 4 (1872). When Professor SAYCE restudied these articles in 1880 he came to the conclusion that the " Hittite " hieroglyphs in the centre of the " boss " were the equivalents of the cuneiform inscription which ran round them, and that he had discovered the means whereby the " Hittite " inscriptions might be read and translated. In his paper in the *Transactions* of the Society of Biblical Archaeology (vol. vii, p. 294 f.) he transcribed the cuneiform inscription on the " boss " thus :—

D.P. Tar - rik - tim - me *śar mat Er - me - e*

Tarrik-timme, king of the country of Ermê.

Dr. PINCHES' transcript reads :—

D.P. Tar - Ḳu - u - tim - me *śar mât Er - me - e*

Tarḳû-timme, king of the land of Ermê.

Dr. PINCHES thinks that the forms of the characters are pure Babylonian, possibly slightly modified by Assyrian influence, but that the second (*Tar*), the third (*ḳu*), the fifth (*tim*, which might equally well be *mu*), and the eleventh (*e*), are incorrect, both from the Babylonian and Assyrian point of view (*Proceedings Soc. Bibl. Arch.*, 1885, p. 124). And he would

text, and how the Rev. STEPHEN WESTON read his translation, which was made from the copy of the Stone, published by the Society of Antiquaries of London,[1] before the Society on July 8, 1802 (see above, p. 33).

---

translate the cuneiform part of the inscription "Tarḳû-timme, king of the land of the city of water." It was the irregularities in the writing which Dr. PINCHES has pointed out that bothered RAWLINSON in the last century. MORDTMANN compared the name of Tarḳû-timme with that of the Cilician king Tarkondimotos, and SAYCE with Tarkondêmos, but where and when Tarḳû-timme reigned cannot be said. The inscription on the "boss" here given is made from a silver electrotype given to me by the late Sir WOLLASTON FRANKS, K.C.B., on his retirement from the British Museum. I make no attempt to describe the "Hittite" hieroglyphs on the "boss," about which so much has been said and written, for I lack the necessary knowledge. They have been treated at length by all those who have formulated systems of "Hittite" decipherment, viz., the Rev. C. J. BALL, Dr. R. CAMPBELL THOMPSON, Colonel CONDER, Dr. COWLEY, Dr. JENSEN, M. MENANT, Dr. PEISER and others, and for their works the reader is referred to G. CONTENAU'S *Elements de Bibliographie Hittite*, Paris, 1922, an indispensable work for all students of Hittitology.

[1] The drawings and engravings were the work of JAMES BASIRE. The descriptive title read:—"Has tabulas (V, VI, VII) inscriptionem sacris Ægyptiorum et vulgaribus literis itemque Graecis in lapide nigro ac praeduro insculptam exhibentis ad formam et modulum exemplaris inter spolia ex bello Ægyptiaco nuper reportati et in Museo Britannico asservati suo sumptu incidendas curant Soc: Antiquar: Londini: A.D. MDCCCIII." See also *Vetusta Monumenta*, vol. iv, London, 1815.

A general description of the work done on the Greek and Demotic versions of the Decree of Memphis engraved on the ROSETTA STONE will be found on pp. 49 f. and 76 f., and we therefore pass on to describe the attempts made to decipher the Egyptian hieroglyphs in the years immediately following the discovery of the Stone. The earliest of these appeared in the works of M. le Comte NILS GUSTAF **de Pahlin,** who in 1802 published his *Lettres sur les Hiéroglyphes* (Weimar, with plates), and in 1804 his *Essai sur les Hiéroglyphes* (Weimar, with 24 inscriptions), and an *Analyse de l'inscription en Hiéroglyphes du Monument trouvé à Rosette* (Weimar, with a facsimile of the hieroglyphic text on the ROSETTA STONE). DE PAHLIN thought that the Chinese and Egyptian hieroglyphs were identical in origin and meaning, and, according to YOUNG, he thought that if the Psalms of David were translated into Chinese, and they were then written in the ancient character of that language, the inscriptions on Egyptian papyri would be reproduced. It is easy to see now that if DE PAHLIN had studied the "Lettres" which DE SACY and ÅKERBLAD had published on the Demotic version on the Stone, and followed in their steps, he might have seen that some of the Egyptian hieroglyphs were *alphabetic*, and so might have deciphered the proper names. The mistake he made was in following the dicta of KIRCHER and JABLONSKI. DE PAHLIN was an honest enthusiast, and even the learned were led astray by his apt and specious arguments; but the truth is that, like others, he never understood the problem which he undertook to solve. Many accepted DE PAHLIN'S fantastic translations, and even so sound a scholar as ÅKERBLAD was inclined to regard them as correct.

During the twelve years which followed the publication of DE SACY'S *Lettre au Citoyen Chaptal au sujet de l'inscription Égyptienne du monument trouvé à Rosette*, Paris, An X [1802 *v. st.*], no real progress appears to have been made in the decipherment of Egyptian hieroglyphs. Much was written and said about them by the faddists and cranks, who were usually wholly uneducated men, and whose one idea was to prove that the Egyptian inscriptions were extracts from the Bible. One of them went so far as to declare that the inscription over the portico of the temple of DENDERAH was the CXIXth Psalm! The first really successful attempt to decipher Egyptian hieroglyphs was made by Dr. **Thomas Young, F.R.S.**, in 1814. (**Plate VII**.)

IV.—THOMAS YOUNG AND HIS WORK

Thomas Young was born at MILVERTON in SOMERSETSHIRE on June 13, 1773. He is said to have been able to read fluently at the age of two, and before he was twenty years old he had studied French, Italian, Latin, Greek, Hebrew, Syriac,

PLATE VII.

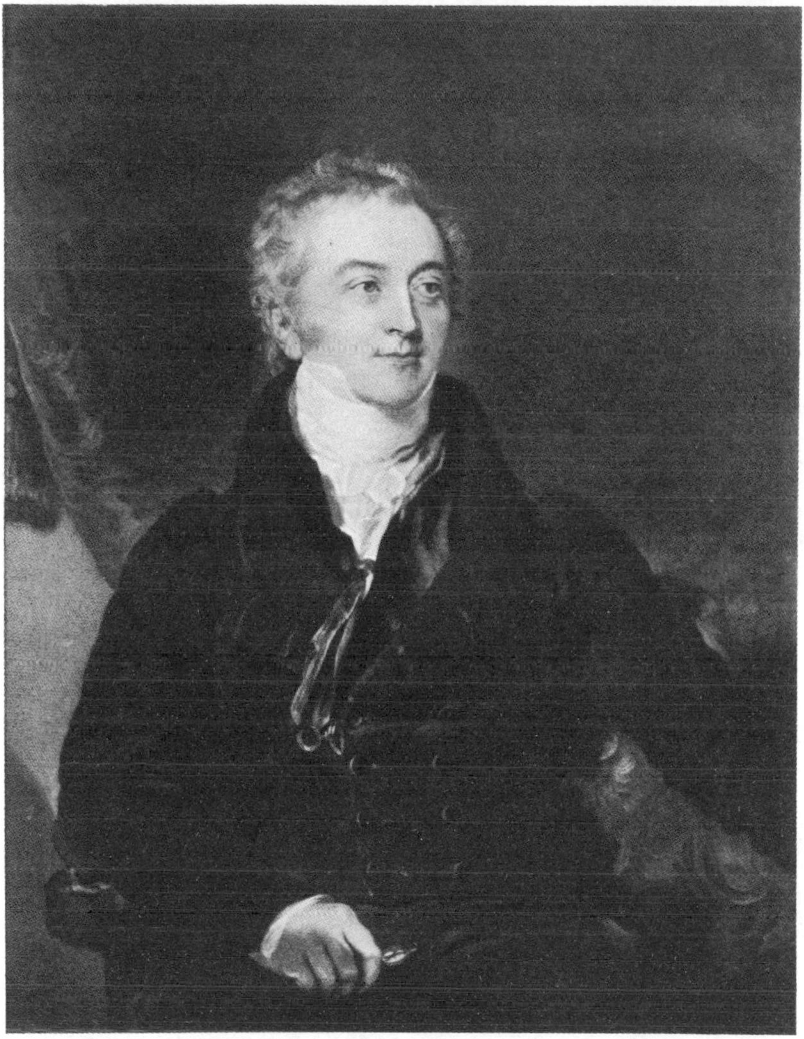

Thomas Young, M.D.
Born June 13, 1773. Died May 10, 1830.

The hieroglyphic inscription of Ptolemy IX on the four sides of the granite obelisk which was found at Philae by G. Belzoni. It was acquired by Mr. J. W. Bankes, who in 1839 set it up in his park at Kingston Lacey in Dorsetshire, where the inscriptions are being injured by the rigours of our English climate.

Chaldee, Samaritan, Arabic, Persian, Turkish, and Ethiopic, to say nothing of Philosophy, Botany and Entomology. In 1793 he entered St. Bartholomew's Hospital as a student; in 1801 he discovered the undulatory theory of light; in 1802 he became Foreign Secretary to the Royal Society, and in 1804 he was elected a Fellow; in 1814 he began to study the inscriptions on the ROSETTA STONE, and four years later published his epoch-making articles on Egyptian hieroglyphs in the *Encyclopaedia Britannica*; in 1818 he was appointed Secretary of the Board of Longitude, and Superintendent of the *Nautical Almanac*; and in 1826 he was elected one of the eight foreign Associates of the Academy of Paris. He died on May 10, 1829, at the comparatively early age of fifty-six. (For further details of his life and studies see G. PEACOCK, *The Life of Thomas Young*, London, 1855.) The above facts will give the reader an idea of the great and varied abilities of this remarkable man, and of the extent of his linguistic and scientific knowledge. It is clear that he was a physicist before everything else; he was only drawn to the study of Egyptian hieroglyphs by accident, as we shall now see. Whilst his friend Sir W. ROUSE BOUGHTON was travelling in Egypt, he purchased at LUXOR a papyrus written in cursive Egyptian characters. This papyrus was broken during its transport to England, and its purchaser submitted the fragments, or copies of them, to YOUNG in the spring of 1814. Why he did this is not clear, for, as far as I know, YOUNG did not occupy himself with the study of Egyptian writing in any form before 1814. BOUGHTON published a *Letter respecting Egyptian Antiquities*, with five plates, London (Parker), 1814, and YOUNG wrote a short article on the papyrus fragments, which was published, with an article by BOUGHTON entitled "Antiquities of Egypt," in *Archaeologia*, vol. xviii (1815), p. 59. YOUNG'S paper, entitled "Remarks on the Ancient Egyptian Manuscripts," was read on May 19, 1814, and was first published in the *Museum Criticum*, pt. vi, p. 15; it was reprinted by LEITCH in *The Works of Thomas Young*, vol. iii, p. 1 f.

YOUNG himself tells us that, having provided himself with a copy of ÅKERBLAD'S "Lettre" to DE SACY, and a copy of the Rosetta Stone, published by the Society of Antiquaries of London (see above, p. 196), he went to WORTHING in the summer of 1814 and then proceeded to work on the three scripts of the famous Decree of MEMPHIS. DE SACY claimed in his *Lettre au Citoyen Chaptal* (Paris, an X = A.D. 1802), that he had identified in the Demotic version the groups of characters which expressed the names of PTOLEMY, ALEXANDER and ALEXANDRIA, and the Swedish scholar J. D. ÅKERBLAD told DE SACY (*Lettre sur l'Inscription Égyptienne de Rosette,*

Paris, an X = A.D. 1802) that he had discovered the groups of characters which represented sixteen other names and words in the same inscription. He also drew up an alphabet, which was generally applicable to proper names, and to them only. But neither DE SACY nor ÅKERBLAD was able to make further progress, and in the following years they contented themselves with watching other scholars attempting to decipher the Egyptian hieroglyphs, and in criticising their efforts. YOUNG availed himself of the results obtained by DE SACY and ÅKERBLAD, and then began to try to translate the texts for himself. He first cut up his copy of the Demotic text into pieces, line by line, and pasted them on sheets of paper, and over each group of signs forming a word he pasted what he believed to be the equivalent of them from the Greek text. Then he treated the hieroglyphic text in the same way, but here a serious difficulty met him, for a very large portion of the hieroglyphic version was wanting. He certainly succeeded in identifying some of the groups of signs in the Demotic version, just as ÅKERBLAD had done, but he could not *read* either the Demotic or the hieroglyphic versions, because he did not realize that some of the characters were used as ideographs, and that some had SYLLABIC and others ALPHABETIC values. At this stage of his work he failed, as DE SACY and ÅKERBLAD had done, and, to tell the truth, his translations, both of the Demotic and hieroglyphic text, were based on guesswork.

But somewhere about this time (1815–16) YOUNG came to the conclusion that if a foreign conqueror of a certain country caused inscriptions commemorating his conquest to be drawn up in the native language of that country, and that language was written with pictorial characters similar to the Egyptian hieroglyphs, the scribes would, in writing the conqueror's name, make use of the PHONETIC values of a number of pictorial characters without any regard for the actual meanings of these characters as pictures.

YOUNG thought that he was the first to arrive at this conclusion, for he says, in enumerating the various points of his discovery, "As far as I have ever heard or read, *not one* of the particulars had ever been established and placed on record by *any other* person, dead or alive." But, as a matter of fact, the same idea had occurred both to BARTHÉLEMY and ZOEGA, a fact which seems to show that YOUNG was unacquainted with the works of two of the ablest and most sensible of the early students of Egyptology. Moreover, as YOUNG was a friend of DE SACY and corresponded with him, it is difficult to think that he was ignorant of the fact that GROTEFEND had partially succeeded in deciphering the names of some of the Persian kings in the great inscription of DARIUS I at BAHISTŪN by deducing the values of the cuneiform signs from the forms of the royal names found in Zend and Pehlevi. We know, too, as a fact that Mr. J. W. BANKES, the discoverer of the obelisk set up at PHILAE by PTOLEMY IX, had furnished him with a copy of the bilingual inscription in Egyptian hieroglyphs and Greek which was inscribed upon it.

Having concluded that the phonetic values of some of the hieroglyphs might be obtained from the cartouches, YOUNG began to work on the name of PTOLEMY, ΠΤΟΛΕΜΑΙΟΣ. Mr. J. W. BANKES had already identified the cartouches of PTOLEMY and CLEOPATRA on the propylaeum of DIOSPOLIS PARVA, and on the obelisk which he discovered at PHILAE (**Plates VIII** and **XIV**), though he was unable to read the characters in them. Now, the name of PTOLEMY is mentioned many times in the Greek version of the Decree on the ROSETTA STONE; we find it some thirteen times in the Demotic version, but only four times, in a complete form, in the hieroglyphic text. In line 6 of the hieroglyphic text we have the name of PTOLEMY written in a cartouche, thus :

1. 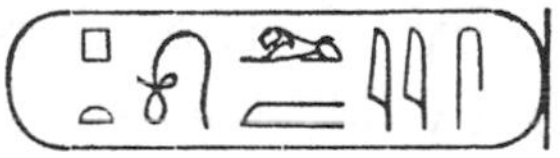

and in the same line and in line 14 we find it written, with additions, thus :—

2. 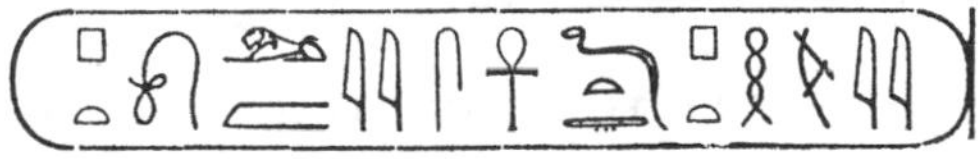.

In the Demotic text the name of PTOLEMY is written in one or other of the three forms here given.

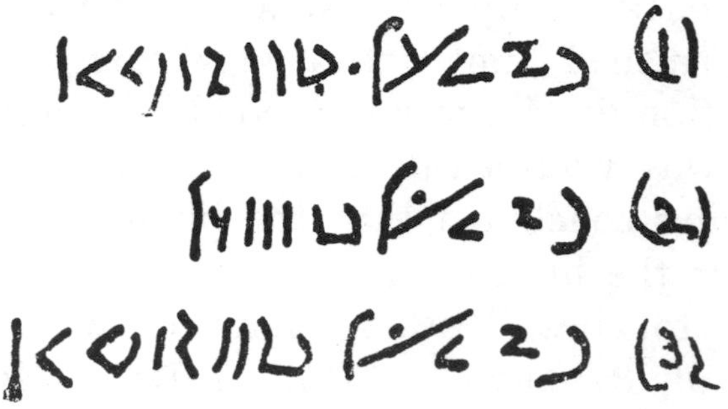

YOUNG argued that any one of the three Demotic forms might be the equivalent of the hieroglyphic form No. 1, and that the hieroglyphic form No. 2 must contain titles of PTOLEMY. He accepted ZOEGA'S view that the cartouche must contain a royal name, and he assumed that only the beginning and end of the cartouche,  and , were written in Demotic, the parallel sides  being omitted. He also assumed that the name began at the rounded end of the cartouche, and he transcribed the first sign by P, the second by T, the third and fourth by OLE, the fifth by M, the sixth and seventh by I, and the eighth by OS or OSH. We now know that he should have transcribed  by U,  by L, and  by S, but in spite of these inaccuracies credit is due to him for assigning correct

PHONETIC VALUES to most of the signs in the hieroglyphic form of the name of PTOLEMY. And in doing this he actually proved that some of the hieroglyphs had ALPHABETIC VALUES, which no one before him had ever done, though BARTHÉLEMY, DE GUIGNES, ZOEGA and Professor VATER had suspected their existence; in fact, YOUNG was the first to decipher any Egyptian hieroglyph correctly. His attempt to decipher the name of BERENICE was not so successful, but even in that he had a certain measure of success, for he assigned the correct value of N to . To sum up: Out of a total of thirteen signs, he assigned correct values to six, namely, , , , ,  and ; partly correct values to three, namely, ,  and , and wrong values to four, namely, , , , and . Some may say that the phonetic values given by YOUNG to the hieroglyphs in the name of PTOLEMY were the result of lucky guesses, and the same may be said of the values which GROTEFEND assigned to the cuneiform characters of which the name of DARIUS was composed; but in each case several of the values were subsequently found to be correct. As the result of his work at this stage YOUNG concluded that "hieroglyphic inscriptions were to be read in the direction in which the characters faced," a statement which will be easily understood from the following words: . In these the reed , and the chicken , and the bird  face to the left, but in reading them the reader must begin with the reed  and read towards the right.

Young continued to work at the decipherment of Egyptian hieroglyphs during the years 1816–18, and though he failed to see that neither the Demotic nor hieroglyphic texts on the Rosetta Stone were literal translations of the original Greek version of the Decree, he discovered many small points which were of considerable interest and importance. He studied the Coptic version of several Books of the Old and New Testaments, for he was well aware of the close affinity which existed between the language of the Demotic text and Coptic, and he drew up an alphabet of Demotic, and added to it what he believed to be the Coptic equivalents of the signs. (**Plate IX.**)

Soon after Young had made his translations of the text on the Rosetta Stone, the editor of the *Encyclopaedia Britannica* asked him to prepare the article Egypt for the new edition. When written, the article filled 38 pages quarto, and was accompanied by five plates, with lists containing 218 words, and "a supposed enchorial alphabet," and "specimens of phrases." The

PLATE IX.

183. MESORE
ⲙⲉⲥⲱⲣⲏ

164. FIRST DAY
ⲥⲟⲩⲁⲓ

185. THIRTIETH
ⲥⲟⲩ ⲙⲁⲃ

I. NUMBERS

186. ONE
ⲟⲩⲁⲓ, ⲟⲩⲓ

187. FIRST
ⲉ ⲟⲩⲓⲧ

188. TWO
ⲥ ⲛⲁⲩ, ⲥⲛⲟⲩⲧ

189. SECOND
ⲙⲁⲉ ⲥⲛⲁⲩ

190. THREE
ϣⲟⲙⲧ

191. THIRD
ⲙⲁⲉ ϣⲟⲙⲧ

192. THRICE
ϣⲟⲙⲧ ⲛⲥⲟⲡ

193. FOUR
ϥⲧⲟ

194. FIVE
ⲧⲓⲟⲩ

195. SEVEN
ϣⲁϣϥ

196. EIGHTH
ⲙⲁⲉ ϣⲙⲏⲛ

197. TEN
ⲙⲏⲧ, ⲙⲏⲧ

198. SEVENTEEN
ⲙⲉⲧϣⲁϣϥ

201. A HUNDRED
ϣⲉ

202. A THOUSAND
ϣⲟ

203. MCDXXVIII
ϣⲟ ⲅⲧⲟ ϣⲉ ⲍⲱⲧ
ϣⲁⲟⲩⲛ

204. SEVERAL
ⲉⲁⲛ...ⲟⲩⲓ   𝟏𝟏.22 Ƶ, ⲯ

K. SOUNDS?

205 Ⲁⲉⲣⲉ   210 ⲕⲉ.ⲕⲏ   215 ⲡ

206 Ⲁⲓⲡ   211 ⲙ.ⲙⲁ   216 ϭ

207 ⲃ   212 ⲛ   217 ⲧ

208 ⲉⲛⲉ   213 ⲟⲗⲉ   218 ⲱ

209   214 ⲡϣ.ⲟⲥ

SUPPOSED ENCHORIAL ALPHABET.

Ⲁ	ⲃ	ⲅ.ⲕ.ϭ	ⲇ	ⲉ	ⲏ	ⲓ	ⲗ	ⲙ	ⲛ

ⲟ	ⲡ.ϥ	ϧ	ⲣ	ⲥ.ϣ	ⲩ	ϫ	ⲱ	ⲍ	ⲝ

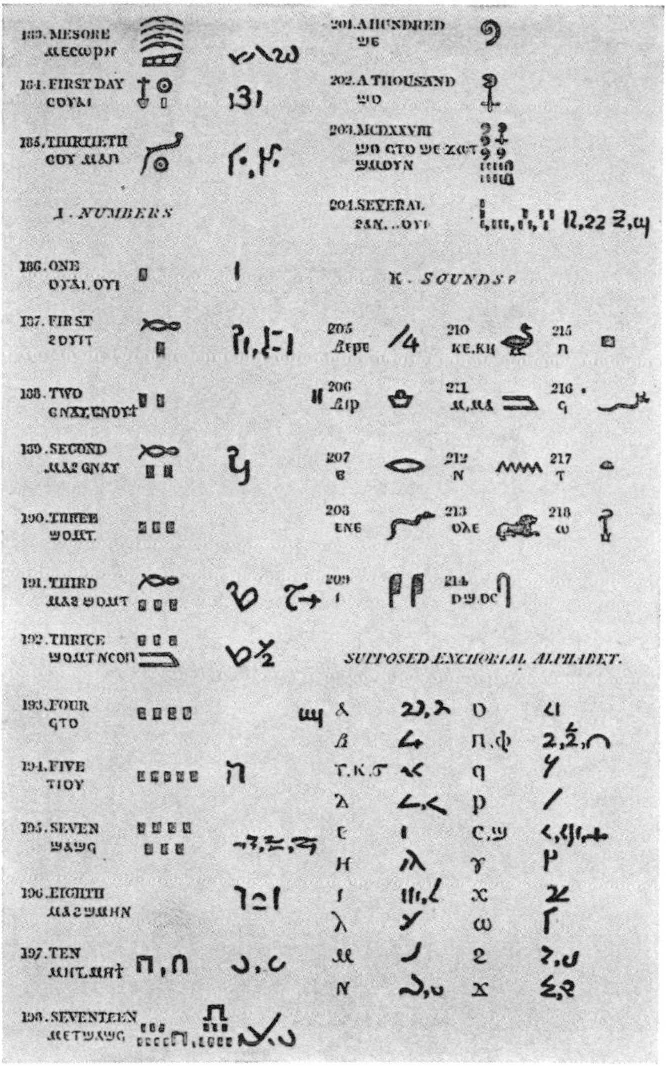

A facsimile of a page of Dr. Young's word-list, with hieroglyphic
and Demotic alphabets. (From the *Encyclopaedia Britannica*,
Supplement, Vol. IV, London, 1818.)

PLATE X.

Jean François Champollion, surnamed "Le Jeune."
Born at Figeac, December 24, 1790. Died March 4, 1832.

article was divided into eight sections, which dealt with—

I.—Recent publications on Egypt.

II.—The Pantheon of Egypt.

III.—The Historiography of Egypt.

IV.—The Egyptian Calendar.

V.—Manners and Customs.

VI.—Analysis of the triple inscription on the ROSETTA STONE.

VII.—Rudiments of a Hieroglyphic Vocabulary.

VIII.—The General Characters and Subjects of the Egyptian Monuments.

The article was printed in Part I of Vol. IV of the *Supplement* to the *Encyclopaedia Britannica*, and was published in 1819. It is the most important of YOUNG'S philological works, and is, practically, the foundation of the science of Egyptology, because in it he shows (I) the "original identity of the enchorial [*i.e.* Demotic] with the sacred characters [*i.e.* hieroglyphs];" and (II) because he gave in it a number of "alphabetical Egyptian characters, to which, in most cases, he had assigned correct phonetic values." The method which he followed was the correct one, for it established the "phonetic principle," and, as CHABAS rightly said, "Cette idée fut, dans la realité, le FIAT LUX de la science" (*Inscription de Rosette*, p. 5). YOUNG was perfectly conscious of the fact that the Egyptian hieroglyphic text contained many more letters than those to which he had assigned correct values, and he himself says that a "continued application of the same method to other monuments" would have resulted in the recovery of the whole alphabet. It is impossible not to ask why, since he felt this with such certainty, he did not continue the application of his method to the cartouches of the Persian kings of Egypt, and those of the Roman CAESARS? His great rival CHAMPOLLION claimed in 1822 that he was the first to identify the cartouche of CLEOPATRA, but this had already been done by Mr. J. W. BANKES in 1816. Had YOUNG studied the variant forms of the cartouche he could have read most of the hieroglyphics in it without difficulty. And had he noted the form of the name of BERENICE II 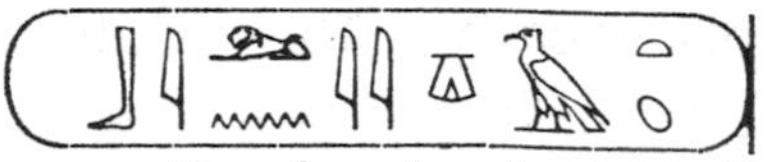 he would have read it correctly, for he knew all the hieroglyphs in it except .

An examination of the five plates which accompanied YOUNG's article in the *Supplement* in the *Encyclopaedia Britannica* shows that he did more than discover the values of the alphabetic hieroglyphs in the name of PTOLEMY. He showed that the numerals were expressed by strokes, ı = 1,

II = 2, III = 3, IIII = 4, and so on up to = 9, and that ∩ = 10, = 100, and = 1000. He knew too that the sign was placed before ordinal numbers, thus = first, = second, and = third, and he deduced the value of from the Coptic ⲙⲁϩ. Plurals were formed by repeating the hieroglyph three times, or by writing three strokes after a hieroglyph, thus = god, or = gods; the signs marked the feminine, *e.g.* = goddess. He identified the names of the gods and goddesses, ISIS, NEPHTHYS, HATHOR, APIS, ANUBIS, PTAḤ, THOTH, OSIRIS, RĀ, etc., though, of course he only knew the Coptic forms of their names. He identified correctly the prenomens of AMENḤETEP III  and SETI I , though he could not read the hieroglyphs. In some cartouches of PTOLEMY two of the king's honorific titles follow the name, thus:—

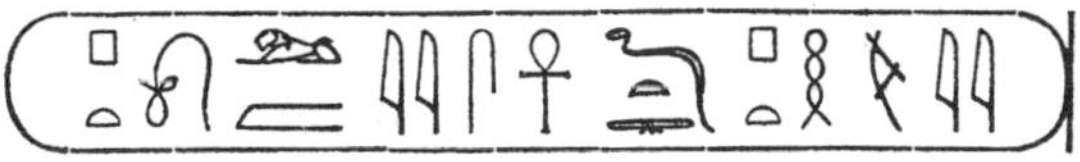

The original Greek text is ΠΤΟΛΕΜΑΙΟΥ ΑΙΩΝΟΒΙΟΥ ΗΓΑΠΗΜΕΝCΥ ΥΠΟ ΤΟΥ ΦΘΑ "PTOLEMY, the everliving, the beloved of PTAḤ." YOUNG had no difficulty in finding the name of PTAḤ, for the first two letters of it, 𓊪𓏏 *Pt,* begin the name of PTOLEMY; this done, it followed that 𓎛 had a phonetic value something like H. His dictionary told him that the Coptic word for "to love" was ⲙⲉⲣ *mer*, or ⲙⲉⲣⲓ *meri*; he therefore gave to 𓌸 the value of *mer*, and he already knew that 𓇌 = I. For the interpretation of the other title 𓋹𓆓𓏏𓇾 "everliving," he had recourse to Coptic, in which language he found that the ordinary word for "life," "living," etc., was *onẖ* ⲟⲛϩ, and the common word for "ever" was *eneẖ* ⲉⲛⲉϩ. Therefore he gave to 𓋹 the meaning of "living," and to 𓆓𓏏𓇾 the meaning of "ever." The Coptic led him astray, as to the reading of the last word, for he assigned the value of *ene* to 𓆓. This was one of his worst mistakes.

The evidence supplied by the section of YOUNG's article in the *Supplement* entitled "Rudiments of a Hieroglyphical Vocabulary" shows that he had made out the correct meaning of many words in the hieroglyphic text on the ROSETTA STONE, though he was unable to transliterate them. The

Coptic words which he adds are not always the correct equivalents of the words in hieroglyphs. Examples of these are :—

		COPTIC.
	strength	ϫⲟⲙ
	stability	ⲧⲁϫⲣⲟ
	condition, office	
	priest, libationer	
	good, beautiful	
	name	ⲣⲁⲛ
	saviour, deliverer	ⲉⲑⲛⲟϩⲉⲙ
	stand, set up	
	and	ⲟⲩⲟϩ
	with, together	ⲛⲉⲙ
	over, upon	ⲉϫⲱ
	day	ⲉϩⲟⲟⲩ
	month	ⲁⲃⲟⲧ
	year	ⲣⲟⲙⲡⲉ
	gold	ⲛⲟⲩⲃ
	image	ⲥⲙⲟⲧ

 crown of the Upper Country

 crown of the Lower Country

 shrine

, and  king

 temples

 of

 in, from

The more the work of YOUNG is studied the clearer it becomes that he never realized the fact that the Decree of the priests inscribed on the ROSETTA STONE was originally written in *Greek*, and that some parts of the Demotic and hieroglyphic versions were paraphrases and not literal translations. Thus the Greek word for "Egyptians" is rendered in hieroglyphs by "those who [dwell] in Ta-Mer-t" 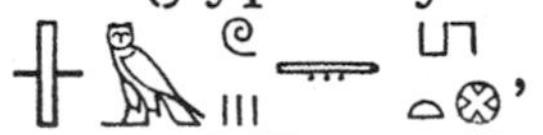, and in Demotic by *rmt kmi* "men of Egypt." The Greek word for king is rendered by *Pr-ăa* (), *i.e.* Pharaoh in the Demotic text, and by  in the hieroglyphic text (l. 5). The meaning is substantially the same, but, strictly speaking,  = King of the South, and  = King of the North. The correct reading of  *nesu bȧt* was only discovered a few years ago. The title EPIPHANES is rendered in the Demotic text by *ntr pr*, and in the hieroglyphic by  *ntr pri*, i.e. " the god who appeareth." The Demotic rendering of εὐχαρίστῳ (l. 36) is *nti na-ān tai-f mṭ-nfr-t* " he whose goodness is splendid," and the hieroglyphic is  *neb neferu* " lord of good [deeds]." In some cases the Demotic and hieroglyphic renderings of the Greek are bald and insufficient, *e.g.* ὁ κυριώτατος Θεὸς τοῦ ἱεροῦ " the most important god of the temple " is rendered by *pa ntr ta nu-t* " the god of the city " in the Demotic, and by  *ntr nu-t* " god of the city " in hieroglyphs. The renderings of ἐν τῶ ἐπιφανεστάτῳ τόπῳ are interesting; the Demotic has (*n*) *pa maā nti ōnḥ n pa arpi* " in the place which is prominent in the temple," but the hieroglyphic text has 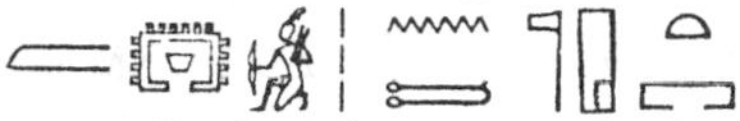 " in the hall of the soldiers of the house of the god." " Queen Arsinoë," βασιλίσσης 'Αρσινόης is rendered in the Demotic *Pr-āa-t Arsina*, " Pharaoh (fem.) Arsina," and in hieroglyphs by 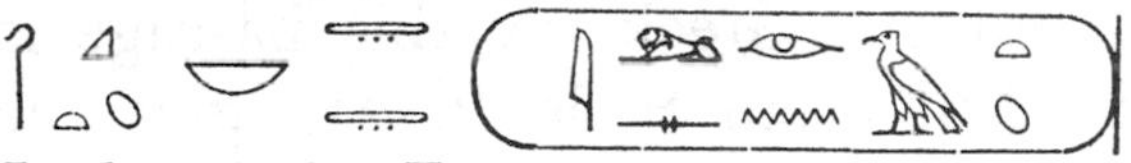 " Governess, Lady of the Two Lands, Arsina."

The dates of the festivals cannot have been understood by the first students of the ROSETTA

STONE, for the Egyptians divided their year into three seasons, each containing four months. The Greek text ordering the five-day festival in the month of THOTH (l. 49) is rendered in Demotic *tpi aḫ ssu I shaā hru V* and in hieroglyphs  "from the first day of the first month of the season Akhat until the fifth day."

These few examples will be sufficient to indicate the difficulties which the Egyptian scribes encountered in translating the Greek text of the Decree into Demotic and hieroglyphs, and they help to show why the translations of DE SACY, ÅKERBLAD and YOUNG were little more than guesswork. And we may note, too, that there is no evidence in their translations that they recognized the fact that the Demotic text contained passages for which there are no equivalents in the Greek. This is specially noticeable in the account of PTOLEMY'S attack on LYKOPOLIS. The Demotic text (ll. 13 and 14) says of the rebels, *àu-u ḥaā pa mit n pa āsh-sḥn n Pr-āa àrm pa āsh-sḥn* [*n-na*]*ntru*, "they had forsaken the path of the command of PHARAOH and the command of the gods," but the Greek for this passage is wanting. The Nubayrah Stele (l. 21) gives as the equivalent of the Demotic 
 "they

had invaded the path beloved of His Majesty, and the ordinances of the gods." Referring to the great and costly military works which Ptolemy had carried out for the protection of Egypt, the Demotic text says, *r bn rkh na Pr-āau ḥatiu ȧr-s m-ḳd-s,* "former kings did not know how to do the like of this," but the Greek for this passage is also wanting. The hieroglyphic text renders this passage by  "former kings had never done the like." The reader who will take the trouble to compare carefully the versions of the Decree of Memphis on the Rosetta Stone will find in the Greek version many words the meanings of which were not clearly understood by the scribes who drafted the Demotic and hieroglyphic texts; this being so, it is not a matter to wonder greatly at that the early Egyptologists failed to decipher the Egyptian texts on the Rosetta Stone.

In the preceding paragraphs I have tried to show where Young succeeded in his attempts to decipher the Egyptian inscriptions and where he failed. We must remember that he was a physicist and not a philologist, and that his knowledge of any Oriental language was not profound. After the publication of his article Egypt in the *Encyclopaedia Britannica* he abandoned the study of hieroglyphs, most probably because he felt he was not equipped with adequate philological knowledge to continue the study successfully. Whether this be so or not matters little. The important fact to remember is that by his decipherment of the name of PTOLEMY he opened the door of a chamber of philological mystery, and indicated the path to be followed by those who entered the chamber. We may now consider the labour of CHAMPOLLION, who was one of the first to realize and to make use of YOUNG's discoveries, which he developed with extraordinary ability and success.

V.—JEAN FRANÇOIS CHAMPOLLION AND HIS WORK

JEAN FRANÇOIS CHAMPOLLION (**Plate X**), surnamed "Le Jeune," to distinguish him from his brother CHAMPOLLION-FIGEAC, was born at FIGEAC on December 23 (or, 24), 1790, and died on March 4, 1832. When still a boy he made rapid progress in classical studies, and though he devoted much time to the study of botany and mineralogy, his chief interest was centred in Oriental languages. At the age of thirteen he is said to have possessed a fair knowledge of Hebrew, Syriac and Chaldee. In 1805 CHAMPOLLION-FIGEAC took him to PARIS, and obtained admission for him to the School of Oriental Languages, and introduced him to DE SACY. Soon after his arrival in PARIS he began to study the inscriptions on the ROSETTA STONE, and in writing to CHAMPOLLION-FIGEAC on the subject DE SACY said, " Je ne pense pas qu'il doive s'attacher au dechiffrement de l'*inscription de Rosette*. Le succès, dans ces sortes de recherches est plutôt l'effet d'une heureuse combinaison de circonstances que celui d'un travail opiniâtre, qui met quelquefois dans le cas de prendre des illusions pour des réalités " (AIMÉ CHAMPOLLION-FIGEAC, *Les Deux Champollion, leur vie et leurs œuvres*, Grenoble, 1887, p. 155). In 1812 CHAMPOLLION became Professor of Ancient History in the Faculty of Letters at GRENOBLE, and he continued to prosecute his Oriental studies. Later, when he came to PARIS, he found that the students of hieroglyphs were still wedded to the view that they formed a symbolic language; in attempting to verify this fact he wasted a whole year, for he found it impossible to come to a decision on the subject.

About this time (1812–13) CHAMPOLLION began to contemplate the publication of an encyclopaedic work on Egypt in several volumes. He intended it to treat of :—(1) Geography; (2) Religion; (3) Language; (4) The Writing and History of EGYPT up to the Invasion of CAMBYSES. He computed that the undertaking would occupy fifty years! A sort of specimen of the proposed publication appeared at GRENOBLE in 1811 with the title of " Introduction," but only thirty copies of it were printed, and none of them were sold to the trade. The first part of the great work, which dealt with the Geography of EGYPT, was entitled *L'Égypte sous les Pharaons*; it appeared at PARIS in two volumes in 1814. These were presented to the king, to whom the whole work was to be dedicated, but no further section was published. In the Preface, CHAMPOLLION speaks of the reading of Egyptian MSS., and he goes on to say that the first and easiest step to be taken with a view of arriving at a satisfactory rendering of such MSS. is the "reading of the Egyptian text (by which he probably meant the enchorial, or Demotic version) of the inscription of ROSETTA. I have had the happiness to see my efforts crowned with an almost complete success; several passages in the Egyptian text are quoted in the two volumes which I now publish (p. xvii). . . . The results which I have obtained ought equally to apply to the reading of the alphabetic MSS.; my first impressions do not permit me to have any doubt on this subject (p. xviii)." The reader who will take the trouble to examine the references to the Demotic text on the ROSETTA STONE which are given by CHAMPOLLION in this work will find that his knowledge of the text was not in advance of that of ÅKERBLAD and DE SACY, a fact which need not surprise us.

In 1821 CHAMPOLLION published his work *De l'écriture Hiératique des Anciens Égyptiens* at

GRENOBLE. In it he refers to BARTHÉLEMY, ZOEGA and DE HUMBOLDT, all of whom agreed that Egyptian writing was ALPHABETIC, that is to say, that it was composed of signs which were intended to recall the sounds of the spoken language, and then goes on to say, " A long study, and, above all, an attentive comparison of the hieroglyphic texts with those of the second kind, which are regarded as alphabetic, has led us to a contrary conclusion." He then states :—

1. The writing of the Egyptian MSS. of the second kind (hieratic) is not alphabetic.

2. The second system is only a simple modification of the hieroglyphic system, and differs merely through the form of the signs. This kind of writing is that called " hieratic " by the Greek writers, and must be considered as hieroglyphic tachygraphy.

3. Finally, the hieratic characters are *signs of things and not signs of sounds.* [The italics are mine.]

Statement No. 3 proves beyond all doubt that when CHAMPOLLION wrote the work in question he did not only *not* believe in the *alphabetic character* of any of the Egyptian signs, but also that he never suspected the possibility of such a thing.

On September 17, 1822, CHAMPOLLION read his *Mémoire* on the hieroglyphs, and exhibited his

"Hieroglyphic Alphabet," with its Greek and Demotic equivalents, before the Académie des Inscriptions; this paper created a great sensation among the learned throughout Europe, and stirred up much interest in Egyptology generally. In the same year he published his "*Lettre à M. Dacier, relative à l'alphabet des Hiéroglyphes phonétiques employés par les Égyptiens pour inscrire sur leurs monuments les titres, les noms, et les surnoms des souverains grecs et romains* (Paris, 1822, avec 4 planches)." This "Letter" is a well and carefully written pamphlet of 52 pp., in which the author, following on the path already indicated by YOUNG, and making use of the alphabetic values of the hieroglyphic signs which occur in the names of PTOLEMY and BERENICE, which YOUNG discovered in 1818, and published in 1819, successfully deciphered the names of several other Greek and Roman rulers of Egypt and their titles. On p. 5 CHAMPOLLION gives a description of the three classes of Egyptian writing, hieratic, Demotic and hieroglyphic, and in it we find the following:—"lettre troisième espèce d'écriture, *l'hiéroglyphique* pure, devait avoir aussi un certain nombre de ses signes doués de la faculté d'exprimer les sons; en un mot, qu'il existait également une série *d'hiéroglyphes phonétiques*."

Now this statement shows that towards the close of the year 1822 CHAMPOLLION held an opinion diametrically opposed to that which he had held in 1821, for up to 1821 he did not believe that Egyptian hieroglyphs *could* possess alphabetic values. This being so, students of the history of the decipherment of the Egyptian hieroglyphs naturally ask, " What was it that made CHAMPOLLION change his opinion, and adopt in 1822 a theory which he had rejected wholly in 1821 ? " Judging by the facts derived from the extracts from the letters of YOUNG, DE SACY and ÅKERBLAD (written in 1814 and 1815), and are printed by LEITCH in vol. iii of his edition of *The Works of Thomas Young*, London, 1865, CHAMPOLLION changed his opinion because he had either read[1] or had had read or explained to him, the system of decipherment which had been initiated by YOUNG and was described by him in his article EGYPT in the *Supplement* to the *Encyclopaedia Britannica*, and in earlier works.

We may now describe briefly how CHAMPOLLION, following YOUNG'S method, discovered the phonetic values of other letters of the hieroglyphic

[1] YOUNG had corresponded with CHAMPOLLION-FIGEAC, as we may see from DE SACY'S letter to YOUNG dated July 20, 1815 :—" Monsieur,—Outre la traduction Latine de l'inscription Égyptienne que vous m'avez communiquée, j'ai reçu postérieurement une autre traduction Anglaise imprimée, que je n'ai pas en ce moment sous les yeux, *l'ayant prêtée à M. Champollion sur la demande que son frère m'en a faite d'après une lettre qu'il m'a dit avoir reçu de vous.*" [The italics are mine.]

alphabet. Among the royal names and titles which he studied were the following:—

1. CLEOPATRA 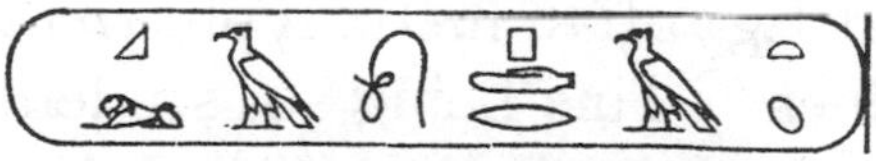.—

The Greek text of the Philae Obelisk made it certain that this cartouche contained the name of Cleopatra. YOUNG had shown that 𓃭 = R or L, 𓄿 = A, 𓍯 = U or O, 𓊪 = P, 𓂋 = R, and that 𓏏𓆇 was always added at the end of a female proper name. The two letters of unknown value were 𓈎 and 𓂧, and their position in the cartouche showed that they must represent K and T.

2. PHILIP  and .—The two letters of unknown value in these cartouches were  and 𓉔, but it was clear that  must = 𓋴 S, and as CHAMPOLLION guessed that 𓊪𓉔 = the Greek letter Φ, it followed that 𓉔 = H.

3. PTOLEMY.—The variant forms of the name of PTOLEMY showed that 𓂧 = 𓏏 T, 𓍯 = 𓅱 𓍢 U.

4. ALEXANDER 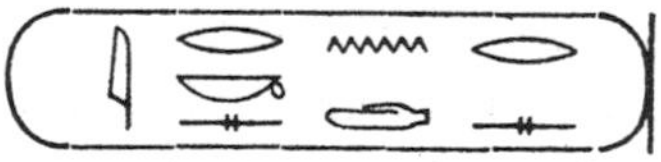.—The letters of unknown value here are 𓇋, 𓎡

and , but the Greek form of the name Alexandros shows that  = A,  = K, and  = S.

5. BERENICE 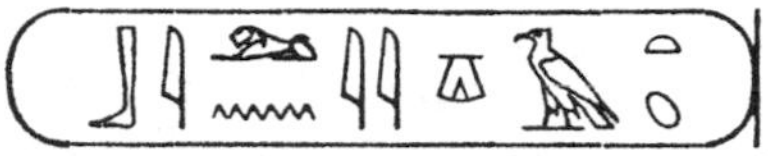.—In this cartouche the unknown signs were  and , but the Greek form of the name shows that  = B and  = K. The variant form 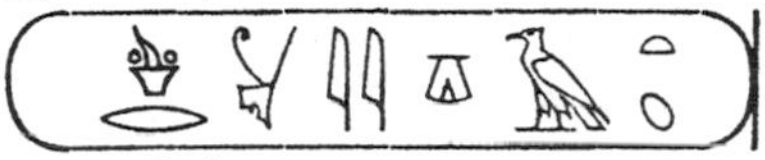 proves that  = B, and  =  = N.

6. AUTOCRATOR 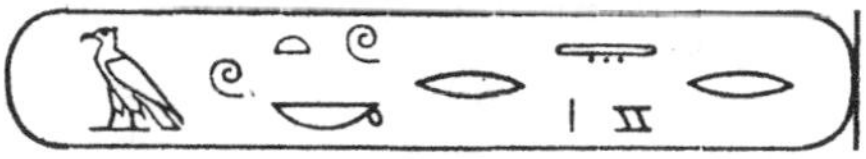, 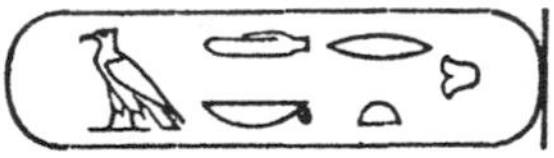, 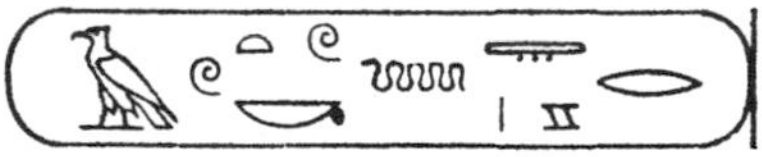.—From these variants we obtain the values,  = T,  = R, and  = R.

7. CAESAR , 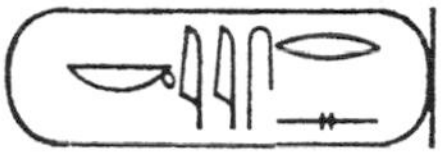, , , 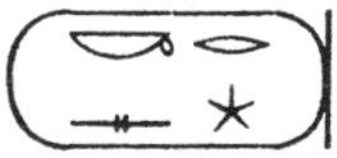, 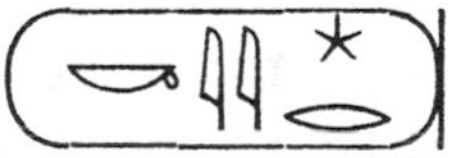.—From these variants we obtain the values  = K, and  = S.

8. HADRIAN 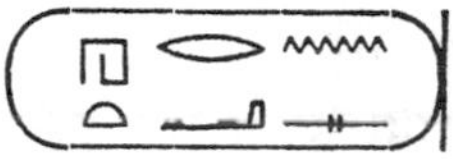.—The only sign with an unknown value here is ; CHAMPOLLION assigned to it the value of I.

Collecting the results which he had obtained, CHAMPOLLION was able to construct the following alphabet :—

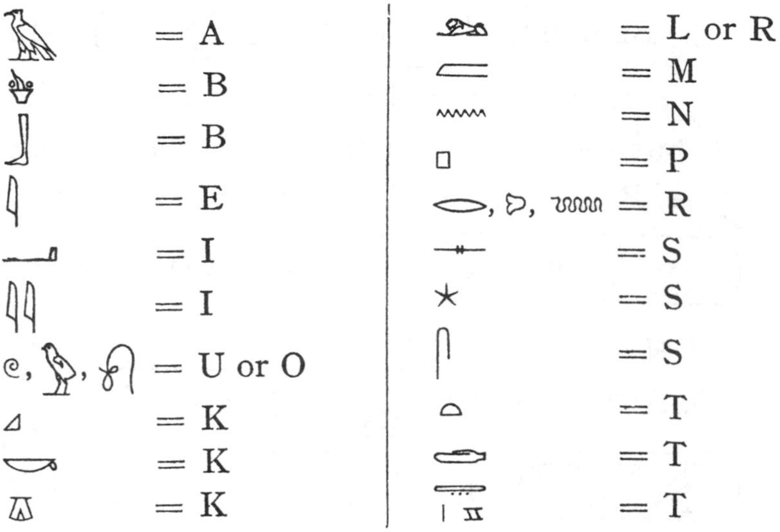

Further study enabled him to discover the values of a number of *syllabic* hieroglyphic signs, and to recognize the use of hieroglyphs as *determinatives*. In cases where the Greek text supplied him with the meaning of hieroglyphs of which he did not know the phonetic values, his knowledge of Coptic enabled him frequently to suggest values which he found subsequently to be substantially correct. Further reference to determinatives and the importance of parallel passages and texts will be made later on in this work.

Between 1822 and 1824 CHAMPOLLION worked incessantly, and was enabled to modify much of his earlier views, and to develop his *Alphabet*; and he evolved some rudimentary principles of Egyptian Grammar. The results of his studies at this period he published in his *Précis du Système Hiéroglyphique*, Paris, 1824, wherein he took special pains to inform his readers that his system had nothing whatever to do with that of Dr. YOUNG. In 1824 he went to TURIN and studied the Egyptian papyri preserved there, whence he passed on to ROME and NAPLES. The French Government sent him out to EGYPT in 1828 to copy the inscriptions on the tombs and temples, and he collected there a vast amount of material, and discovered in the duplicate texts the phonetic values of many syllabic signs and new words. His copies of inscriptions, made with his own hand, filled 2,000 pages (*Les Deux Champollions*, p. 75). He returned from Egypt in March, 1830, and began to arrange the material which he had collected, and to describe the antiquities which he had brought with him, and to translate the inscriptions upon them. But before he could finish the work, he collapsed suddenly and died on March 4, 1832. His brother CHAMPOLLION-FIGEAC, to whose wise counsels and guidance he owed much of his success, at once took in hand the arrangement of the great mass of literary material which he had left behind, and in due course published the famous *Grammaire Égyptienne* (Paris, 1836–41) and the *Dictionnaire Égyptien* (Paris, folio, 1843).

CHAMPOLLION-FIGEAC published a detailed account of his brother's work in *Les Deux Champollions, Leur vie et leurs Œuvres*, Grenoble, 1887 ; and a still more elaborate work on the same subject in two volumes, each containing more than 600 pages, has been written by H. HARTLEBEN, *Champollion, sein Leben und sein Werk*, Berlin, 1906.

But, notwithstanding the general accuracy of CHAMPOLLION'S Egyptian alphabet, many students of Egyptology viewed it with suspicion and doubted his interpretations of words. F. A. W. SPOHN and G. SEYFARTH maintained that the Egyptian language was sacred and mystic, and that all the hieroglyphs were symbols (*De Lingua et Literis veteris Aegyptiorum*, Leipzig, 1825–31). SEYFARTH divided hieroglyphs into three classes, Euphonic (phonetic), Symphonic (enclitic), and Aphonic (ideographic). J. KLAPROTH described them as "Akrologic" (*Examen Critique*, Paris, 1832) ; J. G. H. GREPPO accepted CHAMPOLLION'S system (*Essai*, Paris, 1829), as did F. SALVOLINI, who translated the account of the Battles of RAMESES II against the KHETA from a papyrus belonging to M. SALLIER of Aix with considerable success. R. LEPSIUS, while accepting the system generally, analysed it with great skill and learning. As a result of his criticisms and modifications (see the *Annali dell' Istituto Archeologico di Roma*, tomo ix), and description of the structure of the ancient Egyptian Language, scholars generally took the view that the true method of deciphering the hieroglyphic inscriptions of Egypt had been found.

The early followers of CHAMPOLLION found themselves hampered for want of material, *i.e.* copies of texts to work upon, but this deficiency was soon remedied, for the Governments of Italy and France soon began to publish large volumes of facsimiles of texts. The British Museum published lithographic copies of the SALLIER and ANASTASI papyri, and WILKINSON and BONOMI collected and published many important historical and religious texts. Great impetus was given to the new study in Germany by CHEVALIER BUNSEN. BIRCH, HINCKS, OSBURN, PETTIGREW, BURTON, GOODWIN and others were pioneers of the new science in England, and thanks to Mr. GLIDDON'S lectures and writings CHAMPOLLION'S system obtained a firm footing in AMERICA. With the publication of his *Précis* CHAMPOLLION seems to have abandoned the further study of the ROSETTA STONE, and this is not to be wondered at. After all, the fourteen incomplete lines of hieroglyphs which are found on it gave him little scope to develop his system of interpretation, and he must have felt that he needed more material. And he knew that the text on the Stone was, comparatively speaking, a modern document, and that the Egyptians had used the hieroglyphic system of writing some three or four thousand years before a PTOLEMY sat on the throne of EGYPT. During the years 1825–30 he was too busy in copying texts in ITALY, EGYPT and NUBIA to have much time to complete his system and to reduce it to writing, and the result was that he left it in a very imperfect state. CHAMPOLLION-FIGEAC did not print the MSS. as his brother had left them, but he sorted and classified them, and added supplementary matter, and edited them in a scholarly and systematic manner. He lacked his brother's brilliant intellect, but he was a sound scholar, and the young science of Egyptology owed much to him.

VI.—THE DECIPHERMENT OF EGYPTIAN HIEROGLYPHS

There is little doubt that the system of hieroglyphic writing which is made known to us by the inscriptions of the dynastic period found in EGYPT is a development of the more primitive picture-writing which was in use among the predynastic dwellers in the Valley of the NILE. This primitive writing was probably indigenous, and may have developed naturally into the hieroglyphic system with which we are now familiar, but some think that the development was assisted, or was entirely due to some influence emanating from peoples living in India. It is obvious that pictures alone cannot be regarded as writing in the correct sense of the word, and true writing only begins when the pictures are grouped solely for the sake of their *sounds*, without any reference to the objects which they represent. Let us assume that a king of some foreign country came to visit the king of EGYPT in predynastic times, and that the royal scribe of the day wished to record the event, and to preserve in writing the names of the foreign king and his country. To do this he would have to write down two series of pictures, the sounds of which, as words, would reproduce the sounds of the foreign names, without reference to the objects which these sounds represented. This also was the case when Egyptian hieroglyphs were concerned. ALEXANDER, a Macedonian, became king of EGPYT, and the Egyptian scribes reproduced his name:

A—L—K—S—A—N—T—R—S.

Now  represents an eagle,  a lion,  a bowl,  a bolt,  a reed,  water,  a hand, and  a mouth, and the sounds of the words of these pictures grouped represent the Greek name ALEXANDROS.

The Egyptian scribes soon found out that pronouns, prepositions and conjunctions were absolutely necessary for grammatical purposes, and in consequence they set aside a number of pictures which they used phonetically. Thus Egyptian hieroglyphic writing is both PICTORIAL and PHONETIC, a fact which was first demonstrated by YOUNG and CHAMPOLLION, and it was the latter who showed that it was the phonetic characters employed with the pictures, or hieroglyphs, that made grammatical constructions possible. On the other hand, there are certain hieroglyphs which are placed at the ends of words to indicate their general meanings and are known as DETERMINATIVES, and others are used in words to assist the reader in pronouncing them. These last are called PHONETIC COMPLEMENTS. Some hieroglyphs (ideographs) have more than one phonetic value, in which case they are called POLYPHONES; many different ideographs have similar values, in which case they are called HOMOPHONES. In arriving at the facts summarized above, CHAMPOLLION was greatly helped by his study of texts other than that found on the ROSETTA STONE, and by his good knowledge of Coptic. In the primitive picture-writing, and often in the later hieroglyphic writing, the plural is expressed in the following ways: by writing the picture-sign or ideograph three times, *e.g.*  fields,  offerings,  great ones; by writing the determinative three times, *e.g.* 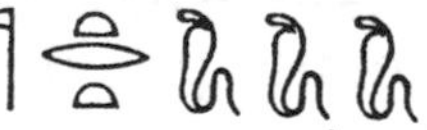 goddesses,  nomes; by adding  to the ideograph written once, *e.g.* 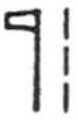 gods, with the variants , , and on the ROSETTA STONE we have gods and goddesses. The word "temple" is expressed by two ideographs thus, , or , "house of the god," or "god's house"; the word "queen" by two, thus "king['s] woman"; and from two others Per-āa, literally "house great," we obtain the word "Pharaoh."

As examples of the sounds of ideographs which have become mere SYLLABLES in other words may be quoted. *men* in breast, *mes* in ear, skin, *mer* in unguent, *shen* in tempest.

DETERMINATIVES assist the reader greatly in reading the texts; the following are examples:—

to call.

man seated.

to eat, to think, to speak.

be inert, lazy, to rest.

woman.

people, company.

to bear, to carry.

foe, enemy, death.

to be old.

to fight, do something with violence.

to exult, to glorify.

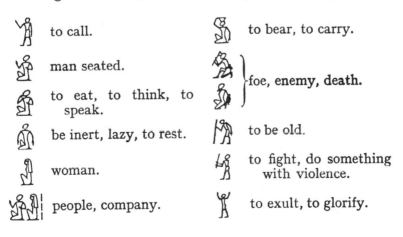

 to worship, to praise.

 to be young, a child.

 God, divine person.

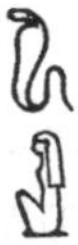 goddess.

 mummy, dead person.

 the dead, a sacred person.

 to hide.

 a priest.

 libationer.

 a great number.

 to fall down.

 to swim.

 to be pregnant.

 to give birth.

 hair.

 to breathe.

 to see.

 to weep.

 to paint the eyes.

 to hear.

 to nurse.

 to vomit.

 flesh.

 to embrace.

 to paddle.

 to fight.

 to rule, to reign.

 to give.

 handicraft, craftsmanship.

 to do a thing with strength.

 to wash.

- to grasp.
- to be in the middle.
- to take.
- to beget.
- female.
- to go, go in, go forward.
- go back, return.
- to walk, to run, to flee.
- to invade, transgress.
- to thirst.
- to be angry.
- the front.
- the end.
- to repeat.
- quadruped.
- to shoot.
- bird, insect.
- to be little.
- to hover, flutter.

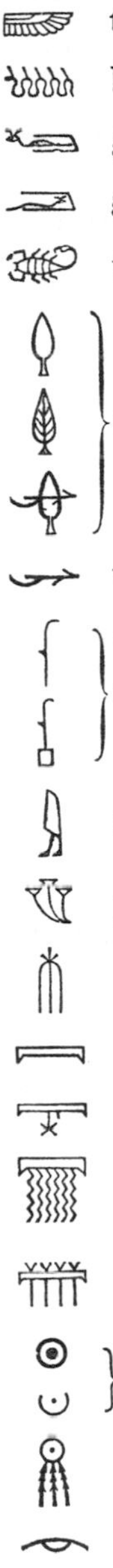

- to fly.
- bad, wicked.
- go out.
- go in.
- to breathe.
- tree.
- wood.
- to blossom.
- to go.
- plant.
- to give birth.
- sky, heaven.
- night.
- rain, dew.
- storm, hurricane, lightning.
- Sun, time.
- shine, illumine.
- moon.

star.

land.

desert, foreign land.

mountain.

way, path, road.

stone.

water.

river, canal, lake.

lake, pool.

to go.

walled village or town.

house.

wall, fort, strong place.

to overthrow.

fortress.

door.

to go up.

pyramid.

obelisk.

to open.

boat, ship, to travel.

to overthrow, wreck.

to sail.

wind, air, breeze.

to steer.

to lie, sleep.

sarcophagus, tomb.

to squeeze out.

apparel, linen.

to fan.

cord, rope.

to untie, unravel.

string.

bag, case.

grain.

bushel.

to be permanent.

mineral, powder.

foreigner.

to hack, to hew wood.

to guide.

to cut.

spread out.

to smite, beat.

to hack to pieces.

dig up.

plough, to plough.

rub down.

to shave.

to go in a circle.

carry off.

to embalm, the dead, unguent, to count up.

strong smelling substance.

pot, jar.

unguent pot.

to bring.

abstract idea.

to write, to polish.

to divide up.

to break.

The following will illustrate the use of determinatives in words :—

uāb priest.

surȧ to drink.

skha to remember.

qnn feeble, exhausted.

ānḫ flower.

sua make to travel, depart.

Rthnnu Syria.

bḫnu house.

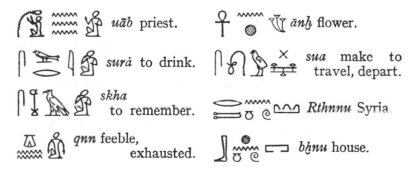

 *āḍau* violence.

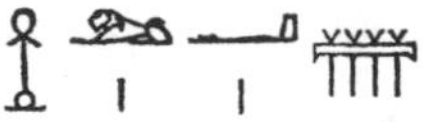 *shenrā* tempest.

 *peḥ* arrive.

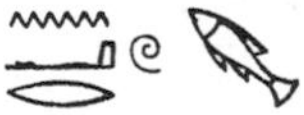 *nāru* fish.

 *āḥā* to stand.

 *rek* time.

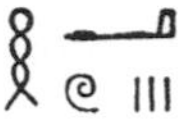 *ḥāu* flesh.

 *rṭ* sandstone.

 *pnnu* mouse.

 *apṭ* duck.

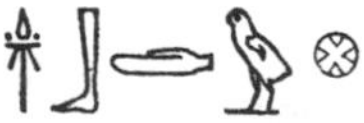 *Ȧbṭu* Abydos.

Some words have two determinatives, *e.g.* 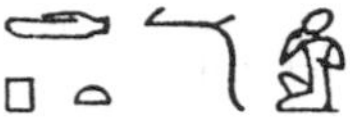 *ṭp-t* taste,  *qbḥ* cool water, and some three, *e.g.*  *shāṭ* slay,  *qbḥ* bath.

In the following passage from an inscription at Bani Ḥasan the determinatives are marked with * and the syllables with † :—

Not a daughter [of] a poor man did I harm ;

not a widow did I oppress ;

not a field-labourer did I repulse him ;

not a shepherd did I quarrel with ; not was there the chief

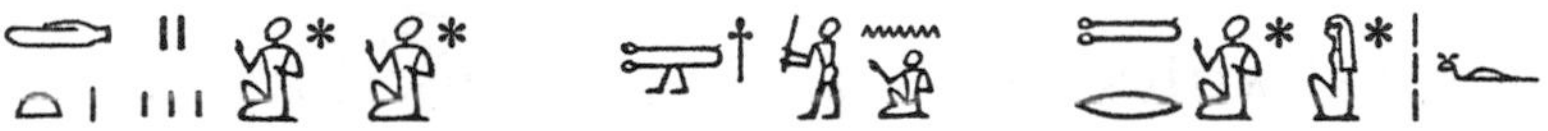

of a gang of 5 men [from whom] I took away his men

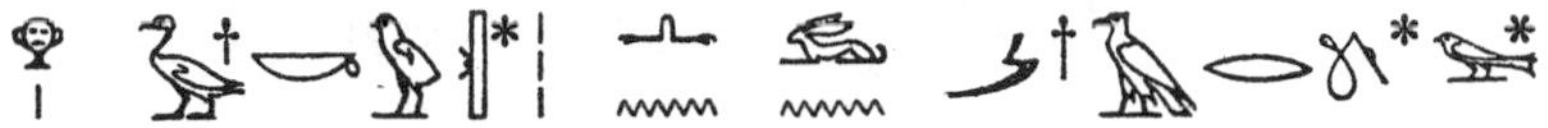

for the corvée ; not existed oppression

in my time ; not [was there] a hungry man

in my time ; [when] came years

hungry I stood up, I ploughed

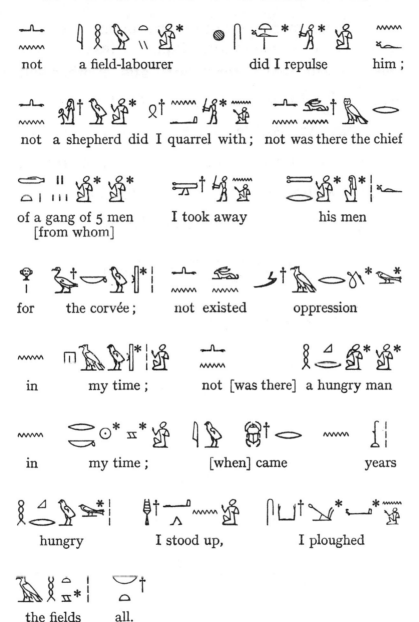

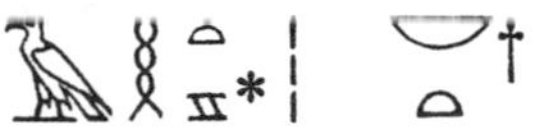

the fields all.

CHAMPOLLION found out the true phonetic values of many signs by comparing duplicate texts. Thus one text will give  for "day," and another will give  *hru*, and so supply the true reading. One text writes the name of the god , and another transcribes it thus,  *Ḫprȧ*; one text writes , and another transcribes it thus,  *Udat*. Other examples are :—

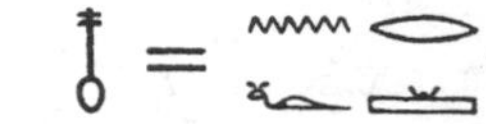 *nfr* good, beautiful.

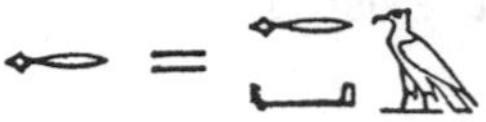 *āa* great.

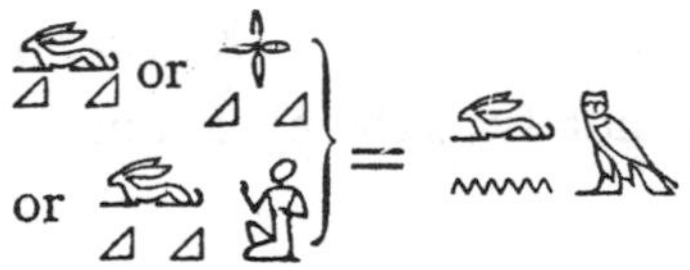 *unem* to eat.

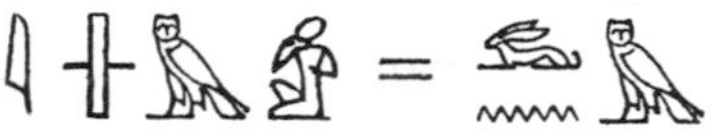 *unem* to eat.

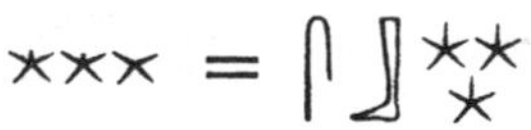 *sebu* stars.

 *ānḫ udja snb*

"life, strength, health [to him]"
i.e. the king.

 *ḏṭ meṭu* speak words.

 *àab-t* west.

 *reḫit* men and women.

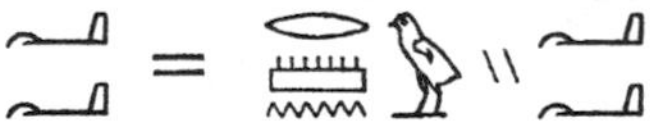 *rmnui* the two arms.

Both YOUNG and CHAMPOLLION knew that the numbers 1 to 9 were represented by strokes, *e.g.* III = 3, III III III = 9, and so on, and that ∩ = 10, 𓍢 = 100, and  = 1,000, but they did not know how to read them. This is now possible, as the following shows.

I	= 1		*uāu*	III III	= 6		*su*
II	= 2		*senui* (dual)	III IIII	= 7		*sfḫ*
III	= 3	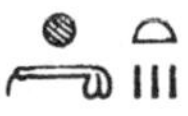	*ḫmt*	IIII IIII	= 8	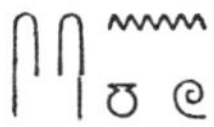	*ḫmnu*
IIII	= 4		*fṭu*	III III III	= 9		*psḏ*
IIIII or ★	= 5		*ṭuau*	∩	= 10		*meṭ*

The feminine is formed by adding 𓏏 *t* to each of these.

 = 100  *shaā*

 = 1,000  *ḫa*

 = 10,000  *ḏbā*

 = 100,000  *ḥfn*

 = 1,000,000  *ḥḥ*

Ordinal numbers are formed by adding  *nu*, *e.g.*  *sn-nu* the second,  *ḫmt-nu* the third, and so on. Rameses III is said to have given

bread cakes large 900,000 + 90,000 +

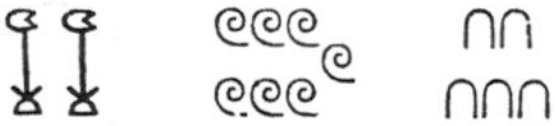

2,000 + 700 + 50

i.e. 992,750 large loaves to one of the temples.

We have seen how useful the determinatives are in arriving at the meanings of certain words, and how the readings of variant texts help us to ascertain the true values of many syllables and alphabetic signs, but there remains a large number of words the exact meaning of which it is extremely difficult to discover from the hieroglyphic texts themselves. The earlier decipherers of the cuneiform inscriptions, when once they had obtained the alphabetic and syllabic values of the signs, could rely on their knowledge of cognate languages for assistance. In working out the Persian version of the Bahistûn Inscription RAWLINSON had Zend and Ṣanskṛit to help him, and NORRIS found much assistance from Hebrew and Syriac when translating the Babylonian version. The only cognate language to which YOUNG and CHAMPOLLION could appeal was COPTIC, *i.e.* that form of the Egyptian language which was written in Greek letters, and has been preserved for us chiefly in the translations of the Scriptures and the writings of the Fathers in use among the Egyptian Christians. But we must remember that the Decree of Memphis was written B.C. 197–196, and that there is very little Coptic literature which can be assigned with any degree of certainty to a period earlier than A.D. 300. CHAMPOLLION did undoubtedly find that his great knowledge of Coptic stood him in good stead, but Coptic represented the ordinary language of the people rather than the literary language used by the scribes in drawing up official documents, and its use for comparative purposes is strictly limited. Still, when the Greek gave the meanings of certain groups of hieroglyphs the Coptic was very useful, in respect of common words, in suggesting probable readings. This is clear from the following examples. The reader will note that, as the result of phonetic decay, the final consonants of many old Egyptian words are not found in their Coptic equivalents.

Hieroglyphs.			Coptic.
	*pt*	heaven	ⲫⲉ
	*bȧa n pt*	iron	ⲃⲉⲛⲓⲡⲉ
	*bnr*	date palm	ⲃⲉⲛ̄ⲛⲉ
	*ḥqr*	hunger	ϩⲕⲟ
	*surȧ*	to drink	ⲥⲱ
	*rmth*	man	ⲣⲱⲙⲓ
	*ntr*	god	ⲛⲟⲩⲧⲉ
	*nfr*	good, fair	ⲛⲟⲩϥⲉ
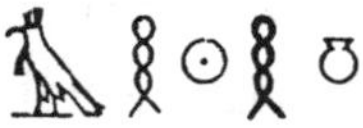	*nḥḥ*	pure oil	ⲛⲉϩ
	*snthr*	incense	ⲥⲟⲛⲧⲉ
	*snḥm*	grasshopper	ⲥⲁⲛⲛⲉϩ
	*sḥur*	to curse	ⲥⲁϩⲟⲩ

	*ḥr*	face	ϩⲣⲁ
	*àtf*	father	ⲉⲓⲱⲧ
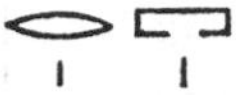	*r pr*	temple	ⲉⲣⲫⲉⲓ
	*khatru*	ichneumon	ϣⲁⲑⲟⲩⲗ

The Greek text on the ROSETTA STONE mentions the names of certain Macedonian months, and these showed CHAMPOLLION that the Egyptians had a system of their own and that they reckoned their months on an entirely different system. We know now that the Egyptian year contained 12 months, each of 30 days, and that to these 360 days they added 5 so-called "epagomenal" days, making 365 days in all. The 12 months were divided into 3 seasons, each containing 120 days. As a year of 365 days was nearly a quarter of a day short of the true solar year, it came to pass that the festivals were celebrated later and later each year, and when a sufficient number of years had passed, the festivals that ought to have been celebrated in the summer were actually celebrated in the winter. PTOLEMY III, in order to remedy this state of affairs, ordered that one day was to be added to the calendar every four years. The three seasons were called AKH-T , PER-T , and SHEMU , and the four months of each season were called the first, second, third and fourth month of that season respectively.

	WINTER.	SPRING.	SUMMER.
The 360 days.	I 𓏤	I	I
	II	II	II
	III	III	III
	IIII	IIII	IIII

The 5 days.   (hieroglyphs)

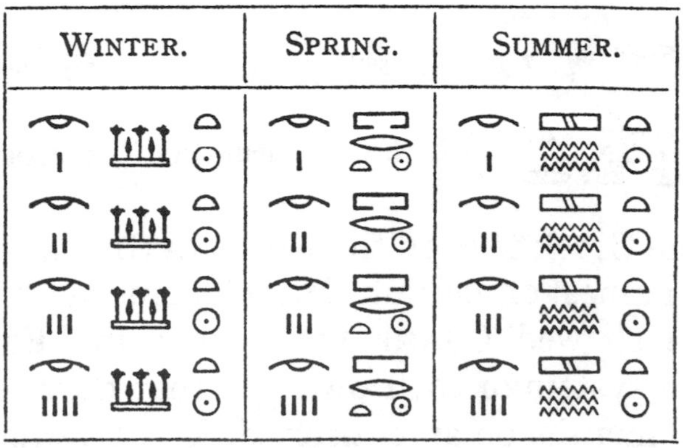

i.e. " days five to be added to the year."

The names given to the twelve months of the Egyptian year by the Greeks and Copts were :—

1	Thoth.	5	Tybi.	9	Pachon.
2	Paophi.	6	Mechir.	10	Payni.
3	Hathyr.	7	Phamenoth.	11	Epiphi.
4	Choiakh.	8	Pharmuthi.	12	Mesore.

These names are corruptions of the names of the festivals which the ancient Egyptians celebrated in the various months. Thus Pachon = (hieroglyphs) " this [is the month of] the god Khonsu "; Paophi = (hieroglyphs) " this [is the month of] the Ap-t (*i.e.* Karnak) ";

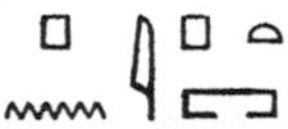

Payni = 𓊪𓈖 𓇋𓆛𓈖𓏏𓈇 "this [is the month of] the Valley"; Phamenoth = 𓊪𓈖 (𓇋𓏠𓈖𓁛𓊵𓏏𓊪) 𓁛 "this [is the month of] King Åmen-ḥetep."

VII.—THE HIEROGLYPHIC ALPHABET[1]

𓄿	A	Heb. א
𓇋	Å	
𓂝	Ā	„ ע
𓇌, 𓏭	I, Y	„ י
𓅱, 𓏲	W, U	„ ו and וּ
𓃀	B	„ ב
𓊪	P	„ פ
𓆑	F	„ פ, Coptic ϥ
𓅓	M	„ מ
𓈖	N	„ נ
𓂋	R and L	„ ר and ל
𓉔	H	„ ה
𓎛	Ḥ	„ ח, Arab. ح
𓐍	KH (or Ḫ)	Heb. ח, Arab. خ, Copt. ϧ and ϩ
𓊃	S	Heb. ס
𓋴	S	„ שׂ and שׁ
𓈙	SH	„ שׁ
𓈎	Ḳ or Q	„ ק
𓎡	K	„ כ
𓎼	G	„ ג or ק
𓏏	T	„ ת
𓍿	TJ	Copt. ϭ or ϫ, Arab. ظ
𓂧	Ṭ or D	Heb. ט
𓆓	TI	Copt. ϯ
𓆓	DJ or Ṣ (?)	„ ϫ

[1] In German works 𓄿 is transliterated by ꜣ; 𓇋 by ỉ, 𓂝 by ʿ (inverted comma), 𓐍 by ḫ, 𓊃 by h̲, 𓋴 by ś, 𓈙 by š, 𓈎 by ḳ, 𓍿 by ṯ, 𓆓 by tj, 𓂧 by d, and 𓆓 by ḏ.

Strictly speaking, all the letters of the Egyptian Alphabet are consonants, just as are the letters of the Hebrew, Syriac and Arabic Alphabets, but certain of them, viz., 𓄿, 𓇋, \\, 𓅱 and 𓂝 (ע) are treated as vowels, although they are in truth weak consonants. BIRCH and BRUGSCH, and some of the early Egyptologists, transcribed these weak consonants as vowels, because in the transcription of Greek and Roman proper names they were used as vowels. In reading a text the Egyptian reader himself supplied the vowels, and it is for this reason that we shall never know accurately how the Egyptians pronounced their words. We find the word 𓄤𓆑𓂋 NFR in a text, and know that it means "good," but it is impossible to pronounce this word without the help of some vowels. The word occurs in Coptic, but in five different forms, viz., *nofre, nofra, nofri, nabre,* and *nafre.* In transliterating Egyptian words I have often added an *e,* as the Copts seem to have done, for otherwise the words are unpronounceable. This is especially the case in proper names, *e.g.* Ptḥḥtp = Ptaḥ-ḥetep. And if we use the German system of transliteration the difficulty is increased; compare the name of the queen ʿnḫnsnfrʾibrʿ = Ānkh (or ḫ)-nes-nefer-ȧb-Rā and the prenomen of Thothmes III, Mnḫprrʿ = Men-kheper-Rā.

VIII.—THE COPTIC ALPHABET

The Coptic Alphabet contains 24 Greek letters, and 7 which are derived from demotic forms of hieratic characters to represent sounds for which the Greek alphabet contained no equivalents.

Coptic	Name.		Coptic	Name.	
ⲁ	alpha	A	ⲣ	ro	R
ⲃ	bida	B	ⲥ	sima	C
ⲅ	gamma	G	ⲧ	tau	T
ⲇ	dalda	D	ⲩ	ue (ḥe)	U
ⲉ	ei	E	ⲫ	phi	ϕ
ⲍ	zita	Z	ⲭ	chi	χ
ⲏ	êta	Ê	ⲯ	psi	Ψ
ⲑ	thita	TH	ⲱ	au	O
ⲓ	iauta	I	ϣ	shei	SH
ⲕ	kappa	K	ϥ	fei	F
ⲗ	laula	L	ϧ	h̲ei, or, ḫei	*Kh*
ⲙ	mi	M	ϩ	h̲ei, or, ḫei	Ḫ
ⲛ	ni	N	ϫ	djandjia	DJ
ⲝ	xi	X (KS)	ϭ	tjima	TJ
ⲟ	o	O	ϯ	ti	TI
ⲡ	pi	P			

PLATE XI.

Philae. The Colonnade from the South. The famous Obelisk of Ptolemy IX was found in this Courtyard. (From Colonel Lyons' *Philae*, Plate 45.)

PLATE XII.

Ptolemy I Soter, 305–282 B.C.

Ptolemy II and his wife Arsinoë II, 283–245 B.C. Ptolemy I and his wife Berenice I.

Arsinoë II Philadelphus.

Ptolemy III, 247–221 B.C.

Berenice II, wife of Ptolemy III.

Coins of the Ptolemies.

PLATE XIII.

Ptolemy IV Philopator, 221–203 B.C.

Arsinoë, wife of Ptolemy IV Philopator.

Ptolemy VI(?) Philometor.

Ptolemy V Epiphanes, 203–181 B.C.

Ptolemy XI Auletes, 80–51 B.C.

Coins of the Ptolemies.

PLATE XIV.

The Temple of Edfû founded by Ptolemy III. View from the Pylon looking northwards.
(From a photograph by the late A. Beato of Luxor.)

APPENDIX

I

THE DECREE CONFERRING ADDITIONAL HONOURS ON PTOLEMY III EUERGETES I (B.C. 247–221) WHICH WAS PASSED BY THE PRIESTHOOD OF ALL EGYPT ASSEMBLED AT MEMPHIS ON THE SEVENTEENTH DAY OF THE MONTH OF TYBI IN THE NINTH YEAR OF THE KING'S REIGN

II

THE DECREE CONFERRING HONOURS ON PTOLEMY IV PHILOPATOR (B.C. 221–203) WHICH WAS PASSED BY THE PRIEST-HOOD OF ALL EGYPT ASSEMBLED AT MEMPHIS ON THE FIRST DAY OF THE MONTH OF PAOPHI IN THE SIXTH YEAR OF THE KING'S REIGN.

THE DECREE OF CANOPUS

The copies of the Greek and hieroglyphic versions of the Decree of Canopus printed in this book are taken from the famous " Stele of Canopus " which was discovered on April 15, 1866, at ṢĀN AL-ḤAGAR (*i.e.* TANIS or ZOAN) by a party of German savants, which included Professors R. LEPSIUS, S. L. REINISCH, E. R. ROESLER and Herr WEIDENBACH. The Stele is a fine limestone slab measuring 7 ft. 4 in. in height, 2 ft. 8 in. in width, and 13½ inches in thickness. On the upper half of the front are cut 37 lines of hieroglyphs, of characteristic Ptolemaïc form, and below these are 76 lines of Greek uncials ; on the right-hand edge of the Stele are 74 lines of Demotic text.

The monument is preserved in the Egyptian Museum in Cairo, and there is a good cast of it, presented by the Khedive, Isma'îl Pâshâ, in 1871, in the British Museum (see the *Guide*, p. 258, No. 957 [1081]). The Greek and hieroglyphic texts were published by:—REINISCH and ROESLER, *Die zweisprachige Inschrift von Tanis*, Vienna, 1866 ; by K. R. LEPSIUS, *Das bilingue Dekret von Kanopus*, Berlin, 1866 (with a translation of the Greek text and a transliteration and translation of the hieroglyphic text); by P. PIERRET, *Le décret trilingue de Canope*, Paris, 1881; by S. SHARPE, *The Decree of Canopus*, London, 1870; and by BUDGE, *The Decrees of Memphis and Canopus*, London, 1904, 3 vols. See also H. BRUGSCH, *Thesaurus inscriptionem Aegyptiacarum*, Leipzig, 1883–91, part vi, p. 1554 f.; and SETHE, *Urkunden*, II, p. 125 f.

The Demotic text has been published by E. REVILLOUT, *Chrestomathie démotique*, Paris, 1880, p. 125 f.; by W. N. GROFF, "Le décret de Canope," in *Rev. Egyptologique*, Paris, 1891; *Les deux versions démotiques du décret de Canope*, Paris, 1888; by J. KRALL, *Demotische Lesestücke*, II, Leipzig, 1908; by H. BRUGSCH, *Thesaurus*, part v, p. 1554; and by SPIEGELBERG, *Kanopus und Memphis* (Rosettana), Heidelberg, 1922. English translations of the Greek text have been published by BIRCH (*Trans. Soc. Lit.*, London, 1870, vol. 14, pp. 349–95; and *Records of the Past*, London (no date), vol. v, pp. 81–90); by BUDGE, *The Decrees of Memphis and Canopus*, London, 1904, vol. III; by J. P. MAHAFFY, *The Empire of the Ptolemies*, p. 208 f.; and E. BEVAN, *The Ptolemaïc Dynasty*, p. 208 f.

In 1881 a duplicate of the Stele of Canopus was found by MASPERO at Kom al-Hisn (see G. MILLER, "Nouvelle copie du décret de Canope," in *Comptes rendus*, série iv, tome 11, pp. 85–90). The new Stele is of white limestone, and is 2 m. 22 cm.

in height and 78 cm. in width, and is inscribed with 26 lines of hieroglyphs, 20 lines of Demotic, and 64 lines of Greek uncials. It is preserved in the Egyptian Museum in Cairo, where it bears the No. 22186, and has been described by AHMAD BEY KAMAL, *Catalogue général,* Cairo, 1905, p. 182, plates LIX, LX and LXI. The Greek text has been published in *Journal des Savants,* 1883, pp. 214–40; and the Demotic text by GROFF, KRALL, BRUGSCH (*Thesaurus,* vi, p. 1575 f.), and SPIEGEBERGL; and the variants of the hieroglyphic text have been given by SETHE. A portion of a second duplicate of the Stele of Canopus is preserved in the Louvre, and it contains parts of ll. 29–37 of the hieroglyphic text.

I

THE DECREE OF CANOPUS

THE GREEK TEXT: ENGLISH RENDERING

I.—THE DATING OF THE DECREE

In the reign of PTOLEMY (III), the son of Ptolemy and Arsinoë, the Brother God and Sister God, the ninth year, APOLLONIDES, the son of Moschion, being priest of Alexander, and of the Brother and Sister Gods, and of the Well-Doing Gods, MENEKRATEIA, the daughter of Philammon, being Kanephoros of Arsinoë Philadelphos, on the seventh day [of the month] Apellaios (December) [which is] the seventeenth day of the month of Tybi[1] of the Egyptians.

II.—INTRODUCTION AND DECREE

DECREE

The high priests and the prophets, and those who go into the holy place (*i.e.* the shrine) to array the gods in their apparel, and the bearers of feathers, and the sacred scribes, and the rest of

[1] March 6, 237 B.C., according to Dr. E. Bevan.

the priests who gathered themselves together from the temples throughout the country for the fifth day of [the month of] Dios,[1] whereon are celebrated the birthday festivals of the King, and for the twenty-fifth day of the same month, whereon he received the sovereignty from his father, having assembled on this day in the temple of the Well-Doing Gods in Canopus, spake [thus] :—

III.—THE BENEFITS CONFERRED ON THE TEMPLES BY PTOLEMY III AND HIS SISTER-WIFE BERENICE

Inasmuch as King PTOLEMY, the son of Ptolemy and Arsinoë, the Brother God and Sister God, and BERENICE, his sister and wife, the Well-Doing Gods, are at all times performing very many and great deeds of benevolence for the temples throughout the country; and are multiplying exceedingly the honours of the gods,

IV.—THEIR MAJESTIES ENDOWED THE SHRINES OF THE SACRED ANIMALS, AND BROUGHT BACK THE STATUES OF THE GODS FROM PERSIA TO EGYPT

and for APIS and for MNEVIS, and for the other sacred animals which are worshipped in the country, they take the greatest care in every way possible, with great expense and provisions in

[1] October-November.

abundance; and the sacred images which had been carried off from the country by the Persians, the King having made an expedition outside Egypt, brought them back safely unto Egypt, and restored [them] to the temples wherefrom they had been carried off originally;

V.—THE KING PROVIDED FOR THE PROTECTION OF EGYPT, AND WAGED WAR IN FOREIGN LANDS

and hath preserved peace in the country, fighting battles on its behalf against many peoples and those who were their overlords; and hath provided good government for all those who live in the country (*i.e.* the natives), and for all those who are in subjection to Their Majesties (*i.e.* Syrians, Nubians, etc.);

VI.—THE KING'S FAMINE-RELIEF MEASURES

and when on one occasion the river [Nile] did not rise [adequately], and all those who were in the country were terror-stricken because of what had happened, and they recalled to their memories the calamities which had taken place under some of the earlier kings, when it fell out that those who dwelt in the country were in distress because of their lacking water; and how they (*i.e.* Their Majesties) helped and showed care for those who lived in the temples, and those who dwelt in the country, and by taking much forethought, and by

PLATE XV.

The Decree of Canopus, Greek Text, lines 1–38.

PLATE XVI.

The Decree of Canopus, Greek Text, lines 39–75.

giving up no small amount of their revenues in order to save men's lives, having brought into the country corn from Syria, and Phoenicia, and Cyprus, and from many other regions, where prices were high, they saved those who lived in Egypt, and so leave behind them a deathless deed of kindness, and of their own merit a great memorial, both to present and future generations, in return wherefor the gods have given to them (*i.e.* Their Majesties) firmly established sovereignty, and they shall give unto them all other good things for ever and ever.

VII.—THE PRIESTS DECIDE TO INCREASE THE HONOURS DUE TO THEIR MAJESTIES AND THEIR ANCESTORS

WITH FORTUNE'S FAVOUR (*i.e.* with Good Luck) It is [hereby] decreed by the priests everywhere in the country :—

To multiply the honours which are at present [paid] in the temples to King PTOLEMY and Queen BERENICE, the Well-Doing Gods, and to those who begot them, the Brother Gods, and to their forebears the Saviour Gods ; and the priests who are in each and every temple throughout the country shall, in addition [to their other titles] be called "priests of the Well-Doing Gods," and the priesthood of the Well-Doing Gods shall be inscribed in all their deeds (or, legal instruments), and added to the engraving upon their rings ;

VIII.—THE PRIESTS DECREE THE FORMATION OF A FIFTH ORDER OF PRIESTS

And there shall be established in addition to the four tribes of the company of priests which already exist in each and every temple, another tribe which is to be named the "Fifth Tribe of [the priests of] the Well-Doing Gods,"

IX.—THE SELECTION OF THE NEW TRIBE AND THEIR PRIVILEGES AND STATUS

since it hath happened through the favour of fortune, that the birth of King PTOLEMY, the son of the Brother Gods, took place on the fifth day of the month of Dios, which became the source of very many good things for all mankind; and among this Tribe shall be entered the priests who have been born since the first year, and those who are to be inscribed among them, up to the month of Mesore, in the ninth year, and those who shall be begotten by them for ever; and those who were priests up to the first year shall continue in the Tribes wherein they were. And, similarly, the children who shall be begotten by them shall be entered among the Tribes wherein their fathers were; and instead of the twenty councillor-priests, who were elected each year from the four Tribes of priests which already exist, five from each Tribe, there shall be five and twenty councillor-priests, and the five additional priests shall be taken from the Fifth Tribe of the Well-Doing Gods; and the priests of the Fifth Tribe of the Well-Doing Gods shall take their part in the religious services, and also in everything else which is in the temples, and there shall be a chief of the Tribe (Phylarch), even as there is in the other four Tribes.

X.—A FESTIVAL IN HONOUR OF THE WELL-DOING GODS SHALL BE CELEBRATED ON THE DAY OF THE RISING OF SOTHIS (SIRIUS, THE DOG-STAR)

And inasmuch as there are celebrated in the temples each month festivals of the Well-Doing Gods, according to the DECREE which was passed originally, namely, on the fifth day, and the ninth day, and the twenty-fifth day; and since festivals and processions generally are celebrated in honour of the other great gods each year; a general festival and procession shall be celebrated each year, both in the temples and by the people throughout the country in honour of King PTOLEMY and Queen BERENICE, the Well-Doing Gods, on the day whereon the star of Isis riseth, which, according to the holy books, is regarded as the New Year and is now, in the ninth year, kept on the first day of the month of Payni, wherein the Greater and Lesser festivals of Bubastis are celebrated, and the garnering of the fruit and the rise of the River [Nile] take place;

but if it fall out that the rising of the star shall, in the course of four years, change to another day, the festival and procession shall not be changed, but they shall be celebrated on the first day of Payni, even as they were celebrated originally on that day in the ninth year; and the festival shall last for five days, and crowns (or, garlands) shall be worn, and sacrifices and libations [shall be made], and whatsoever ought to be done shall be done.

XI.—A SIXTH EPAGOMENAL DAY SHALL BE ADDED TO THE CALENDAR EVERY FOUR YEARS

And that the seasons of the year may coincide wholly with the present settlement (or, constitution of the world), and that it may not happen that some of the popular festivals which ought to be held in the winter come to be celebrated in the summer, [owing to] the Star (*i.e.* the Sun) changing one day in the course of four years, and that festivals which are now kept in the summer come to be celebrated in the winter in times to come, even as hath formerly happened, and would happen at the present time if the year continued to consist of three hundred and sixty days, and the five additional days which it is customary to add thereto; from this time onward one day, a festival of the Well-Doing Gods, shall be added every four years to the five additional days, before the New Year, so that all [men] may know that the error of deficiency which existed formerly in respect of the arrangement of the seasons, and of the year, and of the views usually believed concerning the general ordering of the heavens, hath been rectified and filled up satisfactorily by the Well-Doing Gods.

XII.—THE CEREMONIAL MOURNING OF THE PRIESTS FOR THE SUDDEN DEATH OF THE PRINCESS BERENICE

And since it hath happened that the daughter who was born of King PTOLEMY and Queen BERENICE, the Well-Doing Gods, and was called "Berenice," who was straightway proclaimed Queen, being a virgin, departed suddenly into the everlasting world, whilst there were with him the priests who were wont to gather themselves together to the king every year, who made great mourning straightway because of that which had happened, and having made supplication to the King and to the Queen, they persuaded them to establish the Goddess ["Berenice"] with Osiris in the temple of Canopus, which is not only among the temples of the first class, but is also held in the greatest reverence, both by the King and all the people throughout the country, and the bringing up of the sacred bark of Osiris to this temple from the temple in the Herakleion taketh place each year, on the twenty-ninth day of the month of Choiach, when all [the priests] from the temples of the first class offer up sacrifices upon the altars which they have set up for each of the temples of the first class on each side of the dromos. And after this they performed all the things which were connected with her deification, and brought to an end the mourning ceremonies with all the magnificence and great care which it is wont to show [at the burials] of Apis and Mnevis.

XIII.—DIVINE HONOURS SIMILAR TO THOSE WHICH ARE PAID TO THE DAUGHTER OF THE SUN-GOD RĀ ARE TO BE PAID TO THE PRINCESS BERENICE

It is decreed :—

To pay to Queen BERENICE, the daughter of the Well-Doing Gods, everlasting honours in all the temples throughout the country; and inasmuch as she departed to the gods in the month of Tybi, wherein, in the beginning, the daughter of Helios departed from life, whom her loving father at one time called his "crown," and at another his "sight," and they celebrated in her honour a festival and tow round the sacred boat of Osiris in procession in the greater number of the temples of the first class in this month; wherein her apotheosis took place originally, and to celebrate for Queen BERENICE also, the daughter of the Well-Doing Gods, in all the temples throughout the country, in the month of Tybi, a festival and a procession for four days, from the seventeenth day, wherein the procession and the conclusion of the lamentation for her originally took place;

XIV.—A GOLDEN STATUE OF THE PRINCESS BERENICE, TO BE CARRIED IN PROCESSION, WITH A SPECIAL CROWN, IS TO BE MADE

and to make of her a sacred statue of gold, set with precious stones, in each of the temples of the first and second class, and to set it up in the most holy place, and a prophet, or one of the priests who go into the sanctuary to dress the gods, shall carry it in his arms, when the journeyings forth [of the gods] on the festivals of the other gods are celebrated, so that being seen by all it may be adored and bowed down to under the name of "Berenice, the Queen of Virgins"; and, moreover, the crown which shall be placed upon the head of her statue shall be different from that which is placed upon the statue of her mother, Queen BERENICE, and it shall be [formed] of two ears of corn between which shall be a serpent-shaped crown, and behind this shall be a sceptre, papyrus-shaped, [similar to those] which the goddesses are wont to hold in their hands; and round this [sceptre] the tail of the serpent crown shall be wound, so that from the arrangement of the crown the name of BERENICE shall be indicated according to the distinguishing signs of the hieroglyphs;

XV.—A SECOND GOLD STATUE OF BERENICE SHALL BE SET UP, AND THE PRIESTLY VIRGINS SHALL PAY HONOUR TO IT

and when the Kikellia are celebrated in the month of Choiach before the procession (Periplus) of Osiris, the daughters of the priests shall make ready another statue of Berenice, the Queen of Virgins, whereto likewise they shall offer up sacrifices, and shall perform all the other things which it is customary to perform at this festival; and it shall be lawful, after the same manner, for other virgins who desire to perform the ceremonies which it is customary to perform to the goddess, so to do; and hymns shall be sung to her, both by the holy virgins who are specially chosen, and by those who minister unto the gods, and who shall put on their heads the crowns which are peculiar to the gods, whose priestesses they are held to be; and when the early harvest is nigh, the holy virgins shall bear the ears of corn which are to be set before the image of the goddess; and both at the festivals and in the panegyrics of the other gods the singing men and the singing women, shall sing unto her daily the songs which the sacred scribes, having written them down, shall give to the singing master, whereof copies shall be inscribed in the sacred books;

XVI.—PROVISION SHALL BE MADE FOR THE DAUGHTERS OF THE PRIESTS. THE "BREAD OF BERENICE"

and when supplies of food are given to the priests out of the revenues of the temples, whensoever they are brought for the whole company [of the priests], there shall be given to the daughters of the priests out of the revenues of the temples, [reckoning] from the day when they were born, the subsistence which hath been calculated by the Councillor-priests in each of the temples according to the amount of the revenues of the temples; the bread which shall be given to the wives of the priests shall have a special form, and shall be called the "Bread of Berenice."

XVII.—THE MANNER OF PUBLICATION OF THE DECREE

The governor who hath been appointed to each temple, and the high-priest, and the sacred scribes in each temple shall engrave a copy of this Decree upon a stele of stone or bronze in hieroglyphic characters, and in Egyptian and in Greek characters, and shall set it up in the place where it will be most seen in the temples of the first, and second, and third class, so that the priests throughout the country may show that they hold in honour the Well-Doing Gods, and their children, as is most right.

THE DECREE OF CANOPUS

THE DEMOTIC TEXT: ENGLISH RENDERING

[I.—THE DATING OF THE DECREE]

1 [In] the ninth year, [on] the seventh day of
[the month] Aplis, [which is the seventeenth
day of the first month of the season Per-t], of
Pharaoh (life, strength, health [to him!])
Ptolemy, the everliving, the son of Ptolemy,
2 and Arsinoë, the Gods-Brothers—the priest
of Alexander, and of the Gods-Brothers, and
of the Gods-the-Well-doers, was
3 Apollonides, the son of Moschion, [when]
Menekrateia, the daughter of Phil-Ammon,
was the bearer of
4 the basket (Kanephoros) before Arsinoë, the
Brother-lover.

[II.—INTRODUCTION OR PREFACE]

5 [On this day] Decree:—
The high-priests, and the ministers of the gods
(prophets), and the priests who go into the
holy place (*i.e.* sanctuary) to array the gods in
their apparel, and the scribes of the House of
Life (*i.e.* the great College of the priests), and
the scribes of
6 the Books of the God, and the other priests,
who had come from the temples of Egypt, on

PLATE XVII.

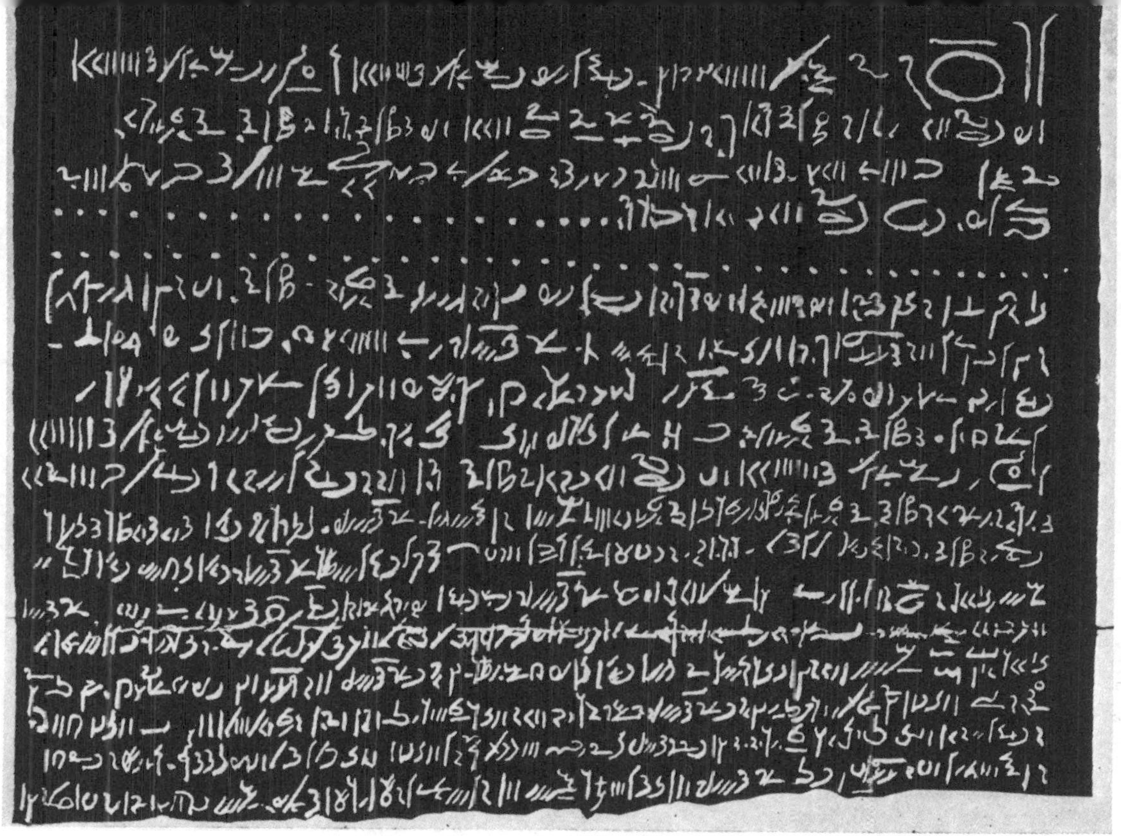

The Decree of Canopus, Demotic Text, lines 1–17. (From a cast in the British Museum.)

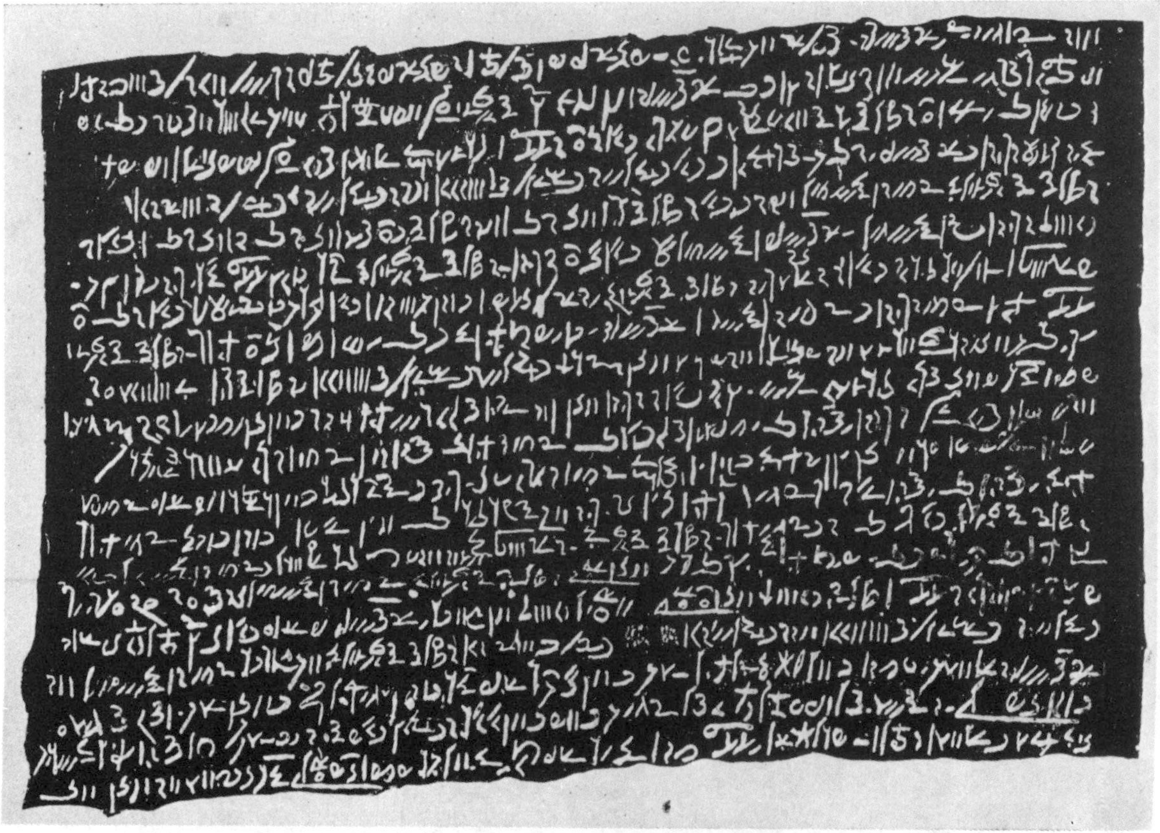

The Decree of Canopus, Demotic Text, lines 18–37. (From a cast in the British Museum.)

the fifth day of the month Tis, on which day was celebrated the Birthday
7 of Pharaoh (life, strength, health [to him !]), and on the twenty-fifth day of the month aforesaid on which day he received the exalted rank (of sovereign) from the hand of his father, and had assembled in the
8 house of the god of the Gods, the Well-doers, in Pn-guti (Canopus), they decreed [thus]:—

[III.—DESCRIPTION OF THE BENEFACTIONS OF PTOLEMY III AND ARSINOË]

Inasmuch as it hath happened that Pharaoh (life, health, strength [to him !]) Ptolemy
9 the everliving, the son of Ptolemy (IV) and Arsinoë, the Gods-Brothers, and the Pharaoh (fem.), Queen Berenice,
10 his sister and his wife, the Gods, the Well-doers, have made very many great benefactions to the temples of Egypt on every occasion [possible] and they have multiplied exceedingly the
11 honours [to be paid] to the gods;

[IV.—THEIR CARE FOR THE CULT OF APIS AND MNEVIS; THEIR RESTORATION OF THE STATUES OF THE GODS TO EGYPT FROM PERSIA]

and have at all times taken care to provide all that is necessary for the [cult of] Apis, and Mnevis, and the other sacred animals that

are worshipped in EGYPT ; and they laboured and made great preparations
12 in respect of the statues of the gods which the men of PERSIA had carried away from EGYPT. Pharaoh (life, health, strength [to him !]) marched out into foreign territories to rescue them (*i.e.* the statues), he brought them [back] to EGYPT,
13 he [re]placed them in their temples wherefrom they had originally been taken.

[V.—THEY HAVE PROTECTED EGYPT AGAINST FOREIGN FOES]

He hath protected the territory [of EGYPT] against war, whilst carrying on war in lands outside [EGYPT] which were remote,
14 and against many foreign lands, and the men who ruled over them. And they (*i.e.* PTOLEMY and his Queen) made the Law (or, the Right) to be kept by everyone in EGYPT, and the other peoples who were under their august rule.

[VI.—HOW THEY FED THE PEOPLE DURING A PERIOD OF FAMINE]

When there was a low Nile-flood (*i.e.* Inundation),
15 during their reign, and there was a period of scarcity (or, famine), and it happened that all the people of EGYPT were terrified because of that which had happened, and they thought

of the calamity which had taken place during the reigns of some of
16 the earlier Pharaohs, when the people of EGYPT [suffered] through the want of [the waters of the Nile] which took place in their time. Then they (*i.e.* PTOLEMY and his Queen) took care, with warm affection of heart, for those who were in
17 the temples, and the other people who were in EGYPT, and they pondered much, casting all consideration for themselves in their many undertakings,[1] with the intention of making men to live.
18 They caused grain, which was purchased at a price higher than that of silver, to be brought from the region of ÅSHER (SYRIA), [and] from the territory of the people of KHAR, [and] from the Island of SALMINA (CYPRUS),
19 and from many other places. They saved the people who were in EGYPT, [thus] leaving behind them benefactions for all time, and a great (or, splendid) example of their exalted [virtue], both for those who are now alive, and
20 for those who shall come after. Wherefore the gods have given unto them as a reward the stablishment of their exalted sovereignty, and have given unto them every kind of good thing for ever and ever.

[1] The literal translation of Spiegelberg reads "sie ihre sandalen in Bezug auf sich Einnahmen hinter sich wurfen."

[VII.—THE PRIESTS DECIDE TO MULTIPLY THE HONOURS PAID TO THEIR MAJESTIES]

With the health and the strength!

21 It hath entered the heart of the priests who are in EGYPT to add to the honours which are paid to PHARAOH (life, strength, health [to him!]), PTURMIS and the Queen (life, strength, health [to her!]) BERENICE,
22 the Gods, the Well-doers, in the temples, and those which are paid to the Gods-Brothers, who begot them, and those which are paid to the Gods-Saviours, who caused them to come into being those who begot them.

[VIII.—A FIFTH ORDER OF THE PRIESTS OF THE GODS, THE WELL-DOERS, IS TO BE ESTABLISHED]

23 The priests who are in the temples of EGYPT, in every temple, shall be called "Priests of the Gods, the Well-doers," in addition to their other priestly names, and they shall write it
24 on all their official documents, and they shall set "Priest of the Gods, the Well-doers," on the rings which they wear, and shall engrave it upon them. And they shall create
25 another order among the priests, who are in the temples of EGYPT, in addition to the four orders which exist at the present time, and it shall be called the fifth order of the Gods, the Well-doers.

[IX.—THE CONSTITUTION AND RIGHTS OF THE NEW ORDER OF PRIESTS]

26 Since it hath happened that a propitious event hath taken place with health and happiness, [and] Pharaoh (life, strength, health [to him !]), Pturmis, son of the Gods-Brothers, was born on the 5th day of the month of Tis,
27 the day aforesaid being the beginning of the working of much happiness for all men, the priests who were made priests from the first year, and those which were made priests up to the first day of the fourth month of the season Shemu, shall be placed in this [new] order,
28 and their children for ever. The priests who were priests up to the first year shall remain in the order in which they were; so likewise shall it be
29 with their children from this day onwards, and their [names] shall be enrolled in the order wherein are their fathers. In the place of the 20 councillor-priests, which are selected yearly from among the four
30 orders, which already exist, and from each of which 5 [priests] are selected, there shall be 25 councillor-priests. The 5 shall be drafted from the 5 orders of the priests
31 of the Gods, the Well-doers. They shall share in the things which belong to the 5 orders of

[priests of] the Gods, the Well-doers, and in the offerings which are made, and in everything which is in the temples. And they
32 shall have a master of their order, even as have the four other orders.

[X.—A FESTIVAL SHALL BE CELEBRATED ON THE DAY OF THE RISING OF SIRIUS]

Moreover, since it happeneth that festivals are celebrated in honour of the Gods, the Well-doers, in the temples each month on the 5th day, and on the 9th day, and on the 25th day,
33 in accordance with the decree which was written in former times, and the people are wont to celebrate great festivals in honour of the other gods, in EGYPT yearly, a great festival shall be celebrated yearly in honour of
34 PHARAOH (life, strength, health [to him !]), PTURMIS, and the PHARAOH (*sic*) (life, strength, health [to her !]), BERENICE, the Gods, the Well-doers, in all the temples and in
35 all EGYPT on the day on which the star SPṬ-T (SOTHIS, or the DOG-STAR) riseth, which is called the beginning of the year in the writings of the [College of the] House of Life, which shall be celebrated in the 9th year of the 1st day of the second month of the season of Shemu (*i.e.* Summer)
36 on which are celebrated the festival of the goddess BAST and the great festival procession

of Bast, which is the period when the crops are gathered in, and the inundation of the Nile taketh place. But although it happeneth
37 that the rising of the star delayeth a whole day every four years, the day on which the afore-mentioned festival is celebrated shall not be changed, but the festival shall be celebrated on
38 the 1st day of the second month of the season of Shemu, on which day already in the 9th year it hath been celebrated. And the festival shall be celebrated for a period of 5 days, during which the people shall wear garlands and libations shall be made, and burnt offerings shall be offered up,
39 and all the other things which it is meet and seemly to do shall be done.

[XI.—THE ADDITION OF A SIXTH EPAGOMENAL DAY TO THE CALENDAR]

And also in order to make it happen that the seasons of the year may always do what appertaineth to them in accordance with the constitution of the heavens as it existeth at the present day, and in order that it may not happen that some of the festivals
40 which are celebrated in Egypt, and which ought to be celebrated in the winter, come to be celebrated in the summer, the luminary (*i.e.* the star) changing his place by one day in every

41 four years, and the other festivals which are
now celebrated in the summer come to be
celebrated in the winter, which hath actually
42 happened in past times, and would happen
again [now], with the year consisting of 360
days, and the five days which are appointed
to be added at the end of them. There shall
be added one
43 day as a festival to the Gods, the Well-doers,
every four years to the 5 additional days
which are added before the beginning of the
New Year, so that
44 all men may know that what was lacking in
the seasons of the year, and in the year
[itself], and the things which must be known
concerning the motions of the heavenly bodies
(*i.e.* the laws of astronomy), and what taketh
place with them, have been corrected and
arranged
45 by the Gods, the Well-doers.

[XII.—THE SUDDEN DEATH OF PRINCESS BERENICE, AND THE STABLISHING OF HER CULT]

And moreover since it hath happened that the daughter which was born to Pharaoh (life, strength, health [to him!]), Pturmis and the Pharaohess (*i.e.* Queen) (life, health, strength [to her!]), Berenice, the

PLATE XIX.

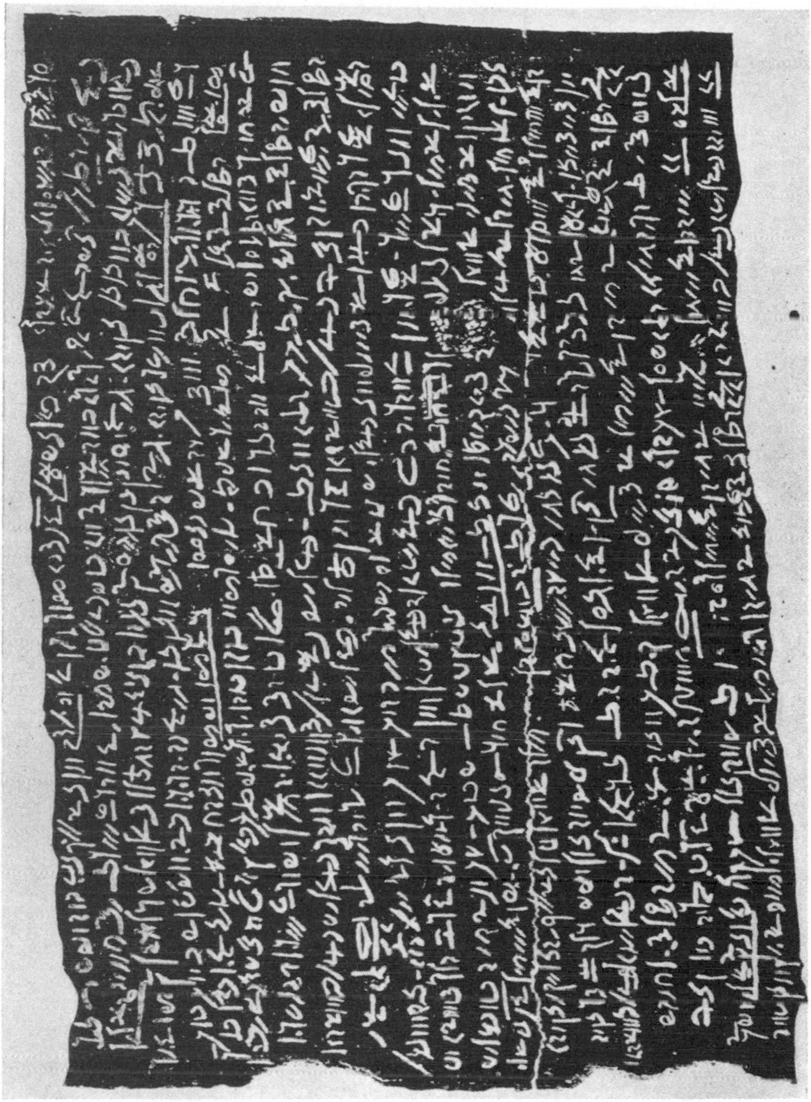

The Decree of Canopus, Demotic Text, lines 38–57. (From a cast in the British Museum.)

PLATE XX.

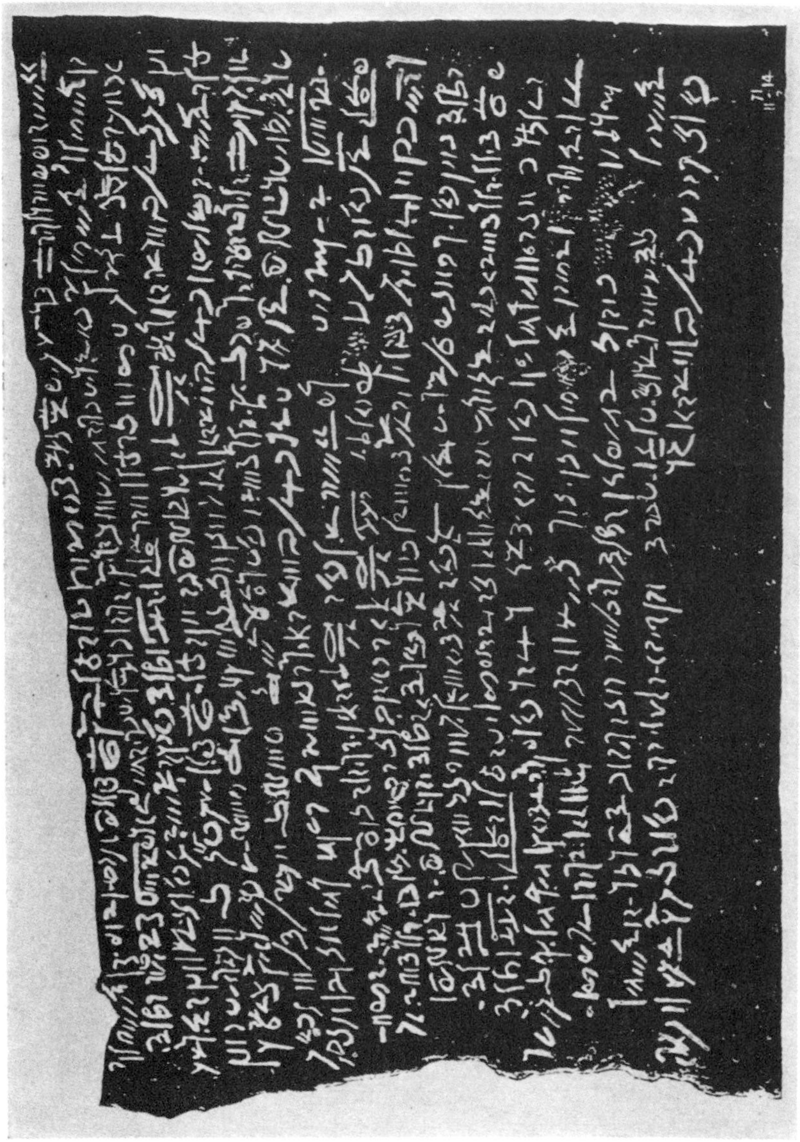

The Decree of Canopus, Demotic Text, lines 58–74. (From a cast in the British Museum.)

46 Gods, the Well-doers—they gave to her the name of BERENICE, and made her to appear as a Pharaohess (*i.e.* Queen)—being a virgin departed suddenly

47 to heaven, the priests of Egypt who came to PHARAOH (life, health, strength [to him !]), annually, to the place where he was, forthwith made great mourning on account of that which had taken place,

48 and they made entreaty before PHARAOH (life, strength, health [to him !]), and the PHARAOHESS, and the desire had entered their hearts to make the goddess (*i.e.* BERENICE) to rest with

49 OSIRIS in the house of the god (*i.e.* temple) of PJEYN-GUTI (CANOPUS), which is not only a temple of the first class, but is also one of those to which PHARAOH (life, strength, health [to him !])

50 and all the men of EGYPT pay honour. When it happeneth that they make OSIRIS in the SEḲTI-BOAT to enter into the afore-mentioned temple annually,

51 in the house of the god of the temple of ÅMEN of GRB, on the 29th day of the fourth month of the season of Akhet, then all those who are in the temples of the first rank shall offer up burnt-offerings upon the altars, which they have made for

52 the temples of the first order for each of the temples, on both sides of the court of the temple. After these things they shall do what is ordered to be done by the law for the deification [of the princess] and the purification of her mourning,

53 and they shall pay honour to her, their hearts being hot within them, and they shall do for her what they are accustomed to do for Apis and Mnevis.

[XIII.—HONOURS SHALL BE PAID TO PRINCESS BERENICE SIMILAR TO THOSE WHICH ARE PAID IN THE SAME MONTH TO THE DEAD DAUGHTER OF THE SUN-GOD]

[The priests decided] to pay everlasting honours to the Pharaohess Berenice,

54 the daughter of the Gods, the Well-doers, in all the temples of Egypt. Since it happened that she entered among the gods in the first month of the season Per-t,

55 which was the month wherein in times of old the mummification of the daughter of the Sun-god Rā took place, whom he called his uraeus (*i.e.* cobra), and gave her the name of his eye, because he loved her, and they make in her honour,

56 in the afore-mentioned month, processions of boats in most of the temples of the first rank, because in that month in times of old the

deification of the goddess took place, they shall celebrate a festival and make a
57 procession of boats in honour of the Pharaohess BERENICE, the daughter of the Gods, the Well-doers, in all the temples of EGYPT on the 17th day of the first month of the season Per-t, and they shall celebrate her
58 festival procession of boats and the purification of her mourning for four days on the first occasion.

[XIV.—A GOLDEN STATUE OF THE PRINCESS, WEARING A SPECIAL CROWN, SHALL BE MADE AND SHALL BE CARRIED IN HER FESTAL PROCESSIONS]

And they shall set up a divine statue of gold, inlaid with [semi-precious] stones, in the temples of the first rank, [and]
59 in the temples of the second rank, in each and every temple. And it shall rest in the sanctuary (or, shrine), and the minister of the god (*i.e.* prophet) or one of the priests who shall be chosen for the sanctuary in order to dress the gods in their apparel, shall bear it before him
60 on his breast when they come to celebrate the festal processions and the festivals of the other gods, so that all men may see it and may pay honour to it,

61 and they shall call it " BERENICE, the Lady of Virgins." The crown of gold which is on the head of the divine statue when the priests exhibiteth it, shall be different from that which they shall place

62 on the statue of the Pharaohess BERENICE her mother when they exhibit her. The crown shall be made of two ears of wheat, and between them there shall be an uraeus, and there shall be behind it

63 a stalk of papyrus, of the same size as that which is in the hand of the goddesses. And the tail of this uraeus shall twine itself round the papyrus, so that it may come to pass

64 that the name of the afore-mentioned crown may be read " BERENICE " in accordance with the characters of the writing of the House of Life. When men are about to celebrate the days

65 of the ritual ceremonies of Isis, in the fourth month of the season of Akhet, before the boat procession of OSIRIS, the daughters of the priests who are virgins shall make another statue [of BERENICE, the Lady of Virgins, and they shall offer up burnt offerings to it, and they shall do in her honour the other things which it is customary to do][1] on the days of

[1] The words in brackets are added from the second version of the Decree.

66 the afore-mentioned festival. And the other virgins also shall be at liberty to do that which it is customary to do according to the regulations which are set down in writing.

67 And she shall also be praised by the Shmāiu priestesses who have been chosen for the service of the gods, they being crowned with the crowns of

68 the various gods to whom they minister as priestesses. The first ears of corn which shall ripen, the Shmāiu priestesses shall carry away and shall bring them

69 to the divine image of the goddess. And the male singers, and the female singers, shall sing to her daily praises, both on the days of the festivals and on the days of the festivals of the other gods,

70 in accordance with the hymns which the scribes of the House of Life shall write, and they shall give them to those who teach the singers, who shall make copies of them on the rolls of papyrus of the House of Life.

[XVI.—THE BREAD OF BERENICE]

Now, inasmuch as it is customary

71 to give food from the temple-revenues to the priests in the temples as soon as they are made priests, so let food be given to the daughters of the priests, from the day of

72 their birth, from the revenues of the temples of the gods, according to the measure which the revenues of the temple (*i.e.* the offerings to the gods) will permit the councillor-priests in each of the temples

73 to allot to them. The bread which shall be given to the women of the priests shall be [made] in a form different [from that of other bread],

74 and " Bread of Berenice " is the name which shall be given to it.

[The following is supplied from the text found at Kom al-Hisn :

XVII.—THE PUBLICATION OF THE DECREE]

This DECREE, let the scribes of the market gate which are attached to each temple, and the chief priests, and the scribes of the house of the god, write it upon a slab of stone or copper (bronze ?) in the writing of the House of Life, [and] in the writing of books, and in the writing of the Greeks. And they shall set up the slab in a prominent place in the temples of the first rank, [and] in the temples of the second rank, [and] in the temples of the third rank. Thus will be made manifest clearly that the priests and their children honour the Gods, the Well-doers, even as it is right and proper to do.

THE DECREE OF CANOPUS

EGYPTIAN TEXT: RUNNING TRANSLATION

I.—THE DATING OF THE STELE

1 On the seventh day of the month of Apellaios, in the ninth year, [which is the equivalent of] the seventeenth day of the first month of the season of Per-t[1] for the inhabitants of Egypt, under the Majesty of the King of the South and the North (*i.e.* Upper and Lower Egypt), PTOLEMY, the everliving, the beloved of Ptaḥ, son of Ptolemy (II) and Arsinoë, the two Brother Gods,—

[when] the priest of Alexander, the deceased, and of the two Brother Gods, and of the two Well-Doing Gods, was Apollonides, **2** the son of Moschion, and Menecrateia, daughter of Philammon, was the bearer of the basket (*i.e.* canephoros) before Arsinoë, the Brother-loving (*i.e.* Philadelphus).

[1] The Coptic ⲧⲱⲃⲉ.

II.—INTRODUCTION

This day a DECREE [was passed].

The overseers of the temples, the ministers of the god (prophets ?), the priests who presided over the mysteries, the priests who wash (?) **3** [and] array the gods in their apparel, the scribes of the BOOK OF THE GOD, the sages, the fathers of the gods, and the libationer priests, in all their grades, who came from the two sides of Egypt (*i.e.* from the Eastern and Western banks of the Nile), and from the South and North of Egypt, [for] the fifth day of the month of Dios, on which the festival of the new year (*i.e.* birthday) of His Majesty is celebrated, and [for] the twenty-fifth day of the same month, whereon His Majesty received **4** his great office from his father, and assembled in the house of the god of the two Well-Doing Gods, which is in Peguti (Canopus), and they decreed thus :—

III.—THE BENEFITS CONFERRED ON THE TEMPLES BY PTOLEMY III AND HIS SISTER-WIFE BERENICE

Inasmuch as the King of the South and of the North, PTOLEMY, everliving, beloved of Ptaḥ, the son of Ptolemy and Arsinoë, the two Brother Gods, and Queen BERENICE, his sister and wife, the two Well-Doing Gods, have at all times conferred many great benefits **5** on the temples of Egypt and magnify the majesty of the gods in the greatest manner possible.

IV.—THEIR MAJESTIES ENDOWED THE SHRINES OF THE SACRED ANIMALS, AND BROUGHT BACK THE STATUES OF THE GODS FROM PERSIA TO EGYPT

Moreover, they take care to provide at all times for the things (*i.e.* the cult) of Apis, [and] Mnevis, [and] the sacred beasts which are revered in every temple in Egypt, and they gave (*i.e.* spent) great riches, and very many provisions **6** to maintain them in a fitting state. [And] the statues of the gods which the debased (or, vile) men of Persia carried away from Egypt—His Majesty marched into the lands of Asia, he rescued them, [and] brought them back to Egypt, [and] set them in their places in the temples, wherefrom they had been carried off previously.

V.—THE KING PROVIDED FOR THE PROTECTION OF EGYPT AND WAGED WAR IN FOREIGN LANDS

He protected Egypt against those who would fight **7** and at the same time he himself waged war outside its [frontiers] in remote valleys against foreigners of many lands, and [against] their captains who ruled over them. They (*i.e.* PTOLEMY and his Queen) governed righteously all the inhabitants of Egypt, and all the natives of every land who were in subjection to Their Majesties.

VI.—THE KING'S FAMINE-RELIEF MEASURES

Now, there came a year when there was a low Nile in **8** the time of Their Majesties. And the hearts of all the inhabitants of Egypt became sad when they remembered the calamities which had taken place in days of old, in the time of the early kings, and had fallen on the dwellers in Egypt when a low Nile took place in their time. Then did His Majesty himself and his sister **9** pay good heed to the matter, and their hearts warmed towards those who dwelt in the houses of the gods [*i.e.* temples], and towards all the inhabitants of Egypt. They pondered over the matter very deeply and frequently, and they remitted very many of the taxes with the intention of keeping the people alive. They caused corn to be brought to Egypt from Eastern Retnu (Syria), from the land of Kefth-t (Keftô), and from the Island of Sbinai (Cyprus), which is in the midst of the Green **10** Great (*i.e.* the Mediterranean Sea), and from many other foreign lands. And they (*i.e.* Their Majesties) expended very much money in purchasing [the grain] for which they paid an exceedingly high price, in order to save the lives of the people who were in the land of Egypt—thus they made known for time unending their beneficence and their gracious qualities (or, merits) to those who are living at the present time, and to those who shall come after them. Therefore have the gods made to be permanent their positions as Ruler[s] of the Two Lands, in return for these [deeds], **11** and they have rewarded them with benefits of every sort and kind which they can possibly have for all time.

VII.—THE PRIESTS DECIDE TO INCREASE THE HONOURS DUE TO THEIR MAJESTIES

Strength and health!

The priests of Egypt have determined in their minds to increase in many ways the ceremonial honours paid to the King of the South and of the North, the everliving, the beloved of Ptaḥ, and Queen Berenice, the two Well-Doing Gods, in the temples, and those who are paid to the two Brother Gods, who begot them, and **12** those which are paid to the two Saviour Gods, who created them, and to magnify them.

VIII.—THE PRIESTS DECREE THE FORMATION OF A FIFTH ORDER OF PRIESTS; ALL THE PRIESTS ARE TO BE KNOWN AS THE PRIESTS OF THE WELL-DOING GODS

The priests who are in all the temples of Egypt, all of them, shall [henceforward] be called "Priests of the Well-Doing Gods." [This title] shall be added to the title of their rank as prophets, and it shall be inscribed in all [their] documents, and the title "Prophet of the two Well-Doing Gods" shall be engraved on the rings which they wear

on their hands. And they shall constitute another
13 order of priests from among all the priests who are in the temples, in addition to the four orders of priests which exist at the present day, and it shall be called the "Fifth Order of Priests of the two Well-Doing Gods."

IX.—THE SELECTION OF THE NEW ORDER OF PRIESTS AND THEIR PRIVILEGES AND STATUS

Inasmuch as there took place the lucky event, with strength and health, namely, the birth of the King of the South and of the North, the ever-living, the beloved of Ptaḥ, the son of the two Brother Gods, on the fifth day of the month of Dios, which day was the beginning of **14** great happiness and prosperity for all men; the priests who were inducted by the king into the temples from the first year of His Majesty, and also those who were inducted [by him] up to the fourth month[1] of the season of Shemu (*i.e.* the Summer) of his ninth year, shall be placed in this Order of priests, and likewise their children for ever. And the priests who were priests up to the first year shall remain in the Orders of priests in which **15**
they were up to that time. So likewise shall it be for their children henceforward for ever, being inscribed (or, enrolled) in the Orders of the priesthood wherein their fathers were before them.

[1] In Coptic ⲙⲉⲥⲱⲣⲏ.

And instead of the twenty priest-councillors, who are chosen each year from the four Orders of priests which already exist, five persons from each Order of priests, there shall be twenty-five priest-councillors, **16** and the five priests who are to be added [to the twenty] shall be drawn from the Fifth Order of the Well-Doing Gods. And there shall be given to them a share in what is possessed by the Five Orders of priests of the Well-Doing Gods, and in the offerings, and in the purificatory gifts to the house of the god, and in everything which appertaineth to them in the temples. And this Fifth Order shall have a Director (Phylarch) as prophet, even as have the other four Orders.

X.—A FESTIVAL IN HONOUR OF THE WELL-DOING GODS SHALL BE CELEBRATED ON THE DAY OF THE RISING OF SOTHIS (SIRIUS, THE DOG-STAR)

Inasmuch as there are celebrated festivals **17** in honour of the Well-Doing Gods in all the temples every month, [namely] on the fifth day, and on the ninth day, and on the twenty-fifth day in accordance with a Decree which was written down in time past; and as, moreover, there is also celebrated each year throughout Egypt a festival in honour of the great gods, and a great procession [is made], so likewise there shall be celebrated a great festival, with a procession, each year in honour of the King of the

South and North, Ptolemy, the everliving, the beloved of Ptaḥ, **18** and Queen Berenice, the Well-Doing Gods, in the two halves (*i.e.* the right and left banks) of Egypt, and throughout the whole extent of Egypt, on the day when the star Sept (Sothis, Sirius) appeareth, the name whereof is called in the registers of the House of Life, "The Festival of the Opening of the Year" (*i.e.* the New Year), and which in [this] month is celebrated on the first day of the second month[1] of the season of Summer, in which month is celebrated the Festival of the New Year of Bast (Bubastis), and the great processional festival of the goddess Bast, because the time for the **19** in-gathering of all the crops, and the inundation of the Nile taketh place therein. Now, although it happeneth that the rising of the star Sothis changeth to another day ever four years, the day of the celebration of this festival shall not be changed because of this, but it shall be celebrated on the first day of the second month of the season of Summer, on which day, in [this] ninth year, it was originally celebrated. **20** This festival shall be celebrated for five days, and [the people] shall wear garlands of flowers on their heads, and offerings shall be laid on the altars, and libations shall be made, and every kind of thing which it is customary to offer [in the temples] shall be offered.

[1] In Coptic ⲡⲁⲱⲛⲉ.

PLATE XXI.

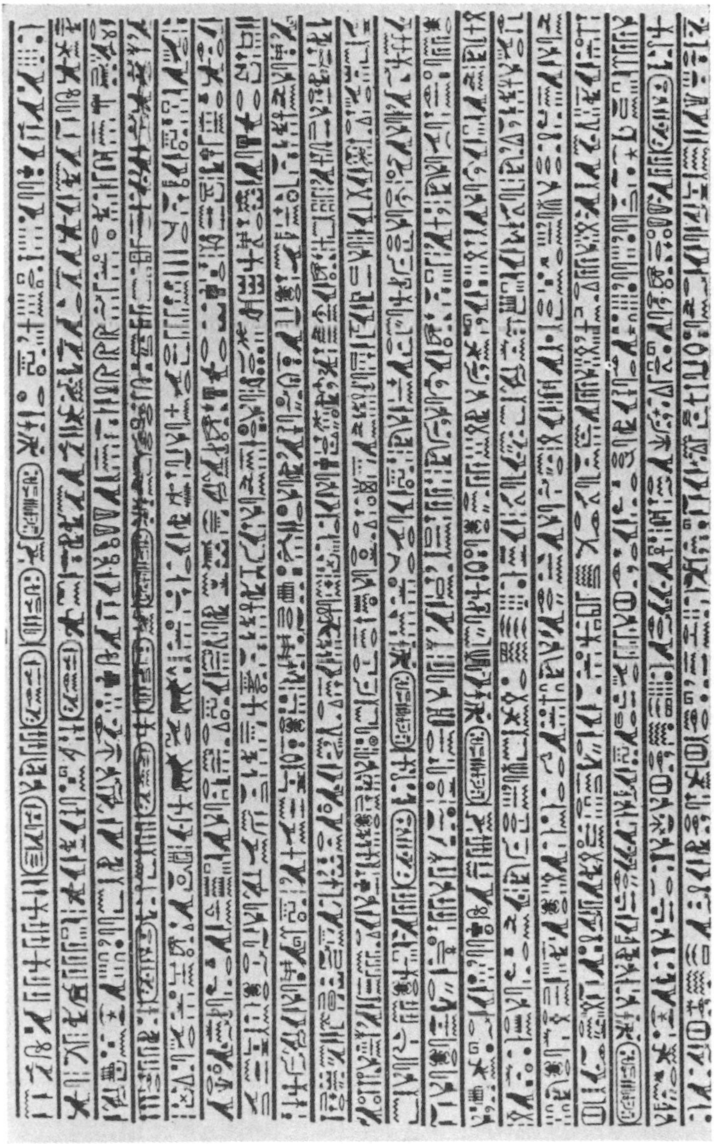

The Decree of Canopus, Hieroglyphic Text, lines 1–19.

PLATE XXII.

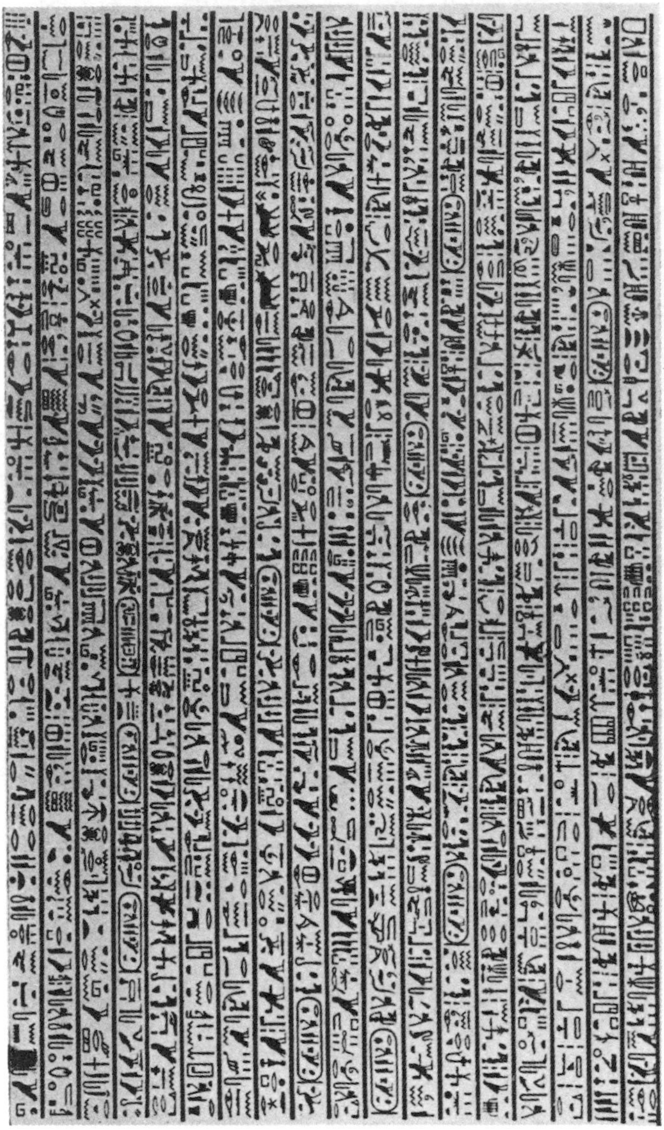

The Decree of Canopus, Hieroglyphic Text, lines 20–37.

XI.—A SIXTH EPAGOMENAL DAY SHALL BE ADDED TO THE CALENDAR EVERY FOUR YEARS

Now in order to make it to happen that the seasons of the year may perform what hath been allotted to them at every period, according to the plan whereby heaven is established at the present **21** day, and in order that it may not happen that the festivals which are celebrated throughout all Egypt in the season of Per-t (*i.e.* the Winter), come to be celebrated some time in the season of Shemu (Summer), because the rising of Sothis changeth one day in every four years, and contrarywise in times to come, those festivals will be celebrated in the season of Shemu (Summer), which at the present time are celebrated in the season of Per-t (Winter), even as they did in the time **22** of the ancestors. And this would happen now if the year consisted of three hundred and sixty days, and the five days which it hath been decided to add to them, at the[ir] end. Therefore from this day there shall be added one day to the festival of the two Well-Doing Gods every four years, and it shall be added to the five days which are added before the Festival of the New Year. Thus it shall happen that all men shall know that the little [time] which was lacking in the fixing of the seasons, **23** and the year, and the matters which [concern] the laws of the knowledge of the roads of the heavens, have been set in order and made correct in so far as it is possible to do so, by the Well-Doing Gods.

XII.—THE CEREMONIAL MOURNING OF THE PRIESTS FOR THE DEATH OF PRINCESS BERENICE

Now the King of the South and of the North, Ptolemy, the everliving, the beloved of Ptaḥ, and the Lady of the Two Lands (Egypt), Berenice, the two Well-Doing Gods, had a daughter, who was called by her name Berenice, and she was raised [to the rank of] Queen, **24** and it happened that this goddess, who was a virgin, entered heaven suddenly. And the priests, who came from [all parts of] Egypt to the King year by year, came to the place where His Majesty was, and they straightway made a great mourning because of the event which had happened (*i.e.* the death of the Princess). They made supplication before the King and Queen—having the intention in their hearts—to allow **25** this goddess to rest with Osiris in the temple of Pegut, which is among the temples of the first order, because it is the greatest temple of them all, and because it is the principal place of worship of the King and the inhabitants of Ta-Mer-t, all of them. Now when Osiris in the Sektt Boat is [permitted] to enter into this temple, at the [appointed] time of the year, from the temple of Åmen of Garb,

26 from Re-ḥent,[1] on the twenty-ninth day of the fourth month[2] of the season Akht, all those who are in the temples of the first rank offer up burnt offerings upon the altars of the temples of the first rank, on the right hand and on the left in the forecourt of this temple. [And] after these things everything which it is customary to do was done, in respect of the deification of the Princess, and they performed on her behalf the purification of her mourning **27** in splendid fashion (or, in a worshipful manner). Their hearts were on fire even as is customary for Apis and Mnevis.[3]

XIII.—DIVINE HONOURS SIMILAR TO THOSE WHICH ARE PAID TO THE DAUGHTER OF THE SUN-GOD RĀ, ARE TO BE PAID TO THE PRINCESS BERENICE

They (*i.e.* the priests) came to a decision to pay perpetual honours to Princess Berenice, the daughter of the two Well-Doing Gods, in all the temples throughout Egypt. For it happened that she entered in among the gods in the first month of the season Per-t,[4] and it was in this same month **28** that, in times of old, the daughter

[1] A name for the mouth of the Canopic arm of the Nile.

[2] In Coptic **χοιαϩκ**.

[3] *I.e.* they regarded the dead princess as holy, and they buried her with the same care as they would have buried an Apis Bull or a Mnevis Bull.

[4] In Coptic **τωβε**.

of the Sun-god Rā entered heaven—now he called her name "Eye of Rā" and "Meḥent," the uraeus on his forehead, because he loved her, and they (*i.e.* the priests) in days of old celebrated festivals in her honour, and made processions of boats, in the great temples among the temples of the first order in this month, wherein the deification of Her Majesty (*i.e.* the daughter of Rā) took place. And a festival, and a boat-procession, shall be made for Princess Berenice, the daughter of **29** the two Well-Doing Gods, in all the temples throughout Egypt, in the first month of the season Per-t, beginning on the seventeenth day, and the boat-procession shall last four days, and the ceremony of the purification of her mourning shall be [performed] as on the first occasion.

XIV.—A GOLD STATUE OF THE PRINCESS BERENICE, TO BE CARRIED IN PROCESSIONS, WITH A SPECIAL CROWN, IS TO BE MADE

And they shall set up a divine statue of this goddess [made] of gold and inlaid with every kind of precious stone, in every temple of the first order and in every temple of the second order, and its **30** pedestal (?) shall be placed in the house of the god. A Ḥem priest, or one of the priests who are selected for [service] in the august holy place, to array the gods in their apparel, shall on the day of the festival in which the gods are carried in procession, and at the festivals of all the gods, carry the statue in the procession held in the embrace of his arms, so that all the people may see how the statue is adored in its sanctity. The name of the statue shall be called " Berenice, **31** Queen of the Virgins." The crown which is on the head of the divine statue shall not be like that which is on the head[s] of the statues of her mother, the Horus Berenice.[1] It shall be made of two ears of corn, with an uraeus between them. Behind the uraeus shall be an upright stalk of papyrus, similar to that which the goddesses hold in their hands. The tail of the uraeus shall be twined round **32** this stalk so that the appearance (?) of the crown shall proclaim the name of Berenice according to the characters [found] in the writings of the House of Life.[2]

XV.—A SECOND GOLD STATUE OF BERENICE SHALL BE SET UP, AND THE PRIESTLY VIRGINS SHALL PAY HONOUR TO IT

Moreover, when the days of the Gaȧugaȧu [mysteries of Isis ?] are celebrated in the fourth month of the season of Akht, before the boat-procession of Osiris, the virgins and women of

[1] Ptolemy was called Horus, and Berenice was the female Horus .

[2] The characters referred to are clearly hieroglyphs, but it is equally clear that they must have had in Ptolemaïc times phonetic values different from those given to them in Pharaohic times.

the priests shall cause another statue of Berenice, the Queen of Virgins, to be made, and burnt offerings shall be offered up, **33** and all the other offerings which it is customary to make on days of festival shall also be made. And it is [permitted] to other virgins to act in a similar manner in respect of these things for this goddess at their good pleasure. And this goddess shall be hymned also by the Shemāit priestesses who are chosen to minister to the gods, and they shall be crowned with the crowns of the gods whose priestesses they are. When also the harvest cometh these priestesses shall take first of all ears of corn and shall carry them forward and **34** present them to the divine statue of this goddess. And her KA shall be praised by companies of singers, both men and women, daily, and at all the festivals and processions of the gods, with the hymns which have been composed and chosen by the sages of the House of Life, and have been given to the directors who train the singers, and are written likewise upon the rolls [of papyri] of the House of Life.

XVI.—PROVISION SHALL BE MADE FOR THE DAUGHTERS OF THE PRIESTS. THE "CAKES OF BERENICE"

Now seeing that [food from] the divine offerings is granted to the priests in the temples, when they are introduced **35** by the King into the house of the god, it is permitted to give subsistence to the women-children of the priests [from the day when they are born] from the divine offerings of the gods, together with the food which is allotted [to them] by the priestly stewards in all the temples, in proportion to the offerings [made]. The bread which is given **36** to the women of the priests shall be made and distinguished as *qefen* bread, and its name shall be called " Bread of Berenice."

XVII.—THE MANNER OF PUBLICATION OF THE DECREE

Let this Decree be written (or, copied) by councillors (or, directors, or stewards) in the temples, and the governors of the temples, and the scribes of the house of the god. And let it be engraved upon a tablet **37** of stone or copper (brass ?) in the writing of the House of Life (*i.e.* in hieroglyphs), and in the writing of books (*i.e.* Demotic), and in the writing of the Greeks. [The tablet] shall be set up in the courtyard of the people, in [each of] the temples of the first order, and in the temples of the second order, and in the temples of the third order, so that every person whatsoever may be made to see the honour which is paid by the priests of the temples of Egypt to the two Well-Doing Gods and to their children in the manner which is right and customary.

II

THE DECREE OF THE PRIESTHOOD ASSEMBLED AT MEMPHIS IN HONOUR OF PTOLEMY IV PHILOPATOR

The existence of this DECREE became known to the learned world through the purchase of a fragment of a copy of it cut upon a grey granite stele which the Egyptian Museum in CAIRO acquired from a native dealer in 1902. It is now numbered 35635. The texts on the fragment were published by AHMAD BEY KAMÂL and W. SPIEGELBERG in the *Catalogue générale*, in the section of that work entitled *Stèles ptolémaïques et romaines*, Cairo, 1904–5, vol. i, p. 218, and vol. ii, plate LXXIV, No. 31088 (see notes 2 and 3 in H. GAUTHIER and H. SOTTAS in their *Décret trilingue*, Cairo, 1925, p. v). In April, 1923, some natives of ABÛ SUWÊR, who were digging out soil at TALL AL-MASKHÛṬAH, to use as top-dressing for their fields, discovered by accident a large fragment, about one-half, of a sandstone stele inscribed with portions of the versions of the Decree in Greek, Demotic and hieroglyph. This monument is now in the Egyptian Museum in Cairo, and bears the No. 47806, and is commonly known as Pithom Stele, No. II.

On the rounded portion of the stele is sculptured the winged disk of Horus of Beḥuṭt and Horus of Mesen, and below the disk is a vertical cartouche containing the name and titles of Ptolemy IV Philopator. On the left are figures of the King and his sister-wife Arsinoë. The King is mounted on horseback, and is spearing with his long Macedonian lance a kneeling prisoner, who is thrust towards him by the god Tem, or Atem. This god, who is styled " life of Tjeku,  " (Succoth ?), is promising to give to the King long life, and power, and many Seṭ Festivals. Behind Temu are figures of Osiris, Ḥer-smai-taui, Horus of Ān, Hathor and Isis. The hieroglyphic text is cut below the sculptured portion of the stele, the Demotic is on the back, and the Greek on the side. For a full description see Gauthier and Sottas, *Un Décret trilingue en l'honneur de Ptolémée IV*, Cairo, 1925.

Curiously enough, the Demotic version of the Decree, which contains 42 lines, is in an almost complete state, and from it the general historical contents of the Decree can be ascertained, though there are words and passages in it which have not, up to the present, been translated satisfactorily. The first scholar to work at it was Sottas, who published a facsimile of the text with a transliteration, and a French translation, and an elaborate commentary in the work mentioned above (pp. 32–64). A German translation of the Demotic text was made and published by W. SPIEGELBERG under the title of "Beiträge zur Erklärung des neuen dreisprachigen Priesterdekretes zu Ehren des Ptolemaios Philopator" (see the *Sitzungsberichte der Bayerischen Akademie der Wissenschaften, Philosophisch-philologische und historische Klasse,* Jahrgang 1925, 4 Abhandlungen, München, 1925). From the translation of the last-named scholar the following English rendering has been made :—

PRIESTLY DECREE IN HONOUR OF PTOLEMY IV PHILOPATOR

[I.—THE DATING OF THE DECREE]

1 On the first day of the month of ARTEMESIOS, which is, according to the reckoning of the Egyptians, the first day of the month of PAOPHI, in the sixth year of the Young HORUS, the strong one, whom his father caused to appear as the PHARAOH (KING), the lord of the uraei (*i.e.* the two crowns, each with a cobra), whose might is great,

2 who is pious of heart towards the gods, who protecteth men (or, mankind), who is over his enemies,[1] who maketh EGYPT happy and illumineth the temples with light, who

[1] The allusion is to HORUS, who, having conquered Seṭ, stood upon his back.

stablisheth the laws which THOTH, the Great-Great, the lord of the Seṭ festivals,
3 like unto PTAḤ, the Great, the Pharaoh like unto PHRE (the Sun-god Rā), Pharaoh of the Upper Country and of the Lower Country (Upper and Lower Egypt), son of the Gods, the Well-doers (*i.e.* PTOLEMY III and Queen BERENICE), whom PTAḤ hath chosen [to be Pharaoh], to whom PHRA hath given victories, the living image [of ÅMEN],
4 the Pharaoh PTRUMIS (PTOLEMAIOS), the ever-living, beloved of ISIS—when PTOLEMY, the son of AEROPOS, was priest of Alexander, and of the Brother Gods, and of the Gods, the Well-doers, and [RHODA (?)],
5 daughter of PURN, was canephoros of the brother-loving Arsinoë.

[II.—THE ASSEMBLING OF THE PRIESTS AT MEMPHIS]

On this day DECREE:
The chief priests, and the prophets, and the priests, who enter into the holy-of-holies to robe [the gods],
6 and the writers of the BOOKS OF THE GODS (*i.e.* the fan-bearers), and the scribes of the House of Life (*i.e.* the sacred scribes), and the other priests who have come from the temples of EGYPT to MEMPHIS to stand before the

Pharaoh at the time when he returned to EGYPT in order to present to him bouquets of flowers, and the Talismans . . .

7 and to offer sacrifices, and burnt offerings, and libations, and to perform the other things which it is customary to perform on the occasion of such a festival, these having gathered themselves together in the temple of MEMPHIS declare, [saying],

[III.—THE REASONS FOR MAKING THIS DECREE]

Inasmuch as it hath happened that the beneficence of Pharaoh, [PTOLEMY, the son of]

8 PTOLEMY and the (Pharaohess) (Queen) ARSINOË (*sic*),[1] the Gods, the Well-doers, hath conferred benefits on the service of the gods, and hath shown concern at all times for that which appertaineth to their worship, it hath come to pass that [all] the gods [of EGYPT]

9 and their goddesses, were present with him, and showed him the road, and protected him at the time when he was marching to the country of the ASSYRIANS (*i.e.* SYRIANS), and the country of the people of KHOR (*i.e.* the PHOENICIANS). They made him see revelations, and made announcements to him, and gave him an oracle through a dream, saying

[1] Read "BERENICE."

that he would overcome his enemies, and [that they would never]
10 be far away from him in times of danger, but would be a protection to him to keep him safe.

[IV.—THE BATTLE OF RAPHIA]

On the first day of the month of Pachons, in the fifth year [of his reign], he marched out from Pelusium and fought with Antiochus at a city called Raphia,
11 near the frontier of Egypt, which lies to the east of Bethelea and Pasanufer. On the tenth day of the same month he defeated him in a great and splendid manner. Those of his enemies who in the course of this fight drew close to him
12 he laid out dead before him, even as in days of old Horus, the son of Isis, had done with his foes. He pressed Antiochus so closely that he was obliged to throw away his crown and his royal hat (helmet ?). He fled with his bodyguard (?), there being only a very few [men] who stayed with him,
13 after his defeat in a miserable and sad manner. The greater number of his soldiers suffered sore want. He saw the best of his friends perish in a miserable fashion. They suffered
14 hunger and thirst. Everything that he left behind him was seized as booty (or, spoil). Only with the greatest exertion was he able to reach his home, and he suffered bitter grief.

[V.—THE SPOIL CAPTURED BY PTOLEMY IV]

Pharaoh took as spoil many people and all the elephants. He made himself master of much gold and silver, and valuable possessions, which

15 were found in the various places which ANTIOCHUS had captured, and which had been brought there under his rule. Pharaoh made them all to be carried to Egypt.

[VI.—PTOLEMY'S TRIUMPHAL PROGRESS THROUGH THE COUNTRY]

Pharaoh made a progress through the other regions which were in his (*i.e.* Antiochus's) kingdom. He went into the temples which were there.

16 He offered burnt offerings and libations, and all the inhabitants who were in the cities received him with joyful hearts, and made feasts, and awaited his arrival with the shrines of the gods—in whose hearts is strength—and they crowned themselves with crowns, and offered up burnt offerings, and offerings of cakes (?).

[VII.—THE HONOURS PAID TO PTOLEMY IV]

17 Many people brought him a gold crown, and announced that they intended to set up a royal statue in his honour, and to build a temple. It came to pass that the King was on the path of a man of God.

[VIII.—PTOLEMY'S CARE FOR THE EGYPTIAN TEMPLES IN SYRIA]

The statues of the gods which were in the temples, and had been damaged by ANTIOCHUS,
18 Pharaoh commanded others to be made in their stead, and set in their places. He gave much gold, and silver, and precious stones for them, and also for the equipment of the temples which those men had carried off, and he concerned himself to have them replaced. The properties
19 which had been given in olden time to the temples, and which had become greatly reduced, Pharaoh commanded to be restored to their original values. In order that nothing might be wanting in respect of that which it was customary to do for the gods, as soon as he heard that much injury had been done to the images (or, bas-reliefs) of the Egyptian gods,
20 he issued a splendid order to the regions over which he ruled outside Egypt, that no man should do them further injury, wishing that every alien should understand the greatness of the consideration which was in his heart for the gods of Egypt. The bodies (*i.e.* mummies) of those (*i.e.* the sacred animals) which were found [there] he caused
21 to be transported to EGYPT, and he caused them to be prepared for burial with honour,

and to be buried in their tombs. Moreover, those which were found to be damaged he caused to be brought back with due ceremony and honour to EGYPT, and conducted into their temples. Moreover, he gave careful thought

22 for the images of the gods, which had been carried out of EGYPT into the territory of the ASSYRIANS (*i.e.* SYRIANS), and the territory of the people of KHOR (*i.e.* PHOENICIA), at the time when the MEDES laid waste the temples of EGYPT. He commanded that careful search should be made for them. Those which were found, in addition to those which his father had brought back to EGYPT, he caused to be brought back to Egypt, and at the same time

23 he celebrated a feast [in their honour], and offered up a burnt offering before them. He caused them to be restored to their temples wherefrom in past times they had been carried off.

[IX.—PTOLEMY ESTABLISHES A FORTIFIED CAMP IN SYRIA]

He caused a fortified camp for his troops to be made, and he remained there as long as

24 his enemies wished to come to fight against him. He passed many days outside that same

place. As soon as they were good again he released his troops. They plundered their cities. As they could not protect them they destroyed them so that it might be apparent to all men that it was the might of the gods which had done this thing, and

25 that it was a sinful thing to fight against him. He marched away from that region, having made himself master of all their settlements in 21 days. After the treason (defection ?) of the officers of the troops he made a treaty with Antiochus for two years and two months. He returned to Egypt

26 on the Feast of Lamps, the Birthday of Horus (October 12 ?), after a campaign of four months. The inhabitants of Egypt welcomed him and were glad because he had protected the temples and had also delivered all the people in Egypt. They did everything which was necessary for his reception, in the lavish and splendid

27 fashion which was appropriate to his heroic deeds. He journeyed through Egypt in a barge (or, ship), and those who were in the temple waited for him at the landing-places (or, quays) with the equipment and the other things which men are accustomed to bring on such a journey, and they were crowned with garlands, and celebrated a festival, and brought

[X.—PTOLEMY RE-ENDOWS THE TEMPLES]

28 burnt offerings, and drink offerings, and many sacrificial gifts. He went into the temples and offered up a burnt offering. He gave many revenues in addition to those which he had given at an earlier period. The images of the gods, which had been for a long time wanting among those which were in shrines, and also those which had been somewhat damaged, he caused

29 others to be set in their places, [and made them to be] as they were formerly. He expended much gold and precious stones on these and on all the other things which they needed. He caused much temple-furniture and equipment to be made of gold and silver, although he had already incurred a vast expense for that campaign, and had given 300,000 pieces of gold in the form of golden crowns

30 to his Army. He bestowed upon the priests, and the dwellers in the temples (temple-servants ?), and the other inhabitants throughout EGYPT many benefactions, and at the same time thanked the gods, that they had fulfilled for him everything which they had promised him.

[XI.—THE DECREE OF THE PRIESTS]

31 WITH GOOD LUCK!

It hath entered into the hearts of the priests of the temples of EGYPT, the honours which are paid to Pharaoh PTOLEMY, the ever-living, the beloved of ISIS, and to his sister, the Pharaohess (Queen) ARSINOË, the Father-Loving Gods, in the temples, and those which are paid to the Gods, the Well-doers, who begot them,
32 and those which are paid to the Brother Gods and to the Saviour Gods, their forefathers, to increase. And a royal statue of Pharaoh PTOLEMY, the everliving, the beloved of Isis, shall be set up, and it shall be called "PTOLEMY, the Avenger of his Father, whose victory is beautiful,"
33 and also a statue of his sister, ARSINOË, the Father-Loving Gods, in the temples of Egypt, in each and in every temple, in the most conspicuous part of the temple, and they shall be made in the Egyptian style. And they shall cause a statue [of the City-god]
34 to be seen in the temple, and they shall set it up by the side of the table of offerings (altar ?) at which the royal statue of the Pharaoh stands, [the City-god] giving him (*i.e.* the Pharaoh) a sword of victory. The priests who are in the temples shall minister to the statues

thrice daily, and shall set the temple equipments before them, and for them

35 shall perform the other ceremonics which are right and proper just as they are performed for the other gods during their festivals and processions and the days appointed [by law]. The figure of the Pharaoh which is painted (*sic*) on the stele, and which shall be painted (*sic*) above the text [of the Decree], shall represent him mounted upon a horse, clad in a suit of armour, and he shall appear wearing the crown of Pharaoh.

36 And he shall be represented in the act of spearing a kneeling figure of a king with a long spear in his hand, which shall resemble the spear which the victorious Pharaoh used in battle. And they (*i.e.* the priests) shall celebrate a festival and [make a] procession in the temples, and in all Egypt, in honour of Pharaoh Ptolemy, the everliving, the beloved of Isis,

37 from the tenth day of the month Pachons, the day whereon Pharaoh conquered his enemy (?), for five days, yearly, and they shall wear garlands, and offer up burnt offerings and drink offerings, and do the other things which it is right and proper to do, and they shall do according to the beautiful command . . .

38 . . . The shrines of the Father-Loving Gods shall be exhibited in procession on these days,

and a bouquet of flowers shall be brought to Pharaoh in the temple on these aforementioned days. Inasmuch as it happened that Pharaoh [PTOLEMY, the everliving, the beloved of ISIS] . . .

39 . . . the Saviour Gods, to whom he had paid honour on that day, having already paid them honour, and the priests shall keep the first ten days in every month as a festival, and they shall offer up burnt offerings and drink offerings, and they [shall do the other things which it is right and proper to do at the other festivals]

40 on these days in each month. That which is prepared for the burnt offerings shall be distributed among [all those who perform service in the temple, . . . the priests, and the scribes . . .]

[The last two lines are much mutilated, but they seem to have contained an order from the priests to the effect that on the ten days burnt offerings, etc., similar to those which it was customary to offer to the great gods on the days of their festivals, must be offered to the statue of Pharaoh PTOLEMY, the everliving, the beloved of Isis, which is called "Pharaoh PTOLEMY, the Avenger of his Father," whose victory is beautiful, so that it may be made manifest to everyone that all who are in EGYPT honour the Father-Loving Gods.]

BIBLIOGRAPHY

ÅKERBLAD, J. D. *Lettre sur l'inscription égyptienne de Rosette*, Paris, 1802.

AMEILHON, H. P. *Eclaircissement*, Paris, 1803.

BAILEY, J. *Hieroglyphicorum origo et natura*, Cambridge, 1816.

BAILLET, A. *Le Décret de Memphis*, Paris, 1905.

BIRCH, S. *Sur quelques groupes hiéroglyphiques*, Paris, 1848.

On the lost book of Chacremon on hieroglyphics, London, 1850.

An introduction to the study of the Egyptian hieroglyphs, London, 1857.

Decree of Canopus, London, 1870.

The Greek inscription on the Rosetta Stone, London, (date ?).

BRIÈRE, DE. *Essai sur le symbolisme antique d'Orient*, Paris, 1847.

BRUGSCH, H. K. *Die Inschrift von Rosette* (Demotic text), Berlin, 1850.

Inscriptio Rosettana hieroglyphica, Berlin, 1851.

BUDGE, E. A. WALLIS. *The Decrees of Memphis and Canopus*, 3 vols., London, 1904 (contains the Rosetta Stone and the Stele of Ṣân).

The Rosetta Stone, London, 1913.

CAUSSIN, N. *De Symbolica Aegyptiorum sapientia*, Paris, 1618.

CHABAS, F. J. *L'inscription hiéroglyphique de Rosette*, Châlon-sur-Saône, 1867.

Le décret de Canope, Paris, 1883.

CHAMPOLLION, J. F. *Lettre à M. Dacier*, Paris, 1822.

Précis du système hiéroglyphique, Paris, 1824.

[A revised and enlarged edition of this work appeared at Paris in 1827–8.]

CHAMPOLLION-FIGEAC, J. J. *Écriture démotique égyptienne*, Paris, 1843.

CORY, A. T. *The hieroglyphics of Horapollo Nilous*, London, 1840.

DITTENBERGER, W. *Orientis graeci inscriptiones selectae*, Bd. I, No. 56.

DULAURIER, E. *Examen de quelques points*, Paris, 1852.

ERMAN, J. P. A. *Die Entzifferung der Hieroglyphen*, Berlin, 1922.

GREPPO, J. G. HONORÉ. *Essai sur système hiéroglyphique de M. Champollion*, Paris, 1829.

GROFF, W. *Les deux versions démotiques du décret de Canope*, Paris, 1888.

Le décret de Canope, Paris, 1891.

GULYANOV, I. A. *Essai sur les hiéroglyphes d'Horapollon*, Paris, 1827.

Archéologie Égyptienne, Leipzig, 1839.

HARTLEBEN, H. *Champollion: sein Leben und sein Werk*, Berlin, 1906.

HESS, J. J. *Der Demotische Teil der Dreisprachigen Inscrift von Rosette*, Strassburg, 1902.

HINCKS, E. *On the true date of the Rosetta Stone*, Dublin, 1841.

An attempt to ascertain the number, names and powers of the . . . Egyptian Alphabet, Dublin, 1848.

HORAPOLLO, N. See CORY, A. T., and LEEMANS, CONRAD.

IDELER, J. L. *Hermapion*, Leipzig, 1841.

JANNELLI, C. *Tabulae Rosettanae*, Naples, 1830.

KIRCHER, A. *Obeliscus Pamphilius*, Rome, 1650.

Oedipus Aegyptiacus, Rome, 1652–1654.

Obelisci Aegyptiaci, Rome, 1666.

Sphinx mystagoga, Amsterdam, 1676.

KLAPROTH, J. H. *Lettre sur la découverte des hiéroglyphes aerologiques*, Paris, 1827.

Seconde lettre, Paris, 1827.

Examen critique, Paris, 1832.

KOSEGARTEN, J. G. L. *De prisca Aegyptiorum litteratura*, Vimar, 1828.

KRALL, J. *Demotische Lesestücke*, Vienna, 1903.

LACOUR, P. *Fragmens*, Bordeaux, 1821.

LEEMANS, CONRAD. *Horapollinis Niloi hieroglyphica*, Amsterdam, 1835.

LEGGE, G. F. *The history of the transliteration of Egyptian*, London, 1902.

LENORMANT, C. *Recherches sur . . . l'utilité actuelle des hiéroglyphes d'Horapollon*, Paris, 1838.

LEPSIUS, R. *Ueber die in Philae aufgefundene Republikation des Dekretes von Rosette*, Leipzig, 1847.

Das bilingue Dekret von Kanopus, Berlin, 1866.

Das Sothisdatum, Leipzig, 1868.

Die Kalenderreform, Leipzig, 1869.

LETRONNE, J. A. *Inscription grecque de Rosette*, Paris, 1840.

MAHAFFY, J. P. *The Rosetta Stone*, Washington, 1902.

MAHLER, E. *Das Dekret von Kanopus*, London, 1893.

ORCURTI, P. C. *Discorso sulla storia dell' ermeneutica egizia*, Turin, 1863.

PALIN, N. G. *Essai sur les hiéroglyphes*, Weimar, 1804.

De l'étude des hiéroglyphes, Paris, 1812.

Nouvelles recherches, Florence, 1830.

PAUTHIER, J. P. G. *Sinico-Aegyptiaca*, Paris, 1842.

PIERRET, P. *Le décret trilingue de Canope*, Paris, 1881.

PLEYTE, W. *Zur Geschichte der Hieroglyphenschrift*, Leipzig, 1890.

REINISCH, S. L., and ROESLER, E. R. *Die Zweisprachige Inschrift von Tanis*, Vienna, 1866.

RENOUF, P. LE PAGE. *Seyffarth and Uhlemann*, London, 1859.

REVILLOUT, EUGÈNE. *Étude historique*, Paris, 1877.

Les deux versions démotiques du Décret de Canope, Leyden, 1885.

Les deux versions hiéroglyphiques du Décret de Rosette, Paris, 1911.

ROSELLINI, I. *Il sistema geroglifico del . . . Champollion*, Pisa, 1825.

ROUGÉ, E. DE. *Lettre à M. de Saulcy*, Paris, 1848.

SACY, A. I. SILVESTRE DE. *Lettre au Citoyen Chaptal*, Paris, 1802.

Notice [a criticism of works by Champollion and Young], Paris, 1825.

SALT, H. *Essay*, London, 1825.

SALVOLINI, F. *Analyse grammaticale*, Paris, 1836.

SAULCY, L. F. J. C. DE. *Analyse grammatical du Texte Démotique du Décret de Rosette*, Paris, 1845.

De l'étude des hiéroglyphes, Paris, 1846.

Examen des écrits de Klaproth, Paris, 1846.

Seconde lettre à M. Letronne, Paris, 1846.

Lettre à M. Ampère, Paris, 1847.

SCHWARTZE, M. G. *Das alte Aegypten*, Leipzig, 1843.

SETHE, KURT. *Zur Geschichte und Erklärung der Rosettana*, Berlin, 1916.

Urkunden des aegyptischen Altertums, Bd. II, No. 36.

SEYFFARTH, GUSTAV. *Rudimenta hieroglyphices*, Leipzig, 1826.

Grammatica Aegyptiaca, Gotha, 1855.

SHARPE, S. *Egyptian hieroglyphics*, London, 1861.

The Decree of Canopus, London, 1870.

SPIEGELBERG, W. *Das Verhältnis der griechischen und ägyptischen Texte in den zweisprachigen Dekreten von Rosette und Kanopus*, Berlin, 1922.

Der demotische Text der Priesterdekret von Kanopus und Memphis (*Rosettana*), Heidelberg, 1922.

SPINETO. *Lectures*, London, 1829.

SPOHN, F. A. W. *De lingua et literis veterum Aegyptiorum*, Leipzig, 1825–31.

UHLEMANN, M. A. *Inscriptionis Rosettanae hieroglyphicae decretum sacerdotale*, etc., Leipzig, 1853.

VALERIANO BOLZANI, G. P. *Hieroglyphica*, Leyden, 1586.

YOUNG, T. *An account of some recent discoveries*, London, 1823.

INDEX

In the transliteration of Oriental proper names and words, Ḥ represents a sharp but smooth guttural aspirate; Ṭ is a strongly articulated palatal T; Ṣ is a strongly articulated S, something like *ss* in *hiss*; Ḳ is a strongly articulated guttural K; an apostrophe before a letter (*e.g.* 'A) is the spiritus lenis of the Greeks, and an inverted comma (*e.g.* ʻA) is a strong guttural, like the Hebrew ע, which is unpronounceable by Europeans. Long vowels are marked by a circumflex.

A CATALOG OF SELECTED

DOVER BOOKS

IN ALL FIELDS OF INTEREST

A CATALOG OF SELECTED DOVER BOOKS IN ALL FIELDS OF INTEREST

THE CLARINET AND CLARINET PLAYING, David Pino. Lively, comprehensive work features suggestions about technique, musicianship, and musical interpretation, as well as guidelines for teaching, making your own reeds, and preparing for public performance. Includes an intriguing look at clarinet history. "A godsend," *The Clarinet,* Journal of the International Clarinet Society. Appendixes. 7 illus. 320pp. 5$\frac{3}{8}$ x 8$\frac{1}{2}$. 0-486-40270-3

HOLLYWOOD GLAMOR PORTRAITS, John Kobal (ed.). 145 photos from 1926-49. Harlow, Gable, Bogart, Bacall; 94 stars in all. Full background on photographers, technical aspects. 160pp. 8$\frac{3}{8}$ x 11$\frac{1}{4}$. 0-486-23352-9

THE RAVEN AND OTHER FAVORITE POEMS, Edgar Allan Poe. Over 40 of the author's most memorable poems: "The Bells," "Ulalume," "Israfel," "To Helen," "The Conqueror Worm," "Eldorado," "Annabel Lee," many more. Alphabetic lists of titles and first lines. 64pp. 5$\frac{3}{16}$ x 8$\frac{1}{4}$. 0-486-26685-0

PERSONAL MEMOIRS OF U. S. GRANT, Ulysses Simpson Grant. Intelligent, deeply moving firsthand account of Civil War campaigns, considered by many the finest military memoirs ever written. Includes letters, historic photographs, maps and more. 528pp. 6$\frac{1}{8}$ x 9$\frac{1}{4}$. 0-486-28587-1

ANCIENT EGYPTIAN MATERIALS AND INDUSTRIES, A. Lucas and J. Harris. Fascinating, comprehensive, thoroughly documented text describes this ancient civilization's vast resources and the processes that incorporated them in daily life, including the use of animal products, building materials, cosmetics, perfumes and incense, fibers, glazed ware, glass and its manufacture, materials used in the mummification process, and much more. 544pp. 6$\frac{1}{8}$ x 9$\frac{1}{4}$. (Available in U.S. only.) 0-486-40446-3

RUSSIAN STORIES/RUSSKIE RASSKAZY: A Dual-Language Book, edited by Gleb Struve. Twelve tales by such masters as Chekhov, Tolstoy, Dostoevsky, Pushkin, others. Excellent word-for-word English translations on facing pages, plus teaching and study aids, Russian/English vocabulary, biographical/critical introductions, more. 416pp. 5$\frac{3}{8}$ x 8$\frac{1}{2}$. 0-486-26244-8

PHILADELPHIA THEN AND NOW: 60 Sites Photographed in the Past and Present, Kenneth Finkel and Susan Oyama. Rare photographs of City Hall, Logan Square, Independence Hall, Betsy Ross House, other landmarks juxtaposed with contemporary views. Captures changing face of historic city. Introduction. Captions. 128pp. 8$\frac{1}{4}$ x 11. 0-486-25790-8

NORTH AMERICAN INDIAN LIFE: Customs and Traditions of 23 Tribes, Elsie Clews Parsons (ed.). 27 fictionalized essays by noted anthropologists examine religion, customs, government, additional facets of life among the Winnebago, Crow, Zuni, Eskimo, other tribes. 480pp. 6$\frac{1}{8}$ x 9$\frac{1}{4}$. 0-486-27377-6

TECHNICAL MANUAL AND DICTIONARY OF CLASSICAL BALLET, Gail Grant. Defines, explains, comments on steps, movements, poses and concepts. 15-page pictorial section. Basic book for student, viewer. 127pp. 5$\frac{3}{8}$ x 8$\frac{1}{2}$. 0-486-21843-0

THE MALE AND FEMALE FIGURE IN MOTION: 60 Classic Photographic Sequences, Eadweard Muybridge. 60 true-action photographs of men and women walking, running, climbing, bending, turning, etc., reproduced from rare 19th-century masterpiece. vi + 121pp. 9 x 12. 0-486-24745-7

ANIMALS: 1,419 Copyright-Free Illustrations of Mammals, Birds, Fish, Insects, etc., Jim Harter (ed.). Clear wood engravings present, in extremely lifelike poses, over 1,000 species of animals. One of the most extensive pictorial sourcebooks of its kind. Captions. Index. 284pp. 9 x 12. 0-486-23766-4

1001 QUESTIONS ANSWERED ABOUT THE SEASHORE, N. J. Berrill and Jacquelyn Berrill. Queries answered about dolphins, sea snails, sponges, starfish, fishes, shore birds, many others. Covers appearance, breeding, growth, feeding, much more. 305pp. 5¼ x 8¼. 0-486-23366-9

ATTRACTING BIRDS TO YOUR YARD, William J. Weber. Easy-to-follow guide offers advice on how to attract the greatest diversity of birds: birdhouses, feeders, water and waterers, much more. 96pp. 5³⁄₁₆ x 8¼. 0-486-28927-3

MEDICINAL AND OTHER USES OF NORTH AMERICAN PLANTS: A Historical Survey with Special Reference to the Eastern Indian Tribes, Charlotte Erichsen-Brown. Chronological historical citations document 500 years of usage of plants, trees, shrubs native to eastern Canada, northeastern U.S. Also complete identifying information. 343 illustrations. 544pp. 6½ x 9¼. 0-486-25951-X

STORYBOOK MAZES, Dave Phillips. 23 stories and mazes on two-page spreads: Wizard of Oz, Treasure Island, Robin Hood, etc. Solutions. 64pp. 8¼ x 11. 0-486-23628-5

AMERICAN NEGRO SONGS: 230 Folk Songs and Spirituals, Religious and Secular, John W. Work. This authoritative study traces the African influences of songs sung and played by black Americans at work, in church, and as entertainment. The author discusses the lyric significance of such songs as "Swing Low, Sweet Chariot," "John Henry," and others and offers the words and music for 230 songs. Bibliography. Index of Song Titles. 272pp. 6½ x 9¼. 0-486-40271-1

MOVIE-STAR PORTRAITS OF THE FORTIES, John Kobal (ed.). 163 glamor, studio photos of 106 stars of the 1940s: Rita Hayworth, Ava Gardner, Marlon Brando, Clark Gable, many more. 176pp. 8⅜ x 11¼. 0-486-23546-7

YEKL and THE IMPORTED BRIDEGROOM AND OTHER STORIES OF YIDDISH NEW YORK, Abraham Cahan. Film Hester Street based on *Yekl* (1896). Novel, other stories among first about Jewish immigrants on N.Y.'s East Side. 240pp. 5⅜ x 8½. 0-486-22427-9

SELECTED POEMS, Walt Whitman. Generous sampling from *Leaves of Grass*. Twenty-four poems include "I Hear America Singing," "Song of the Open Road," "I Sing the Body Electric," "When Lilacs Last in the Dooryard Bloom'd," "O Captain! My Captain!"–all reprinted from an authoritative edition. Lists of titles and first lines. 128pp. 5³⁄₁₆ x 8¼. 0-486-26878-0

SONGS OF EXPERIENCE: Facsimile Reproduction with 26 Plates in Full Color, William Blake. 26 full-color plates from a rare 1826 edition. Includes "The Tyger," "London," "Holy Thursday," and other poems. Printed text of poems. 48pp. 5¼ x 7. 0-486-24636-1

THE BEST TALES OF HOFFMANN, E. T. A. Hoffmann. 10 of Hoffmann's most important stories: "Nutcracker and the King of Mice," "The Golden Flowerpot," etc. 458pp. 5⅜ x 8½. 0-486-21793-0

THE BOOK OF TEA, Kakuzo Okakura. Minor classic of the Orient: entertaining, charming explanation, interpretation of traditional Japanese culture in terms of tea ceremony. 94pp. 5⅜ x 8½. 0-486-20070-1

HOW TO DO BEADWORK, Mary White. Fundamental book on craft from simple projects to five-bead chains and woven works. 106 illustrations. 142pp. 5⅜ x 8. 0-486-20697-1

THE 1912 AND 1915 GUSTAV STICKLEY FURNITURE CATALOGS, Gustav Stickley. With over 200 detailed illustrations and descriptions, these two catalogs are essential reading and reference materials and identification guides for Stickley furniture. Captions cite materials, dimensions and prices. 112pp. 6½ x 9¼. 0-486-26676-1

EARLY AMERICAN LOCOMOTIVES, John H. White, Jr. Finest locomotive engravings from early 19th century: historical (1804–74), main-line (after 1870), special, foreign, etc. 147 plates. 142pp. 11⅜ x 8¼. 0-486-22772-3

LITTLE BOOK OF EARLY AMERICAN CRAFTS AND TRADES, Peter Stockham (ed.). 1807 children's book explains crafts and trades: baker, hatter, cooper, potter, and many others. 23 copperplate illustrations. 140pp. 4⅝ x 6. 0-486-23336-7

VICTORIAN FASHIONS AND COSTUMES FROM HARPER'S BAZAR, 1867–1898, Stella Blum (ed.). Day costumes, evening wear, sports clothes, shoes, hats, other accessories in over 1,000 detailed engravings. 320pp. 9⅜ x 12¼. 0-486-22990-4

THE LONG ISLAND RAIL ROAD IN EARLY PHOTOGRAPHS, Ron Ziel. Over 220 rare photos, informative text document origin (1844) and development of rail service on Long Island. Vintage views of early trains, locomotives, stations, passengers, crews, much more. Captions. 8⅞ x 11¾. 0-486-26301-0

VOYAGE OF THE LIBERDADE, Joshua Slocum. Great 19th-century mariner's thrilling, first-hand account of the wreck of his ship off South America, the 35-foot boat he built from the wreckage, and its remarkable voyage home. 128pp. 5⅜ x 8½. 0-486-40022-0

TEN BOOKS ON ARCHITECTURE, Vitruvius. The most important book ever written on architecture. Early Roman aesthetics, technology, classical orders, site selection, all other aspects. Morgan translation. 331pp. 5⅜ x 8½. 0-486-20645-9

THE HUMAN FIGURE IN MOTION, Eadweard Muybridge. More than 4,500 stopped-action photos, in action series, showing undraped men, women, children jumping, lying down, throwing, sitting, wrestling, carrying, etc. 390pp. 7⅞ x 10⅝. 0-486-20204-6 Clothbd.

TREES OF THE EASTERN AND CENTRAL UNITED STATES AND CANADA, William M. Harlow. Best one-volume guide to 140 trees. Full descriptions, woodlore, range, etc. Over 600 illustrations. Handy size. 288pp. 4½ x 6⅜. 0-486-20395-6

GROWING AND USING HERBS AND SPICES, Milo Miloradovich. Versatile handbook provides all the information needed for cultivation and use of all the herbs and spices available in North America. 4 illustrations. Index. Glossary. 236pp. 5⅜ x 8½. 0-486-25058-X

BIG BOOK OF MAZES AND LABYRINTHS, Walter Shepherd. 50 mazes and labyrinths in all–classical, solid, ripple, and more–in one great volume. Perfect inexpensive puzzler for clever youngsters. Full solutions. 112pp. 8⅛ x 11. 0-486-22951-3

PIANO TUNING, J. Cree Fischer. Clearest, best book for beginner, amateur. Simple repairs, raising dropped notes, tuning by easy method of flattened fifths. No previous skills needed. 4 illustrations. 201pp. 5⅜ x 8½. 0-486-23267-0

DRIED FLOWERS: How to Prepare Them, Sarah Whitlock and Martha Rankin. Complete instructions on how to use silica gel, meal and borax, perlite aggregate, sand and borax, glycerine and water to create attractive permanent flower arrangements. 12 illustrations. 32pp. 5⅜ x 8½. 0-486-21802-3

EASY-TO-MAKE BIRD FEEDERS FOR WOODWORKERS, Scott D. Campbell. Detailed, simple-to-use guide for designing, constructing, caring for and using feeders. Text, illustrations for 12 classic and contemporary designs. 96pp. 5⅜ x 8½. 0-486-25847-5

THE COMPLETE BOOK OF BIRDHOUSE CONSTRUCTION FOR WOODWORKERS, Scott D. Campbell. Detailed instructions, illustrations, tables. Also data on bird habitat and instinct patterns. Bibliography. 3 tables. 63 illustrations in 15 figures. 48pp. 5¼ x 8½. 0-486-24407-5

SCOTTISH WONDER TALES FROM MYTH AND LEGEND, Donald A. Mackenzie. 16 lively tales tell of giants rumbling down mountainsides, of a magic wand that turns stone pillars into warriors, of gods and goddesses, evil hags, powerful forces and more. 240pp. 5⅜ x 8½. 0-486-29677-6

THE HISTORY OF UNDERCLOTHES, C. Willett Cunnington and Phyllis Cunnington. Fascinating, well-documented survey covering six centuries of English undergarments, enhanced with over 100 illustrations: 12th-century laced-up bodice, footed long drawers (1795), 19th-century bustles, 19th-century corsets for men, Victorian "bust improvers," much more. 272pp. 5⅝ x 8¼. 0-486-27124-2

ARTS AND CRAFTS FURNITURE: The Complete Brooks Catalog of 1912, Brooks Manufacturing Co. Photos and detailed descriptions of more than 150 now very collectible furniture designs from the Arts and Crafts movement depict davenports, settees, buffets, desks, tables, chairs, bedsteads, dressers and more, all built of solid, quarter-sawed oak. Invaluable for students and enthusiasts of antiques, Americana and the decorative arts. 80pp. 6½ x 9¼. 0-486-27471-3

WILBUR AND ORVILLE: A Biography of the Wright Brothers, Fred Howard. Definitive, crisply written study tells the full story of the brothers' lives and work. A vividly written biography, unparalleled in scope and color, that also captures the spirit of an extraordinary era. 560pp. 6⅛ x 9¼. 0-486-40297-5

THE ARTS OF THE SAILOR: Knotting, Splicing and Ropework, Hervey Garrett Smith. Indispensable shipboard reference covers tools, basic knots and useful hitches; handsewing and canvas work, more. Over 100 illustrations. Delightful reading for sea lovers. 256pp. 5⅜ x 8½. 0-486-26440-8

FRANK LLOYD WRIGHT'S FALLINGWATER: The House and Its History, Second, Revised Edition, Donald Hoffmann. A total revision–both in text and illustrations–of the standard document on Fallingwater, the boldest, most personal architectural statement of Wright's mature years, updated with valuable new material from the recently opened Frank Lloyd Wright Archives. "Fascinating"–*The New York Times*. 116 illustrations. 128pp. 9¼ x 10¾. 0-486-27430-6

PHOTOGRAPHIC SKETCHBOOK OF THE CIVIL WAR, Alexander Gardner. 100 photos taken on field during the Civil War. Famous shots of Manassas Harper's Ferry, Lincoln, Richmond, slave pens, etc. 244pp. 10⅝ x 8¼. 0-486-22731-6

FIVE ACRES AND INDEPENDENCE, Maurice G. Kains. Great back-to-the-land classic explains basics of self-sufficient farming. The one book to get. 95 illustrations. 397pp. 5⅜ x 8½. 0-486-20974-1

A MODERN HERBAL, Margaret Grieve. Much the fullest, most exact, most useful compilation of herbal material. Gigantic alphabetical encyclopedia, from aconite to zedoary, gives botanical information, medical properties, folklore, economic uses, much else. Indispensable to serious reader. 161 illustrations. 888pp. 6½ x 9¼. 2-vol. set. (Available in U.S. only.) Vol. I: 0-486-22798-7 Vol. II: 0-486-22799-5

HIDDEN TREASURE MAZE BOOK, Dave Phillips. Solve 34 challenging mazes accompanied by heroic tales of adventure. Evil dragons, people-eating plants, bloodthirsty giants, many more dangerous adversaries lurk at every twist and turn. 34 mazes, stories, solutions. 48pp. 8¼ x 11. 0-486-24566-7

LETTERS OF W. A. MOZART, Wolfgang A. Mozart. Remarkable letters show bawdy wit, humor, imagination, musical insights, contemporary musical world; includes some letters from Leopold Mozart. 276pp. 5⅜ x 8½. 0-486-22859-2

BASIC PRINCIPLES OF CLASSICAL BALLET, Agrippina Vaganova. Great Russian theoretician, teacher explains methods for teaching classical ballet. 118 illustrations. 175pp. 5⅜ x 8½. 0-486-22036-2

THE JUMPING FROG, Mark Twain. Revenge edition. The original story of The Celebrated Jumping Frog of Calaveras County, a hapless French translation, and Twain's hilarious "retranslation" from the French. 12 illustrations. 66pp. 5⅜ x 8½. 0-486-22686-7

BEST REMEMBERED POEMS, Martin Gardner (ed.). The 126 poems in this superb collection of 19th- and 20th-century British and American verse range from Shelley's "To a Skylark" to the impassioned "Renascence" of Edna St. Vincent Millay and to Edward Lear's whimsical "The Owl and the Pussycat." 224pp. 5⅜ x 8½. 0-486-27165-X

COMPLETE SONNETS, William Shakespeare. Over 150 exquisite poems deal with love, friendship, the tyranny of time, beauty's evanescence, death and other themes in language of remarkable power, precision and beauty. Glossary of archaic terms. 80pp. 5³⁄₁₆ x 8¼. 0-486-26686-9

HISTORIC HOMES OF THE AMERICAN PRESIDENTS, Second, Revised Edition, Irvin Haas. A traveler's guide to American Presidential homes, most open to the public, depicting and describing homes occupied by every American President from George Washington to George Bush. With visiting hours, admission charges, travel routes. 175 photographs. Index. 160pp. 8¼ x 11. 0-486-26751-2

THE WIT AND HUMOR OF OSCAR WILDE, Alvin Redman (ed.). More than 1,000 ripostes, paradoxes, wisecracks: Work is the curse of the drinking classes; I can resist everything except temptation; etc. 258pp. 5⅜ x 8½. 0-486-20602-5

SHAKESPEARE LEXICON AND QUOTATION DICTIONARY, Alexander Schmidt. Full definitions, locations, shades of meaning in every word in plays and poems. More than 50,000 exact quotations. 1,485pp. 6½ x 9¼. 2-vol. set. Vol. 1: 0-486-22726-X Vol. 2: 0-486-22727-8

SELECTED POEMS, Emily Dickinson. Over 100 best-known, best-loved poems by one of America's foremost poets, reprinted from authoritative early editions. No comparable edition at this price. Index of first lines. 64pp. 5³⁄₁₆ x 8¼. 0-486-26466-1

THE INSIDIOUS DR. FU-MANCHU, Sax Rohmer. The first of the popular mystery series introduces a pair of English detectives to their archnemesis, the diabolical Dr. Fu-Manchu. Flavorful atmosphere, fast-paced action, and colorful characters enliven this classic of the genre. 208pp. 5³⁄₁₆ x 8¼. 0-486-29898-1

MAGIC AND MYSTERY IN TIBET, Madame Alexandra David-Neel. Experiences among lamas, magicians, sages, sorcerers, Bonpa wizards. A true psychic discovery. 32 illustrations. 321pp. 5⅜ x 8½. (Available in U.S. only.) 0-486-22682-4

THE EGYPTIAN BOOK OF THE DEAD, E. A. Wallis Budge. Complete reproduction of Ani's papyrus, finest ever found. Full hieroglyphic text, interlinear transliteration, word-for-word translation, smooth translation. 533pp. 6½ x 9¼. 0-486-21866-X

HISTORIC COSTUME IN PICTURES, Braun & Schneider. Over 1,450 costumed figures in clearly detailed engravings–from dawn of civilization to end of 19th century. Captions. Many folk costumes. 256pp. 8⅜ x 11¾. 0-486-23150-X

MATHEMATICS FOR THE NONMATHEMATICIAN, Morris Kline. Detailed, college-level treatment of mathematics in cultural and historical context, with numerous exercises. Recommended Reading Lists. Tables. Numerous figures. 641pp. 5⅜ x 8½. 0-486-24823-2

PROBABILISTIC METHODS IN THE THEORY OF STRUCTURES, Isaac Elishakoff. Well-written introduction covers the elements of the theory of probability from two or more random variables, the reliability of such multivariable structures, the theory of random function, Monte Carlo methods of treating problems incapable of exact solution, and more. Examples. 502pp. 5⅜ x 8½. 0-486-40691-1

THE RIME OF THE ANCIENT MARINER, Gustave Doré, S. T. Coleridge. Doré's finest work; 34 plates capture moods, subtleties of poem. Flawless full-size reproductions printed on facing pages with authoritative text of poem. "Beautiful. Simply beautiful."–*Publisher's Weekly*. 77pp. 9¼ x 12. 0-486-22305-1

SCULPTURE: Principles and Practice, Louis Slobodkin. Step-by-step approach to clay, plaster, metals, stone; classical and modern. 253 drawings, photos. 255pp. 8⅛ x 11. 0-486-22960-2

THE INFLUENCE OF SEA POWER UPON HISTORY, 1660–1783, A. T. Mahan. Influential classic of naval history and tactics still used as text in war colleges. First paperback edition. 4 maps. 24 battle plans. 640pp. 5⅜ x 8½. 0-486-25509-3

THE STORY OF THE TITANIC AS TOLD BY ITS SURVIVORS, Jack Winocour (ed.). What it was really like. Panic, despair, shocking inefficiency, and a little heroism. More thrilling than any fictional account. 26 illustrations. 320pp. 5⅜ x 8½. 0-486-20610-6

ONE TWO THREE . . . INFINITY: Facts and Speculations of Science, George Gamow. Great physicist's fascinating, readable overview of contemporary science: number theory, relativity, fourth dimension, entropy, genes, atomic structure, much more. 128 illustrations. Index. 352pp. 5⅜ x 8½. 0-486-25664-2

DALÍ ON MODERN ART: The Cuckolds of Antiquated Modern Art, Salvador Dalí. Influential painter skewers modern art and its practitioners. Outrageous evaluations of Picasso, Cézanne, Turner, more. 15 renderings of paintings discussed. 44 calligraphic decorations by Dalí. 96pp. 5⅜ x 8½. (Available in U.S. only.) 0-486-29220-7

ANTIQUE PLAYING CARDS: A Pictorial History, Henry René D'Allemagne. Over 900 elaborate, decorative images from rare playing cards (14th–20th centuries): Bacchus, death, dancing dogs, hunting scenes, royal coats of arms, players cheating, much more. 96pp. 9¼ x 12¼. 0-486-29265-7

CATALOG OF DOVER BOOKS

LIGHT AND SHADE: A Classic Approach to Three-Dimensional Drawing, Mrs. Mary P. Merrifield. Handy reference clearly demonstrates principles of light and shade by revealing effects of common daylight, sunshine, and candle or artificial light on geometrical solids. 13 plates. 64pp. 5⅜ x 8½. 0-486-44143-1

ASTROLOGY AND ASTRONOMY: A Pictorial Archive of Signs and Symbols, Ernst and Johanna Lehner. Treasure trove of stories, lore, and myth, accompanied by more than 300 rare illustrations of planets, the Milky Way, signs of the zodiac, comets, meteors, and other astronomical phenomena. 192pp. 8⅜ x 11. 0-486-43981-X

JEWELRY MAKING: Techniques for Metal, Tim McCreight. Easy-to-follow instructions and carefully executed illustrations describe tools and techniques, use of gems and enamels, wire inlay, casting, and other topics. 72 line illustrations and diagrams. 176pp. 8¼ x 10⅞. 0-486-44043-5

MAKING BIRDHOUSES: Easy and Advanced Projects, Gladstone Califf. Easy-to-follow instructions include diagrams for everything from a one-room house for bluebirds to a forty-two-room structure for purple martins. 56 plates; 4 figures. 80pp. 8¾ x 6⅜. 0-486-44183-0

LITTLE BOOK OF LOG CABINS: How to Build and Furnish Them, William S. Wicks. Handy how-to manual, with instructions and illustrations for building cabins in the Adirondack style, fireplaces, stairways, furniture, beamed ceilings, and more. 102 line drawings. 96pp. 8¾ x 6⅜. 0-486-44259-4

THE SEASONS OF AMERICA PAST, Eric Sloane. From "sugaring time" and strawberry picking to Indian summer and fall harvest, a whole year's activities described in charming prose and enhanced with 79 of the author's own illustrations. 160pp. 8¼ x 11. 0-486-44220-9

THE METROPOLIS OF TOMORROW, Hugh Ferriss. Generous, prophetic vision of the metropolis of the future, as perceived in 1929. Powerful illustrations of towering structures, wide avenues, and rooftop parks–all features in many of today's modern cities. 59 illustrations. 144pp. 8¼ x 11. 0-486-43727-2

THE PATH TO ROME, Hilaire Belloc. This 1902 memoir abounds in lively vignettes from a vanished time, recounting a pilgrimage on foot across the Alps and Apennines in order to "see all Europe which the Christian Faith has saved." 77 of the author's original line drawings complement his sparkling prose. 272pp. 5⅜ x 8½. 0-486-44001-X

THE HISTORY OF RASSELAS: Prince of Abissinia, Samuel Johnson. Distinguished English writer attacks eighteenth-century optimism and man's unrealistic estimates of what life has to offer. 112pp. 5⅜ x 8½. 0-486-44094-X

A VOYAGE TO ARCTURUS, David Lindsay. A brilliant flight of pure fancy, where wild creatures crowd the fantastic landscape and demented torturers dominate victims with their bizarre mental powers. 272pp. 5⅜ x 8½. 0-486-44198-9